THE LIFE OF THE POET

Beginning and Ending
Poetic Careers

LAWRENCE LIPKING

The University of Chicago Press
CHICAGO AND LONDON

LAWRENCE LIPKING is Chester Tripp
Professor of Humanities at
Northwestern University.

THE UNIVERSITY OF CHICAGO PRESS, CHICAGO 60637
THE UNIVERSITY OF CHICAGO PRESS, LTD., LONDON

© 1981 by The University of Chicago
All rights reserved. Published 1981
Printed in the United States of America
5 4 3 2 1   81 82 83 84 85 86 87 88

LIBRARY OF CONGRESS CATALOGING IN PUBLICATION DATA

Lipking, Lawrence I., 1934–
   The life of the poet.

   Includes bibliographical references and index.
   1. Poets—Biography. 2. Poetry. I. Title.
PN1075.L5   809.1 [B]   81–1067
ISBN 0–226–48450–5   AACR2

THE LIFE OF THE POET

"Dante before the fire": Blake's illustration for *Purgatorio* XXVII

Contents

Preface: The Life of the Poet vii
Acknowledgments xv
Beginning: A First Look into Keats 3

I INITIATION
Books of New Life 13
La Vita Nuova 20
The Marriage of Heaven and Hell 34
Per Amica Silentia Lunae 47

II HARMONIUM
The Tradition of One and *Four Quartets* 65
The *Aeneid* 76
Faust 93
Leaves of Grass 114
The Death of Virgil 130

III TOMBEAU
Jonson on Shakespeare 138
Collins on Thomson 146
Auden on Yeats 151
The Tombs of Mallarmé: Poe, Baudelaire, Verlaine 160

Ending: Keats, Lowell, Rilke 180
Notes and Glosses 193
Index 235

PREFACE

The Life of the Poet

We have heard too much about the lives of the poets. When Samuel Johnson supplied *Prefaces, biographical and critical, to the most eminent of the English Poets* (1779–81), he intended to advertise and criticize a collection of poems, not to substitute the biography of each poet for a reading of his verse. But soon enough the prefaces changed into *Johnson's Lives,* divorced from the poems, and ever since then the lives of the poets have tended to sell better than their works. It is not surprising. Readers have always loved gossip, and a nimbus of stories or legends has wrapped poets round throughout history—why Sappho killed herself and how much Li Po drank and what was Lord Byron's secret. But in the last few centuries this casual curiosity has swelled to an open obsession. The Romantics began it, perhaps, by insisting on the uniqueness and eccentricity of genius, the difference of poets from other people. The scholars confirmed it, eventually, with the growth of historical and biographical studies that deflected attention from poems to the facts and circumstances behind them. Today the lives of the poets are better known, and more public, than ever. Yet what does this obsessive interest in poets have to do with understanding poetry?

The question, once raised, has been asked again and again. For much of this century intelligent critics have made a point of not reading the lives of the poets. The poem itself, they have said, must acquire a life of its own. And in recent years this reaction has gone still further: we have begun to hear about the *death* of the poet. The lives of poets must be sacrificed, ruthlessly expunged from our consciousness, according to critics like Roland Barthes, in order to make a place for the reader, or the imperatives of structure, or the needs of society. Down with the tyrant! For too long the supposed intentions of authors have been allowed to dominate their works, repressing and possessing them like so much property. The time has come for liberation of the text and the reader. Hence a great deal of modern criticism may be viewed as an attempt to render poems anonymous; to free them from the lives of the poets. And even those critics who continue to base their interpretations on some version of the author's intention are likely to sound defensive. For two centuries we have been hearing about the lives of the poets, and the law of diminishing returns has set in. We cannot expect to learn much more about the life of Homer or even the life of Dylan Thomas, and literary biographies notoriously tell us less about the work the longer they grow. Perhaps a moratorium is due on the lives of the poets.

Yet the life of the poet—the shape of his life *as a poet*—has not been exhausted. Indeed, it has hardly been studied. We know far more about the facts of poets' lives, their quirks and torments, their singularities, than we do about the life that all poets share: their vocation as poets. How does an aspiring author of verses become a poet? How does a poet, once established, face the challenge of refreshing and deepening his work, instead of being content to write the same poem over and over? What is the legacy that a poet leaves? Obvious as they are, these questions have scarcely been asked in modern times. Thus most biographies of poets present the development of the hero, his struggle to find a poetic identity, as if it were the product of his own individual will—a unique self-making. Yet no poet becomes himself without inheriting an idea of what it means to be a poet. The same patterns recur again and again; the same excited discoveries lead to the same sense of achievement. We cannot ignore the evidence that the development of a great many poets follows a consistent internal logic. Nor need we stray far outside their poems to find the evidence. If the lives of the poets tend to be peripheral to the insides of poems, the life of the poet is often the life of the poem.

The reluctance of critics to consider such issues has led to some very strange consequences. A whole critical vocabulary has had to be invented, for instance, to account for the presence in all Dante's major works of an obtrusive character called "Dante." Doubtless he is a "persona," not to be confused with the author of the *Commedia,* any more than we would confuse the speaker in "Lycidas" with Milton, the protagonist of *The Prelude* with Wordsworth, or the daughter of "Daddy" with Sylvia Plath. Or so critics used to tell us. But the mask-like face of the persona has lately begun to crack, revealing a more human face behind it. The fact is that poems (at least since the time of Hesiod) have always confided something about the life of the poet: not necessarily his personality or even his individuality, but his sense of a vocation and a destiny. Not every poem is obliged to lay bare its poet. But every major Western poet after Homer, I believe, has left some work that records the principles of his own poetic development. Though the playwright Shakespeare may still remain an enigma, the poet Shakespeare devotes many sonnets to exposing his Will. The nature of Western poetry seems to require such exposure, such self-reference. In order to teach us how to see him, the poet must first project himself into his work. Hence the presence of the poet in his poem, in major poetry, is not the exception but the rule. It alerts us to where he stands.

This is a book about the life of the poet: poetic vocations, poetic careers, poetic destinies. It traces a number of great poets through the crucial moments of their development and tries to discern what problems and solutions they have in common. By listening carefully both to what poets say about their works and to what works say about themselves, it hopes to arrive at a clearer understanding of the way that a poem can constitute the experience of a life. And it also hopes to offer new ways of reading poems.

Three points, in particular, will focus the investigation: the moment of initiation or breakthrough; the moment of summing up; and the moment of passage, when the legacy or soul of the poet's work is transmitted to the next generation. I have chosen these points partly because they are so decisive in themselves—every great poet defines himself in such moments—and partly for reasons of clarity. A major author may go through many stages, sometimes as often as every few years, and his career may seem to shift direction with every passing wind. But no poet can avoid the testing moments charted by this book, moments that question whether his work exists, whether it amounts to anything more than the sum of its parts, and whether it will continue to exist. Most poetic careers include poems that not only illustrate these problems but directly confront and debate them. As a result, the study of moments of breakthrough, summing up, and passage allows a career to be foreshortened into a few specific life-giving works. Such studies cannot be exhaustive or conclusive, but at least they can be precise. The poet who claims to have entered a new stage of life brings a witness who cannot lie: the evidence of the poems.

The poems themselves, above all, declare the life of the poet. In this respect my study differs from those that would associate the stages of poetic life with the stages of human life in general. Of course poets share the human lot. But the great poet also makes his own destiny; he makes it, precisely, with poems. Thus the stage of poetic initiation, which resembles in so many ways the initiation ceremonies described by anthropologists, contrasts with them in two crucial respects: it is the poet himself who sets the terms of his ritual ordeal; and the great majority of aspirants do not survive it. When T. S. Eliot called his first book of criticism *The Sacred Wood,* he was suggesting that the world of letters could elevate only one King of the Wood at a time (like the murderer-priest of Nemi in Frazer's *Golden Bough*); a poet-critic could establish himself as master only by killing the others. Yet the anthropology was dubious and the parallel inexact. For the sacred wood of poetry offers no sanctuary. It does not exist outside the work of the poet, nor can any poet inhabit it unless he has made it himself, as Eliot made his own sense of Tradition. Hence every successful poetic initiation occurs only once. When the poet arrives at the innermost shrine, what he finds there is no special wisdom or community but his own beginning work.

Nor does my study resemble those that use the life of the poet to symbolize universal moral and psychological problems or to illustrate lessons imported from Augustine or Freud. Johnson's *Lives of the Poets,* for instance, derive much of their power from holding poets to account, like other men, for the use of their talents. If poets are different, it is only because their special line of work makes them even more susceptible than most sinners to the frailties of mankind: the dangerous prevalence of imagination; sacrificing the duties of life to expectation; hoping for immortality on earth. No poet can afford to overlook these warnings. Yet Johnson, whose own career depended so much on chance and occasion, pays little attention to the internal logic of poetic growth. "The Young Author," written when he was twenty, acknowledges only two stages of a literary calling: vain dreams, followed by a baffled retreat to obscurity. Nor did Johnson's later success significantly change his mind. His morality teaches him all the pitfalls in the life of the poet but almost none of the rewards. A poem may approach perfection, Johnson knows, but a life may not. Hence he rigorously separates the life from the work and comments without sympathy on those passages where Milton, for instance, invokes his own destiny as a poet. Johnson will judge the poems; but a final verdict on the life must be reserved for a higher judge.

This book takes another course. It accepts the testimony of poems as decisive evidence about the way that poets conceive, or invent, their careers. Poets cannot be trusted more than anyone else, of course, to tell the truth about themselves. But the poet's claim to have achieved an identity, to have shaped his life into art, cannot deceive anyone for long. Either the poems themselves prove it, or they do not. Poetry cannot tell us whether the author was a happy person, or a sinner, or justified in his politics, or suffering from bad dreams; but it can tell us all we need to know about the author's ability to convert his experience into vision. Here—not in the creative process or some irrecoverable unconscious—life and poetry intersect. Thus, whatever else we know about Dante's life, we can be certain about one fact: he actually did achieve the vision recorded in the final canto of the *Commedia.* To deny it would be to deny the whole poem—and to deny his life as a poet.

Each of the central chapters of this book, therefore, examines the kind of life expressed by one kind of literary work. I aim to write not the biographies of poets but the biography that gets into poems: the life that has passed through a refining poetic fire. The meaning of that life can be seen only through the eyes of the poet. Hence my formulation of arguments draws constantly on the poet's own point of view. Theory, for the poet, is whatever he can put into practice; history is whatever his poem can transpose to present needs; genres are not collections of laws and precepts but possible ways of solving his problems. This book follows a similar line of thought. Its theories are tied to practice; its sense of history is both diachronic and synchronic, chronological and perennial; the genres it defines are set not by conventions but by problems (thus an "initiation" is a work in which a poet finds himself; "harmonium" includes but is not restricted to various "epics"; a "tombeau" is not a sort of "elegy" but another way of looking at the problems of poetic mortality). Imagining poems as poets first see them, we must put aside our keys and categories and restore some of the uncertainty of their setting-forth.

A related emphasis on the trial of ideas through practice accounts for my selection of poets. To begin with, I have tried to choose figures of stature, from a variety of times and countries, whose work represents the problems of my subject as explicitly as possible. To consider the question of how a poet molds a career, for example, is almost necessarily to consider Virgil, who supplied the pattern of a career to so many later poets. Next, I have chosen figures who offer commentary and explanations of what they have done. *La Vita Nuova* is particularly precious, for instance, because Dante has incorporated in his first great work an unfolding of its meaning. Whether or not we take such evidence at face value, it does lead us further into the poet's ways of thinking. Finally, I have deliberately chosen works that function as counterexamples, that test rather than confirm my arguments. Since Virgil affords the paradigm of a harmonium, he is followed here not by Milton or Pope, who tried to mold their careers to Virgil's specifications, but by Goethe, who repudiated the Virgilian model, by Whitman, who rejected not only Virgil and Goethe but also the very idea of a classical career, and by Broch, who put his recanting of Western civilization into Virgil's own mouth. My choice of examples is limited, of course, by the languages I can read, by the poets I feel some minimal competence to discuss, and doubtless by a certain parochial bias toward my own culture. But I hope it is clear that I have not chosen only the safest and most comfortable examples.

In one respect, however, most of the poets discussed in this book do share, for all their differences, a common creed: a faith in greatness. Their ambition is less to write individual great verses than to become great poets by achieving great poetic careers. Such ambitions may well induce a considerable uneasiness or even hostility. No poet likes to be accused of "careerism." Indeed, for many poets the rejection of anything that resembles a career has always seemed the epitome of poetic virtue. Even before Virgil had finished the *Aeneid,* according to Ezra Pound, the small sharp voice of

Sextus Propertius had denounced him as Caesar's toady. A craftsman disdains such "greatness."

> Out-weariers of Apollo will, as we know, continue their
>   Martian generalities,
> We have kept our erasers in order.

From this perspective the very notion of a great career may look like a conspiracy against the public, a cloak of generalities and pomposities that covers the naked poem. And many modern judges—critics as various as Yvor Winters and Robert Graves—have sustained the conspiracy charge. Poetry, they maintain, consists of poems; not poets, not great names, not careers, not history, certainly not critical ideas, but poems—a few priceless verses winnowed from the chaff. To view a poet's work as a whole is to commit an act of totalitarianism. The muse herself is democratic; no respecter of fame and titles, she descends wherever she pleases, in isolated flashes that strike like lightning. Nor can any amount of previous success or future glory sustain an ill-wrought line.

Clearly the attack on careerism has considerable power. I too suspect the poet who claims attention for what he is rather than what he does; I too disapprove of the reader who trusts the name and reputation of the poet more than his own responses. Yet an indifference to the total achievement of the poet can also carry some distorting ideological biases. First of all, it tends to diminish all poetry to lyrics or collections of lyrics. Winters, Graves, Richards and the New Critics, all turn their instruments of critical analysis most readily on poems that can survive in a vacuum—anonymous poems. And even this mode of analysis requires some suppression of contexts (thus Richards, in *Practical Criticism,* prompted his students to interesting misreadings by suppressing the titles and even some lines of poems). The New Critical triumphs with "Lycidas," for example, were purchased at the cost of ignoring what many readers have found the most thrilling aspect of the poem: that the young poet who suffers through these ruminations on the fate of poets, who dedicates himself to pastures new, would eventually prove to be Milton. Our knowledge of Milton's destination completes his poem. And certainly longer works of art, those epics that summon up the whole of a culture, a history, a career, a myth of creation, demand a reader whose vision stretches beyond the text. Too much mistrust of greatness and ambition, like too much reverence, can result in a systematic perversion of what poems say.

Second, the attack on careerism does not preclude the poet's need to shape some sort of career, some sense of destiny or vocation. Propertius and Pound, Winters and Graves, are not modest authors. Their contempt for "official" poetry and "heroic" careers implies a reverse ambition: a self-consuming devotion to craft. Indeed, one might argue that resistance to orthodox definitions of greatness and public careers itself constitutes a career ideal. Thus a poet like Emily Dickinson, with her unwillingness to publish, her preference for intensity and brevity, her hesitation to try new forms or to "develop," her sublime independence, seems almost too perfect an example of an anti-careerist vocation. To do full justice to the logic of such poetic lives would require another book—a book I hope to write. But this book also is concerned with the expense of greatness. The poet who sets out to achieve a great career may doom himself to a life of unsatisfied hungers and broken poems. That too is part of what a sense of destiny means. Most poets fail. The larger the ambition, the more a poet must learn to live with a consciousness of failure. Propertius did not have to remind Virgil of his inadequacy or of the price that the victor pays; no one knew that lesson better than Virgil himself.

On one point, finally, the enemies of "great careers" and I are in agreement: no view of poetry is worth our attention unless it can throw light on poems. This book must stand or fall on the quality of its readings. Trying to look at poems through poets' eyes, it depends on an effort of understanding that must deal not only with giant ambitions but intimate particulars. The life of the poet, like the life of the poem, comes down to details. Moreover, interpreting poems is not only the method of this book but one of its central themes. It is through rereading their own work, discovering the hidden meanings sown by their younger selves, that poets grow. To repeat this process, finding again what great poets once found and passing it on to others, is the aim and the hope of this book.

Acknowledgments

The idea of a book on poetic careers—the lifework that includes and transforms both individual lives and individual works—has been in my mind almost since I first began to think seriously about poetry. Many kinds of aid were necessary, however, before the idea could take shape. A term as Visiting Fellow at the Wesleyan Center for the Humanities and a grant from the American Council of Learned Societies enabled me to start this book, and a term as NEH Fellow at the Newberry Library and a leave from Princeton University enabled me to finish the first draft. Northwestern University supplied a grant for typing the final draft. I am grateful for all this bounty.

A book on poets from so many times and nations could hardly come about without the help of a large community of scholars. Only a few of my debts can be acknowledged here. In the beginning Miss Mary Ryan taught me Virgil and the late Erich Kahler introduced me to Broch. More recently I have benefited from the advice and encouragement of M. H. Abrams, Walter Jackson Bate, Wayne C. Booth, Gerald Graff, Jean Hagstrum, the late Sheldon Sacks, Theodore Weiss, and especially A. Walton Litz, whose good offices and good judgment were invaluable from first to last. At various stages particular helpful comments have been offered by the late Reuben A. Brower, Richard Harrier, Margaret R. Higonnet, Robert Hollander, Herbert J. Levine, Jerome J. McGann, James L. Olney, Robert von Hallberg, Aileen Ward, and Richard Wendorf. Martin Mueller read the whole manuscript and saved me from several blunders. Of the debts that cannot be repaid, I owe the largest to my wife, Joanna. Many other friends, colleagues, and students deserve thanks. One group will have to stand for all: the NEH Summer Seminar at Princeton, 1978, whose willingness to entertain these ideas persuaded me that they were ready to publish.

Part of the chapter "Initiation" first appeared, in a different form, as "Blake's Initiation: *The Marriage of Heaven and Hell,*" in the volume *Woman in the 18th Century and Other Essays,* edited by Paul Fritz and Richard Morton; I thank Garland Publishing Company for permission to use that material again.

Other debts are recorded in the notes at the back of this book, which are tied to page numbers and key phrases. I have also used those notes to provide arguments and information that supplement the text. All translations in the text are my own unless otherwise noted.

THE LIFE OF THE POET

BEGINNING

A First Look into Keats

Just as the sun rose, one October morning in 1816, a talented young apprentice without a name became the poet Keats. It happened abruptly as a fairytale: a sudden apparition in the dawn; a stranger seen for the first time, yet recognized immediately as a familiar; the presentation of a quest; an orphan boy discovering what he was born to do; the name itself, eventually, speaking of magic. Nor is there any more famous story of how a poet is born. Yet the story continues to ring true despite its air of legend. Its truth is confirmed partly by the way that Keats' friends—Charles Cowden Clarke, the first to feel the magic, and later Leigh Hunt—immediately distinguished "the new poet taking possession"; partly by the way that anyone reading through Keats' early verse, even today, all at once comes upon a poem whose power leaps out from the rest; and most of all by that poem itself, which tells its own story.

> ON FIRST LOOKING INTO CHAPMAN'S HOMER
> Much have I travell'd in the realms of gold,
>   And many goodly states and kingdoms seen;
>   Round many western islands have I been
> Which bards in fealty to Apollo hold.
> Oft of one wide expanse had I been told
>   That deep-brow'd Homer ruled as his demesne;
>   Yet did I never breathe its pure serene
> Till I heard Chapman speak out loud and bold:
> Then felt I like some watcher of the skies
>   When a new planet swims into his ken;
> Or like stout Cortez when with eagle eyes
>   He star'd at the Pacific—and all his men

3

> Look'd at each other with a wild surmise—
> Silent, upon a peak in Darien.

The excitement, as many have noted, responds to something more than a first look at Homer. As the poem itself begins with legend and ends with history—the rumors of gold succeeded by an encounter with an actual new world, the states and kingdoms of poesy swept away by an unimaginably vast uncharted ocean—so the poet catches sight not of someone else's dream but of his own reality. He stares at his future, and surmises that he may be a poet. The sense of possibility is thrilling, the moment truly awesome. Keats has discovered Keats.

What does that mean? It is amazing how confidently we refer to "Keats," or "Homer," or "Dante," or "Goethe," as if the author and all his works were one. Clearly no single name can accommodate such a variety of poems or so many stages of life. "Keats" represents a fiction, a cipher that stands for the whole of the poet's career. But the poet himself, we should remember, was the first to invent that fiction. What Keats said of salvation, in the famous "vale of Soulmaking" letter (April 21, 1819), might equally be said of the way that any poet comes into his own: "There may be intelligences or sparks of the divinity in millions—but they are not Souls till they acquire identities, till each one is personally itself." Nor would he have hesitated to substitute "genius" for "divinity" and "Poets" for "Souls." Great poets forge their own identities. They invent an image—as the young Milton resolved that "he who would not be frustrate of his hope to write well hereafter in laudable things, ought him selfe to bee a true Poem, that is, a composition, and patterne of the best and honourablest things"—and project themselves into it. Thus Keats' ability to grow, like Milton's, depends on a vision of his future self: his range of possibilities, his moment in English poetry, the latent principles of his development, the ideal work he hopes to accomplish, the legacy he hopes to leave. "Keats" is his own truest poem. And it is that poem, the pattern of his work as a whole above and beyond any of its particular manifestations, that posterity tries to read.

Nor has posterity been reluctant to interpret "Keats." Two questions, in practice, intrigue almost every reader of "Chapman's Homer": how did Keats come to write it? and what was the nature of his surmise? Many superb biographies of the poet testify to the perennial fascination of those questions and the difficulty in answering them. Keats seems to hold the key to everything we would like to know about how one becomes a poet. At twenty he was no more promising than any number of other would-be authors; suddenly, just short of his twenty-first birthday, he left all the rest behind. What happened? Keats and his biographers share an interest in finding out. The questions we ask of "Chapman's Homer" correspond to the problems of breakthrough and fulfillment, or beginning and ending:

how does a poet discover himself? and what is it, finally, that he discovers? If we understood the process through which Keats acquired his identity, we might also begin to understand the life of every poet.

The questions may be answered, to be sure, with the help of specific facts. How did Keats happen to write "Chapman's Homer"? He and Cowden Clarke had spent the whole night looking at the book; they parted at "day-spring"; while Keats walked home, "in the teeming wonderment of this his first introduction," verses began to well up; by ten o'clock, when Clarke came down to breakfast, the sonnet was on his table. Moreover, so much of the poet's reading and personal experience enters the poem that its sources can be traced line by line—almost word by word. Not only Chapman's Homer, Robertson's *History of America*, Bonnycastle's *Introduction to Astronomy*, and phrases from Wordsworth and Shakespeare find a place, but even Keats' first sight of the sea, a few months before, or his note to Clarke (October 9) that meeting Hunt will be "an Era in my existence." Fitting these scraps of fact together, a scholar may be forgiven for beginning to think "Chapman's Homer" less a miracle than a jigsaw puzzle. Perhaps Keats himself was a kind of scholar, assembling his sources in the same way that, later, we take them apart. In that case the poem would amount to the exact sum of its circumstances. "Chapman's Homer" begins to look as logical and inevitable, from this point of view, as a well-balanced budget. How could it *not* have been written?

Similarly, the question of how "Chapman's Homer" is related to Keats' work as a whole admits some definite technical answers. A poet reaches Parnassus by the same route a violinist takes to Carnegie Hall: practice, practice. When Keats substituted "deep" for "low" in the sixth line, for instance, he was contriving a subtle richness of vowel sequences ("deep . . . demesne," as opposed to the cruder "low-browed Homer") that would mark all his later verse. Moreover, the firm clear structure of the sonnet reveals a poet able to sustain, for the first time in his life, an argument that does not fall apart into separate images. He would build on these grounds. The reverence toward poetry, the mention of Apollo, the images of sea and star, the resolution of the narrative in a vision bordering on a swoon, and above all the comparative simplicity and directness of language, all witness the future master in embryo. Keats grew through a rational process of self-improvement. To follow that process, perhaps we need only analyze the facts.

Such answers may satisfy someone. They would not have satisfied Keats. Again and again, exploring his own potential, he returned to the mystery of how a poet grows and tried to define himself as a poet in some way not limited to the facts of his experience or determined by the mundane round of cause and effect. What happens at the moment of breakthrough? No gathering of sources, according to Keats, but a leap into the unknown.

"The Genius of Poetry must work out its own salvation in a man: It cannot be matured by law & precept, but by sensation & watchfulness in itself— That which is creative must create itself." How does a poet view his future? Not as a refinement of his talents or an expression of what he is, according to Keats, but as a submission to something greater.

> The faint conceptions I have of Poems to come brings the blood frequently into my forehead—. . . I feel assured I should write from the mere yearning and fondness I have for the Beautiful even if my night's labours should be burnt every morning and no eye ever shine upon them. But even now I am perhaps not speaking from myself; but from some character in whose soul I now live.

The true author of the poems, on this analysis, is not the man himself but the Genius of Poetry within him and around him. Keats regards "Keats"— that "character in whose soul I now live"—as a presence radically indifferent to immediate personal concerns. A young poet must be ready to hazard everything, even his life: "In Endymion, I leaped headlong into the Sea." What he does, what he is, is less important than what he may become. The future will forget all facts except those the poet has put to use. If Keats had a vision of "Keats" on that morning—silent, upon a road from Clerkenwell—what he saw was not only himself writ large. He saw a new world.

The best evidence about what Keats discovered in Chapman's Homer, however, is "Chapman's Homer." The sonnet itself confides a good deal about how it happened. Keats describes the process of his discovery, its background and preparation, as well as its climax. Indeed, half the verses recreate his state of mind *before* Chapman. Nor had he been unaware of what he was looking for. Just as Herschel's discovery of Uranus was anything but accidental, since it resulted (according to Bonnycastle) from "pursuing a design which he had formed of observing, with telescopes of his own construction, every part of the heavens"; just as Balboa's discovery of the Pacific and Cortez' first sight of Mexico City followed directly from native reports of that ocean and that kingdom; so Keats found a Homer he had already dreamed. An enormous will to discovery lies behind the poem. But what Keats discovered, of course, was not a legend but a text—one particular translation of the dream. Like a planet or an ocean, it was real: not so much a poem by the real Homer as a poem really Keats' own.

Two observations may be made upon this discovery. First, it results from reading. Keats emerges into his own career, like many other poets, in the midst of a period of intense critical study of poetry, an immersion that seems to issue not merely in increased knowledge but in a whole new way of reading. The dramatic visual imagery of the sestet—unusual, for Keats, in concentrating on only one of the senses—marks him, at this moment, as a *watcher*. Through "watchfulness" he learns to see. And he learns how

6

to use his reading; an astonishing amount of it suddenly compresses together. Later in his career he would learn to read himself in the same way. "Endymion," for all its weaknesses, contains clues and fragments of virtually every one of Keats' major poems, dormant until, revisiting and rereading it, he saw what he should have meant. He never exhausted such acts of reinterpretation; even the unfinished "Fall of Hyperion" returns to "Hyperion" for a fresh perusal. Poetry matures, for him, by being watched. Part of the answer to the question of how "Chapman's Homer" happened seems to be that Keats had become a better reader.

The theme arises already in the opening lines. To have "travell'd in the realms of gold" implies, in context, three different sorts of mental travel. First of all "the realms of gold" are those fabled new-world El Dorados that once lured the conquistadors and still lure every adventurous spirit; and as the end of the poem reminds us, the quest has not always remained in the realm of fable. Second, the central metaphor associates those realms with all great poetry, the "golden world" that, according to Sidney, only poets deliver, refining it in their imaginations. The glance at "western islands" cleverly refers both to the West Indies and to the heritage of European poetry, along with Keats' hint that his want of languages (Greek certainly, and perhaps Hebrew as well, whose bards hold fealty to another lord than Apollo) has kept the eastern part of the golden world closed to him. But "realms of gold" also has a third, more literal, significance: those gold-embossed books into whose interior every reader travels. Keats imports into his reading the explorer's sense of adventure and the poet's sense of a better, unfallen world.

To travel through a book, however, need not mean that one has read it carefully. The slightly pompous poetic diction of the octave makes the poet sound like a tourist. Nor is "looking into" Chapman's Homer quite the same thing, of course, as reading it through. Like an adventurer or an imperialist, like Cortez himself, Keats seized from the book whatever he could use, without much respect to persons. (The line that brought a delighted stare, according to Clarke—"The sea had soak'd his heart through"—is Chapman's own invention.) All night the two young friends had gone searching for nuggets. They turned at once to "some of the 'famousest' passages" and read them aloud "Till I heard Chapman speak out loud and bold"—presumably in the accents of Clarke. When a young poet "looks into" a book in this spirit, he is likely to carry away two sorts of prize: some fine phrases, and a new rhythm or poetic voice. Keats, it might be argued, took both, borrowing the language of Elizabethan voyages and grafting Chapman's long-winded fourteeners on his own pentameter to achieve a more weighty line. He adjusted his voice to another tempo. That is how a young poet reads: not so much by seeing the text as by learning to breathe it.

"Breathing," of course, is Keats' own image. By exchanging his first thought, "Yet could I never judge what Men could mean," for "Yet did I never breathe its pure serene," he showed how well he had absorbed Chapman's preference for the concrete and physical over the abstract and mental. Moreover, the mixture of senses—he looks until he hears a voice that lets him breathe—is worthy of the later Keats. The poet does not say that he has arrived in Homer's wide expanse but that he has had a whiff of it; and in his excitement all the senses blur. Nor can we doubt how life-giving Chapman's Homer seems to him at this instant—no mere air but poetic oxygen.

Such breathing can be dangerously heady. At the moment when Keats inhaled the pure serene he became a poet; the spirit of Homer literally "inspired" him. The whole poem suspends from that line. Keats enters the sublime breathless stillness that would radiate out from the ending of the sonnet into his larger career. Yet at the same moment the full weight of influence—the consciousness of everything that great poetry can be—penetrated his soul and burdened him with an ideal that would pursue him to his death. Mortals cannot bear very much divinity. The effect of such a "pure serene," which carries no poison in "Chapman's Homer," seems darker in a sister poem, "On Seeing the Elgin Marbles."

> My spirit is too weak—mortality
> Weighs heavily on me like unwilling sleep,
> And each imagined pinnacle and steep
> Of godlike hardship tells me I must die
> Like a sick eagle looking at the sky.

(One thinks of Cortez' wondering eagle eyes.) Keats was to read and breathe the greatest poetry until he died. Once a young poet has truly looked into Chapman's Homer he can never look back.

A second observation about Keats' discovery may follow from the first. The instant he learned how to read, he also found the most characteristic theme and structure of his later poems: realizing a dream. "The Imagination may be compared to Adam's dream," according to a famous early letter, "—he awoke and found it truth." The final image of "Chapman's Homer" probably draws on a similar awakening. When the men of Cortez first saw the vast plain of Mexico, according to Robertson,

> the scene so far exceeded their imagination, that some believed the fanciful descriptions of romance were realized . . . others could hardly persuade themselves that this wonderful spectacle was any thing more than a dream. As they advanced, their doubts were removed, but their amazement increased. They were now fully satisfied that the country was rich beyond any conception which they had formed of it.

Their wild surmise had turned out, in fact, to be true. And Keats knew how to read such passages. Again and again his poems climax in that instant of waking, as the dream and reality, anticipation and fulfillment, become one—"solution sweet." Indeed, the poems themselves may be said to represent such instants, when the imagination finds a body and materializes in words. The end of "Chapman's Homer" proclaims not only "the real Homer is more wonderful than I had dreamed" but also "my dream is real; the poem is done." Keats has marked out the labor of his lifetime: to dream himself a great poet like Homer; to awake, and find it truth.

> Whether the dream now purposed to rehearse
> Be poet's or fanatic's will be known
> When this warm scribe my hand is in the grave.

Not all dreams come true, of course. Keats tests the validity of his dreams in many ways. A true poetic dream, as opposed to mere daydreaming or wish-fulfillment, may be recognized by its power to console men or pour "out a balm upon the world," as well as by the functional test of whether it can produce real poems. But perhaps the ultimate test is historical: a true dream will express the deepest meaning of its time. Hence Herschel had ushered in a new era of astronomy, and Cortez (or Balboa) had paved the way for the era of exploration and empire-building. They were the vanguard. And a poet proves his reality, similarly, by the way that his personal acts of discovery serve to advance the cause of mankind as a whole. His dreams speak for everyone. That is the substance of Keats' parable on the Chambers of Thought. Wordsworth, who has explored those chambers so profoundly, is a genius

> in so far as he can, more than we, make discoveries, and shed a light
> in them—Here I must think Wordsworth is deeper than Milton—though
> I think it has depended more upon the general and gregarious advance
> of intellect, than individual greatness of Mind—. . . It proves there is
> really a grand march of intellect—, It proves that a mighty providence
> subdues the mightiest Minds to the service of the time being.

A mighty poet gathers his strength by embodying the essential thought of his age.

From this point of view, what Keats had discovered in "Chapman's Homer" was not only his own theme but a theme that history itself had chosen: the translation of ancient myths and dreams into living psychological truth. On every side the myths were falling. Long ago Cortez had mapped and looted those fabulous realms of gold, and now philosophy had explained the rainbow away and emptied the haunted air. But the grand march of intellect had also probed the human heart and found there the sources of all myths. Now the time had come to perceive that the gods themselves had a human shape and beauty. Hyperion would yield to Apollo. When Keats heard Homer speak, he grasped in a moment the deepest project of his epoch (as he himself saw it): the metamorphosis of the gods from dreams to reality. All through Europe the best scholars and theologians were learning the lesson that poets had already intuitively grasped. The gods were one; they lived in the human brain. Thus Homer had spoken not about faded legends and superstitions but about realities that any sympathetic hearer could recreate in himself. Homer was real. Perceiving that, so personally and intensely, Keats suddenly joined the general advance of his time. At once he was a poet; he would no longer dream alone.

Few poets come of age so dramatically as Keats; few poets are so obsessed with working out their own poetic salvation. But the pattern we have seen in "Chapman's Homer" recurs again and again, I shall argue, in the careers of poets. Suddenly they learn how to read and how to use their reading; suddenly a vision of the poet they may become, an inexhaustible lifetime project, rises before them.

When Robert Frost, for instance, reread his best early poem, "The Tuft of Flowers," sixteen years later, something about its happy message and pretty language—" 'Men work together,' I told him from the heart, / 'Whether they work together or apart' "—must have struck him as facile. Perhaps nature was *not* so good at carrying messages and men did *not* communicate so well. In that case poetic language would also have to toughen, recording the jar of word against word and man against man. Frost's soliloquy changed to a debate. *North of Boston,* the book that resulted, opens with an explicit statement of intentions, on the page after the table of contents: "*Mending Wall* takes up the theme where *A Tuft of Flowers* in *A Boy's Will* laid it down." Returning to his starting place, Frost sees what no one else could have recognized, a secret story of the way that men are divided and communicate, if at all, only in easily misunderstood symbols. Voices clash against each other. "The Tuft of Flowers" turns into "Mending Wall," "The Mountain," and "The Fear." A harder, broken speech replaces the language of the flowers. And through that act of reinterpretation Frost becomes Frost. That is the way that a poet comes into his own: in constant recoil from his earlier themes, in constant grasping toward the familiar ghost—that face like his but deeply lined—the future poet who has achieved his greatness.

A similar vision also attracts most readers. Just as understanding a poem requires fitting its individual lines, feelings, images into a larger unity that includes them all, so understanding a great poet seems to require fitting his individual poems into the cumulative purpose—the career or destiny—that unites them. We perceive Keats as more than the sum of his poems. And so Keats perceived Homer. The poetic spirit who presides over "Chapman's Homer" is not associated with any specific poem or specific passage. He has grown so far away from his individuality that he speaks in a foreign tongue, in words we cannot hear. Yet the fading-away of the actual Homer, the movement from his own particular island to the fabulous realms of gold, only increases his glamor for a reader. The effect of "Chapman's Homer" entirely depends on our sense of Homer's greatness—a greatness unqualified by any need for quotation or justification. He is a planet, an ocean. To hear him is to change one's life. And most of us, even if we know no Greek and have not read Chapman, respond to the mention of Homer. His identity as a poet transcends the smaller questions of who he was and what he wrote. He lived first in his own imagination and eventually in ours. Hence Keats steers beyond the poems of Homer toward the greater Homer in his mind.

Perhaps no poet ever reaches his destination in the realms of gold. Perhaps no reader ever approaches nearer than to hear a momentary voice, draw in a momentary breath, without quite catching sight of the whole expanse. Yet the image of a fulfilled poetic destiny—the life of the poet—continues to lure both poet and reader. And sometimes that image seems very close. In their best moments most poets, like Keats, feel themselves speaking "from some character in whose soul I now live." To search out that character, the point at which a human life is transformed into a life of poetry, gives this book its own direction: where it begins, and where it hopes to end.

I

INITIATION

Books of New Life

Not long after William Butler Yeats had finished "Sailing to Byzantium," some spirit voices, speaking through a medium named Cooper, directed him to another special place: the bottom shelf of his study, third book from the right, page 48 or 84. The book turned out to be Blake's designs for Dante's *Comedy,* and the pages two images of Holy Fire. On Plate 48 the bite of a serpent sparks a fire that consumes Vanni Fucci, "a man of blood and rage," though immediately he will rise from his ashes like the phoenix. As Dante, Blake, and Yeats agree, the "temporal fire" is merely a delusion. Vanni Fucci, twisting like a Laocoon bowed down to mimic his creeping earthly oppressors—mere transparent worms, as drawn by Blake—turns to the left, away from the pent-up sun or true spiritual fire that could cure him. On Plate 84 (*Purgatorio* 27) an angel invites Dante to enter the wall of fire that surrounds Eden, the Earthly Paradise. Though encouraged by Statius and Virgil, Dante hesitates, clasping his hands, "gazing at the fire and strongly imagining bodies I once saw burned." Meanwhile the angel, placed by the text outside the flames but by Blake within, sings *"Beati mundo corde"*: "blessed are the pure in heart," but here, more accurately, "the refined in spirit." At length the thought of Beatrice's eyes will make the pilgrim risk the fire. In Blake's drawing, the tremendous vertical thrust of aspiration is balanced by a horizontal block of waters capped by a setting sun. As Dante has noted at the beginning of the canto, the spiritual fire is partly obscured in this earthly kingdom; yet in another kingdom, on the other side of the earth—Jerusalem, where the Maker of the sun shed His blood—it has just begun to rise.

Dante and Blake had spoken for the spirit. But for Yeats the crucial matter—the insight that made him shake with excitement—was not his reading of other poets but his sudden knowledge that their designs supplied a key to "Sailing to Byzantium." In the sensual blood and rage of Vanni Fucci, reduced to a caricature of a dying animal by his shortsighted entrapment in the world that is begotten, born, and dies, Yeats recognized his own torture in "that country." In the angel who stands amid the fire, whose singing instructs the pilgrim to be consumed, he recognized those "sages standing in God's holy fire," those "singing-masters" of his soul, to whom he prayed to be gathered "Into the artifice of eternity." Yet most of all he realized that the two plates, whose numbers mirrored each other, were mirror images of a single action. "Certainly," he wrote Olivia Shakespear, "the knowledge was not in my head." Yet how well "it puts my own mood between spiritual excitement, and the sexual torture and the knowledge that they are somehow inseparable!" Sexual torture and spiritual excitement—Vanni Fucci's hot blood and Dante's yearning for Beatrice—are seen by Yeats as one: the old man's rage at his body, the old man's passage through fire and time to be reborn in Eden.

Yeats had been sent a message. A few hours before looking at the plates, he told Mrs. Shakespear, he had revised his early lyric, "A Dream of a Blessed Spirit," into a vision of "The Countess Cathleen in Paradise," immersed in holy fire. "Bathed in flaming founts of duty," she stands amid the angels of heaven, "Flame on flame and wing on wing." An amazing anticipation of Plate 84! "After this and all that has gone before I must capitulate if the dark mind lets me." Was Yeats tinkering a little with the sequence of events? Was it Cooper or his own memory that sent him to that special place, that special book? It does not matter. Whether the images floated up out of Anima Hominis or Anima Mundi, Yeats was right to conclude that Dante and Blake, "his people," had sent him "Sailing to Byzantium."

Indeed, a further clue exists. A passage in Yeats' early essay on "William Blake and his Illustrations to the *Divine Comedy*"—an essay he had carefully reread as recently as 1924—shows just how far his vision of the world of Blake anticipates the poem.

> The kingdom that was passing was, he held, the kingdom of the Tree of Knowledge; the kingdom that was coming was the kingdom of the Tree of Life: men who ate from the Tree of Knowledge wasted their days in anger against one another, and in taking one another captive in great nets; men who sought their food among the green leaves of the Tree of Life condemned none but the unimaginative and the idle, and those who forget that even love and death and old age are an imaginative art.

In the contrast of these two kingdoms—one passing, one to come; each sustained by its own tree; one inhabited by the unimaginative and idle, men who waste their days in anger and sensual captivity; the other, by men who know that love and death and old age are an imaginative art, since "True art is the flame of the Last Day, which begins for every man when he is first moved by beauty, and which seeks to burn all things until they become 'infinite and holy' "—Yeats speaks with the voices of Dante and Blake to prophesy a poem. But almost thirty years would have to pass before he learned what his own words meant: the coordinates of "Sailing to Byzantium." For Yeats, like most creative artists, goes on a circular voyage. His excitement begins when the poem he discovers in a flash of critical insight is his own.

That voyage has been repeated often. A poet who wishes to grow must learn to read his own early work, to explore its secret life and hidden meanings. Even apprentice work often contains some gist of everything to come—if the right eye sees it. The only singing-school, as Yeats would have it, studies monuments of its own magnificence; poetry itself is the source of poetry, poems beget poems. And many poets devote their lives to reinterpreting a few images or phrases, deepening and enriching their significance with each new line they write. Nor is such concentration the sign of any imaginative inertia. Dante, successively unfolding the meaning of Beatrice until her final incarnation leads him to Paradise; Blake, dwelling upon the beauty of innocence until it reveals that love of the created world is death; Yeats, worshiping the mask of a cold goddess who appears now as Beauty, now as Ireland, finally as a woman of flesh—each makes a whole and satisfying poetic world by redeeming the first sources of his inspiration. "In my beginning is my end." Yet a poet who can write such words must first have learned where he began.

How does a poet read his work? Many clues are available, ranging from the manifestos (like Whitman's introduction to *Leaves of Grass*) that preface so many new poetic departures, through direct formal explications of a text (like San Juan de la Cruz' exhaustive commentaries on his "Dark Night"), through informal notes and clarifications (like Rilke's and Stevens' invaluable letters to their translators), to the revisions and corrections of a text that reveal the poet's most fundamental self-criticism. Perhaps the most remarkable of all such expositions, however, occurs in a kind of work that has hardly been recognized, much less classified—a kind of work in which the poet not only expounds his poems but teaches us his methods of reading. Such combinations of poetry and criticism appear in many languages and forms, from Greek to Bengali, from the Arabic *adab* to the Japanese poetic diary, and they are also related to works of fiction (like *The Tale of Genji, Tom Jones,* or *Doktor Faustus*) that draw attention to their own principles of composition. But no examples of the kind are more instructive than some books by those poets we have already met, those poets who pass their work through a refining fire: Dante, Blake, and Yeats.

La Vita Nuova, The Marriage of Heaven and Hell, Per Amica Silentia Lunae agree in one respect at least: critics have never known quite what to make of them. Few works resist definition with such ferocity. Indeed, the bafflement they tend to arouse in students, despite thousands of pages of criticism, is made still deeper by the peculiar genres to which they are supposed to belong. We are told, by very good critics, that *La Vita Nuova* is a "Book of Memory," a set of transcribed reminiscences from a mental scroll, or perhaps an apocalyptic "Book of Revelation"; that *The Marriage of Heaven and Hell* is a *principia,* or else a Menippean satire or *anatomy*—the same form, by a happy coincidence, as *Anatomy of Criticism;* that *Per Amica Silentia Lunae* is an *alphabet,* to use Yeats' own word, or perhaps a "marmoreal reverie." Cumulatively these definitions seem to me very judicious, like the Brobdingnagians' famous decision that Gulliver was a *lusus naturae.* They do not conceal, at any rate, that each work is somehow anomalous, somehow unique.

Unfortunately, such definitions do not reveal much of the work either. Most of them attempt to make sense of a protean form by rooting it in a tradition whose methods of signification can be taken for granted. They read the surface of the work as if its meaning, or its ways of meaning, had already been determined. Yet such works cannot be grasped by the surface; they burn surfaces away and force us to look within. None of the three works can be understood—and each of them at times has been sensationally misunderstood—without a search for principles of interpretation. Interpretation constitutes the essence of each work, its subject and justification. Here if anywhere form adapts itself to meaning. Each work shifts its narrative focus, and even slides from poetry into prose, to accommodate the new truth it finds in every successive instant of revelation. And the reader who would make sense of the book must allow himself to be instructed by it in how to read.

Indeed, so vital is this process of interpretive discovery, the dawn that awakens a whole new world of meanings, that all three works might be called, as Dante's is called, *Books of New Life.* Nor would the religious connotations of such a name be inappropriate (though *vita nuova* in Italian, we should remember, primarily means "youth"). A more precise term for the kind, however, must take account not only of its sense of a beginning but of the ceremony or rite of instruction it performs. Let me christen it The Initiation. The double sense of "initiation"—the starting-out, the gathering-in—accounts for the inner life of many literary works. Dante, Blake, and Yeats, like Goethe in *Wilhelm Meister* or Joyce in his *Portrait,* submit themselves to rituals of initiation. First they undergo a trial by fire where understanding is refined; then they pass to a stage of higher knowledge where past experience will be radically reinterpreted. *La Vita Nuova, The Marriage of Heaven and Hell,* and *Per Amica Silentia Lunae,* as well as many other initiations, draw upon this pattern. And for all their superficial differences, there is much else that they share.

They share, most obviously of all, an extraordinary mixture of verse and prose. In each case part of the work consists of an imaginative vision, often challenging and obscure, and part of prose commentary, often rather direct and explicit. *La Vita Nuova* is a collection of poems (thirty-one in all), each broken down analytically into its literal meaning and further elucidated by a narrative that supplies both an autobiographical context and a tissue of higher, allegorical levels of meaning. *The Marriage of Heaven and Hell* is prefaced by a verse "Argument," explicated to some extent, in the following plate, in prose. Subsequently its poetic proverbs and "memorable fancies" alternate with sections of relatively straightforward exposition; and the book returns to verse at the end, with "A Song of Liberty" that imaginatively gathers together much of what Blake has said. "Ego Dominus Tuus," whose title Yeats drew from *Vita Nuova* 3, stands at the head of *Per Amica Silentia Lunae*. The next part of the book, "Anima Hominis," is an extended "reading" of the poem, progressively unfolding and meditating upon its images; the last part, "Anima Mundi," meditates in turn upon the relation of those images to "the general mind." Formally, the mixture of verse and prose gives each work its character. However disconcerting such hybrids may seem at first—Boccaccio and Rossetti, for instance, both objected to Dante's prose divisions of his poems, and Coleridge remarks the incongruity of the form, like "jewels in a crown of lead or iron"—in these three books they come to seem inevitable. Verse and commentary, reflecting each other, bear the argument between them; none of the works would be conceivable without the interplay of its two modes of discourse. Indeed, one might well argue that Dante, Blake, and Yeats never wrote books more elegant or unified than these.

That unity is fundamental; for every initiation, however small and problematical, comes in the end emphatically to one thing: a book. The very notion of a book—its textual authority, its coherence, even its physical appearance—furnishes each author with his structural design. The poet collects the fragments of his work into a greater whole. Thus the controlling metaphor of *La Vita Nuova,* according to Charles Singleton, is the scribe, who copies out a manuscript from the more random book of memories that lies open before him. Blake's "copying" goes much further: he supervises the making of *The Marriage of Heaven and Hell* at every stage, from the first vision through the process of etching and printing (described on Plate 15), until at last he binds it together, a book to reimagine the bibles of the past and transmit them to future generations. Yeats, who like Blake always aimed to compose books rather than individual poems, took special pains with *Per Amica Silentia Lunae*. The prologue and epilogue to "Maurice," both dated May 11, 1917, suggest that the book has run through a round, like Yeats' thoughts; and for the cover he persuaded Sturge Moore to design a Rose, emblem not only of Intellectual Beauty but of the natural and supernatural folded together in unity of being (or "the transmutation of life into art"). A similar image, small but perfect, might stand before each of the books. Within its little space each contains whole libraries, the microcosm of an infinitely grander creation. Blake's *Marriage* stakes this microcosmic claim most strongly; a parody bible, complete with proverbs and commandments, it offers a complete sacred code in fiercely concentrated form.

Sacred codes, however, need priests to interpret them. Perhaps the center of each initiation, that on which all the rest depends, is its effort to initiate the reader into its own way of meaning. The poems each book contains cannot be understood by ordinary methods, ordinary acts of attention. Rather, the reader must enter the book as if it were an antechamber to certain mysteries, a place where secret ceremonies of reading will be taught. Like the lovers in *The Magic Flute* (another strange mixture of poetry and prose), someone who undergoes this rite of passage is promised a new mode of seeing. Dante offers his reader infallible truth in the guise of love, Blake cleanses the doors of perception with corrosive vision, Yeats invites us to visit the haunts of the dead. The way is prepared by the author himself, our cicerone and mentor, who unravels the secrets of his own dark texts with loving and explicit prose. If successful, therefore, each book will effect a conversion or, rather, will usher the reader into a state of hermeneutic maturity where he sees all texts plain. Northrop Frye has commented on more than one occasion that "learning to read Blake was a step, and for me a necessary step, in learning to read poetry, and to write criticism." Every initiation, given a proper reader, is capable of achieving the same result. Helpfully, insistently, it tells us to open our eyes and change our lives.

But the true initiate, in every case, must be the poet himself. Dante, Blake, and Yeats do not transmit a knowledge they have already learned and codified. Instead their books of initiation crackle with the excitement of new readings that unfold before them. Familiar lines and images, as when a cloud passes from before the sun, are suddenly transfused by strange clear light. The poet becomes his own master.

In almost all initiations, moreover, the excitement derives from the same source: the poet realizes that his own personal history, reflected in his poems, coincides with the universal spiritual history of mankind. This dramatic insight, in the *Vita Nuova,* prompts Dante to arrange and interpret his poems in a narrative sequence that proves Beatrice to have been the emissary of Christ on earth. Blake, similarly, in his own thirty-third year, also the thirty-third year since Swedenborg had announced the advent of the New Jerusalem, writes a last judgment or universal history to fit the revolutionary needs of modern times. And Yeats, abandoning his mind to dreams, discovers there the shape of a Great Memory or Anima Mundi, a tradition more ancient and universal than the Church. Such insights, in the first flush of recognition, seem to confer on the poet some of the creative energy of a prophet.

They also put the poet back in phase. The act of initiation restores not only poetry but the pattern of history itself. In the moment before his transformation, each poet has seemed to be living in a backwater, a province or enclave that time has forgotten. What has history to do with Florence, that low dishonest city in a vulgar century when language itself has fallen from immortal Latin to a Babel of dialects? Who can redeem the curse of London, the very breeding ground of that materialistic philosophy and those dark Satanic mills that cast their shadows over the future of the world? How can the juggernaut of modern times be stalled for even an instant by the most backward country in Europe, a land that drives its own best hopes to the grave—"Romantic Ireland's dead and gone"? History passes by such places, and the poets who live there are doomed to a hollow in time. Yet all at once, in the rush of initiation, the situation reverses. Florence, London, Dublin turn into prototypes of Jerusalem and Rome: the central stage where history plays itself out. Even the warfare that threatens each city becomes an emblem of the great eternal war—a conflict between secular and spiritual forces—whose victor will rule the world. The initiated poet inhabits the focal point of all civilization. Making sense of history at last, he sees into the future.

Indeed, the most remarkable single trait initiations share is that each ends with a prophecy of greater works to come. "The sun is but a morning star." At the close of *La Vita Nuova,* Dante announces a marvelous vision that has determined him to write of Beatrice "that which has never before been written of any woman"—a prediction, most scholars agree, of the *Commedia*. Blake, not hesitant to prophesy, speaks of reading the Bible "in its infernal or diabolical sense which the world shall have if they behave well," and adds, "I have also: The Bible of Hell: which the world shall have whether they will or no." This promise, or threat, can be interpreted in different ways. Possibly the Bible of Hell is the *Marriage* itself, which the world must have because the world already holds it in its hand; possibly Blake refers to work in progress. In any case, the reference to a future infernal Bible clearly sights to Blake's greater prophecies, where the interpretive techniques developed in the *Marriage* will reach their apotheosis. Yeats' predictions in *Per Amica* are far more tentative. At times he suggests that he may become a medium for the *Anima Mundi,* his will to poetry replaced by "some kind of simple piety like that of an old woman." But the spectral voices themselves gave him an answer. In October, 1917, Yeats' new wife began to transcribe messages from an unknown writer, who took his theme from the just-published *Per Amica*. When the poet offered to

19

devote his life to piecing those sentences together, he received a famous reply: "No, we have come to give you metaphors for poetry." The prophetic strain he had discovered in *Per Amica* turned out to be poetry after all. "Sometimes," Yeats wrote more than a decade later, in the Introduction to *A Vision*, "when my mind strays back to those first days I remember that Browning's Paracelsus did not obtain the secret until he had written his spiritual history at the bidding of his Byzantine teacher, that before initiation Wilhelm Meister read his own history written by another, and I compare my *Per Amica* to those histories." After initiation new poems would come.

The ascension to a new phase, therefore, justifies the initiation and makes its claims ring true. Strictly speaking, every work in the form must issue in a greater work, proving that its mastery of interpretation can be turned to account. Dante's prediction of the *Commedia* would be less impressive, at any rate, had he not gone on to write it. (Similarly, Joyce's *Portrait of the Artist*, with all its Dantesque ambition to forge the conscience of a race, requires *Ulysses* to complete the artist's prophecy.) But no work of art can depend wholly on its successor; the best authors, like the best prophets, anticipate all time to come, not only their personal, immediate future. More simply, we might say that every initiation not only describes and prepares but *is* the way to a higher art. Dante's glorification of Beatrice, Blake's anglicized bibles, Yeats' occult vision are all adumbrated—some critics would say fulfilled—in the early books themselves. At the moment of initiation, when the poet learns freshly to read himself and shares his vision with the reader, a stage has been completed. The new mode of understanding receives its purest, most crystalline expression. Indeed, such a moment of rest may never come again, precisely because the complication and articulation of the vision, which will require such monumental and exhausting effort, have yet to descend. The initiation, like every accomplished work, sets the terms of its own success. If we want to comprehend the new life that it holds out to us, we need only pay attention to what passes before our eyes. But first we must be willing to learn how to read.

La Vita Nuova

La Vita Nuova, as the Victorians used to say, is a book about growing up— first love, first sorrow. But the trials of youth are not Dante's main concern, any more than mid-life crisis—the doubts that assail a man who has reached the middle of his journey—accounts for the concerns of the *Commedia*. What grows in both works, rather, is Dante's understanding. Above all, in the little book of memory, he comes to understand the way that poetry can be transformed by love. Poetry stands at the center. Even Love, personified and dressed in various literary guises, appears only by poetic license. In Chapter xxv, Dante admits that he has spoken of love as if "He" were a substance rather than "an accident in a substance," and justifies this philosophical error by citing the authority of the Latin poets: "Therefore, if we see that those poets have spoken to inanimate things, as if they had sense and reason, and made them speak to each other, . . . then it is fitting for a vernacular poet to make them do the same." The rules of verse take precedence over the accidents of life. Nor does Dante tell us more about his life than interpretation of his verse requires. Philosophical and biographical truth must submit to the kind of truth that poems embody. It is there, in poems, that the new life manifests itself. And the subject of *La Vita Nuova* is Dante's growth as a poet, a growth that occurs before our eyes until at last, as poet and reader, he comes magnificently of age.

The collection of poems, however, would tell no story at all were it not for the commentary that encloses them: Dante's *ragione* (reasons). In the web of explanations and reasons for writing, the book acquires its meaning. Indeed, the originality of *La Vita Nuova* consists less in its verse (much of which clearly pays tribute to Dante's mentors Guinizelli and Cavalcanti) than in its decision to group the poems in a significant order and to explain the nature of that significance. Such exegesis seems especially daring to Dante himself because it is lavished on Italian verses, conferring on the vernacular a Latin dignity. The point weighs so heavily with him that Latin is reserved for several of the crucial moments of the book, among them its own christening: *"incipit vita nova"*; and Love talks the same high language. Yet Dante courageously employs his "vulgar" tongue to convey sacred and eternal meanings.

The order of daring here is precisely the same as that required to "translate" Beatrice into a type of Christ. Did Dante's poems really mean at first writing what the *Vita Nuova* now says they mean? The question scarcely differs from the old critical perplexity about whether Beatrice was a real woman. The world assumes its reality, from the poet's point of view, only when we begin to understand the reasons for which God created it. Like the history of the Jews, in medieval terms, the original pales into insignificance beside the light of its interpretation. *La Vita Nuova* deals not with the world of what is begotten, born, and dies but with the world of what is past, or passing, or to come. All times are fixed by it in a significant, permanent relation, as changeless as the number nine. Its story, a tangle of incidents, verses, and speculations, is suddenly gathered into a perfect circle by Dante's interpretive logic. To the initiate, at the instant of initiation everything becomes clear.

The first sonnet of *La Vita Nuova,* "A ciascun'alma presa e gentil core," is a particularly fine example of the way that the act of interpretation transforms whatever it touches. It begins, in fact, by asking the reader his opinion of its meaning.

> A ciascun'alma presa e gentil core
>> Nel cui cospetto ven lo dir presente,
>> In ciò che mi rescrivan suo parvente,
>> Salute in lor segnor, cioè Amore.
>> Già eran quasi che atterzate l'ore
>> Del tempo che onne stella n'è lucente,
>> Quando m'apparve Amor subitamente,
>> Cui essenza membrar mi dà orrore.
> Allegro mi sembrava Amor tenendo
>> Meo core in mano, e ne le braccia avea
>> Madonna involta in un drappo dormendo.
>> Poi la svegliava, e d'esto core ardendo
>> Lei paventosa umilmente pascea:
>> Appresso gir lo ne vedea piangendo.

> [iii. 10–12]

> (To every captive soul and gentle heart
>> Into whose sight these present words may come,
>> That each may answer me with his surmise,
>> I send a greeting in their lord, who is Love.
>> Almost a third part of the hours had passed
>> Of that time when every star is shining on us,
>> When Love appeared before me suddenly,
>> The memory of whose being fills me with horror.
> Merry Love seemed to me, holding
>> My heart in his hand, and in his arms
>> Had wound a wrap about my lady, sleeping.
>> Then he awoke her, and that burning heart
>> To her affrighted, did he humbly feed.
>> Afterwards he passed from vision, weeping.)

What does it all mean? To its first readers such a poem must have seemed little more than a riddle, a sort of scholastic exercise. When the eighteen-year-old Dante finished it, in fact, he also was puzzled. Ingeniously, he sent copies to many famous poets (those gentle captives of love), requesting "opinions" *(parvente)*. An "opinion," in such a context, has a variety of connotations: the scholastic or legalistic adjudication of his "case," or dream; professional judgment on his poetic talents; or, most directly, the criticism appropriate to poets, an answering poem. Three answers (which Dante calls *sentenzie,* opinions or verdicts) have been preserved; the best known, by Guido Cavalcanti, began their friendship, which was to prove so close and fruitful. Nor could an apprentice poet have hoped for a better result. His riddle had won him a place in the company of poets and launched his career.

Taken by itself the sonnet would remain a mystery. Perhaps the "opinion" of Dante da Maiano still speaks for many readers: "all I understand, believe me, is that you were raving." Dante compresses Love's visit into eight vivid lines, more notable for sudden shifts in emotion (horror, joy, fear, sorrow) than explanations. Like a piece of music, the verse moves from allegro to piangendo without pausing for thought. Evidently we must take seriously Dante's contention that the poem describes a dream; and when he tells us that "the true meaning [giudicio, a legal judgment or opinion] of the dream I have spoken was not seen then by anyone," there is no reason to believe that he excludes himself. Inscrutability, the enigma that surrounds every nocturnal visit from a god, is part of the charm of the sonnet. Only the god himself could know why he came, was merry, wept. Though Dante plays with the stock devices of love poetry, he expresses more horror than love. Are we to conclude, because Love wraps the madonna in a cloth and departs weeping, that the dream secretly recounts the death of a lady? Cavalcanti's adroit reply-sonnet ("It seems to me that you beheld all value") explains Love's actions by postulating that "your lady was sinking to death." But speculations can find little internal evidence on which to work.

Indeed, one might well argue that the poem describes a closed circle, whose uncanny images merely reiterate the opening challenge to poets in order to confound them. The vision turns verbal clichés into pictures. Seen this way, the sonnet appears little more than an amplification or literalization of its first quatrain. Love comes to rule Dante in his dream because, as we already know, Love is the lord of poets; the captive soul and gentle heart of poets, referred to in the first line, become alarmingly literal in the dream; Love feeds the poet's heart to his lady, reenacting the making of every poem of love; poetry, as always, tries in vain to interpret the unearthly emotions that Love inspires in his servants. And when his vision ends, the poet like his readers is left in the dark.

More than ten years later, however, when Dante chose this sonnet to begin La Vita Nuova, everything had changed. Now, he tells us, its meaning is perfectly obvious (manifestissimo) to the simplest reader. The source of change, clearly, was La Vita Nuova itself. In Chapter iii Dante wraps the poem in a long and loving commentary, throwing radically new light on many of its details. We learn that the lady in the dream was Beatrice, who earlier that day had greeted Dante for the first time, overwhelming him with bliss—when Dante, in the poem, "salutes" his fellow lovers and poets, he is passing on the memory of that greeting. We learn that nine years had passed since Beatrice's first appearance and that she greeted Dante in the ninth hour of the day (3 P. M.)—the curious reference to time in the sonnet (lines 5 and 6) establishes that the dream occurred in "the first of the last nine hours of the night." We learn that Love came in a cloud like fire and that "he said many things, of which I understood only a few; among which I understood these: *Ego dominus tuus*" (I am thy Lord)—Dante consecrates his life to love, though he still has much to understand. Finally, we are given a much fuller version of the end of the dream: weeping, Love "gathered the lady in his arms, and together it seemed to me they went toward heaven," whereupon Dante woke in anguish. From the beginning of *La Vita Nuova* (ii. 1) we have known that Beatrice, *at present,* is dead, glorified. Superimposed on the poem, this knowledge suggests an interpretation that less privileged readers could never have conceived: the dream prophesies the death of Beatrice and the course of *La Vita Nuova*—ten years before the book was written.

Indeed, the true meaning of the sonnet, and of the other early poems Dante collects, depends absolutely on what the poet now makes of them. *La Vita Nuova* does not remark any disparity between what the poems might once have meant and what they now mean in their bold new context. Rather, it follows the critical principles laid down by Dante elsewhere (most notably in the *Convivio* and the letter to Can Grande): writings should be expounded in multiple (fourfold) senses or levels of meaning, and each part of a work may best be understood by reference to the work as a whole. A firm grasp of these principles of exegesis, the ability to go deeper and deeper in interpretation, distinguishes the poet from the mere rhymer. Dante makes this point explicitly at the end of the longest critical passage in *La Vita Nuova* (xxv. 10): "it would be a great shame for someone to make rhymes garbed in figures or rhetorical colors and then, when asked, not know how to divest his words of such garb in such a way as to disclose their true intention. And my best friend and I know well some people who make rhymes so stupidly." Far from compromising his first inspiration, Dante's second thoughts and laborious explanations prove him a poet.

If difficult and unlikely interpretations are the mark of poetic depth, then the author of *La Vita Nuova* is certainly a very great poet. Few works require a more subtle, more inferential reading. Nor do most critics of the book accept that other critics understand it. But the difficulty of interpretation is not incidental but functional. For the reader it provides a test of mind and heart; only those who are worthy will receive Dante's salute—a word that means both greeting and salvation—of initiation. For the work itself it provides a center where two themes meet: the secret order that rules our lives, and the secret messages we can expound in dreams or poems. The world and the *Vita Nuova* alike, Dante suggests, depend on penetralia, the sweet revelations hidden at the root of things. The Creator has folded his meanings, layer on layer, into the book we live within. To delve into such mysteries is why we were made, and why the poet makes his own secondary creation.

Fortunately, however, the same hand that concealed the penetralia in things has sent guides to reveal them. As Dante guides the reader, so is Dante guided by Love and Beatrice. The story of *La Vita Nuova* (as of the *Commedia*) traces a journey toward understanding, a series of ascents. It is this story, not the story of Beatrice or even of Dante's love for her, that motivates the book. Consider, for instance, the great cataclysm of *La Vita Nuova*, Beatrice's death. To a modern reader this section usually proves the most shocking of the book—not because of what happens but because of Dante's reaction. He does not describe the death itself, for the surprising reason that it does not belong to the present subject *(proposito)*. Nor does he recount, for the moment, his grief. Rather, he launches into a long passage "that fits the subject," an explanation of why, at so many points, Beatrice has been associated with the number nine. And the best answer, the answer to which he comes through deep thought and infallible truth, is that "this number was her very self" *(questo numero fue ella medesima)*. Since the root of nine is three, Father, Son, and Holy Ghost, "this lady was accompanied by this number nine to disclose that she was a nine, that is a miracle, whose root . . . is solely the marvelous Trinity" (xxix. 3). (Incidentally, the key sentence of this section, "questo numero fue ella me- desima," contains exactly twenty-seven letters, Beatrice multiplied by three.) The miracle at the core of *La Vita Nuova* is a matter of interpretation. Dante defines his subject, in Chapter i, not as his memories but as their *sentenzia* (meaning, substance). That is where Beatrice lives, in her meaning: the root of blessedness, the number nine.

Even with the help of revelation, such meanings come only to those who labor for them. Love does not speak plain language to his votaries. Indeed, each of his appearances in *La Vita Nuova* poses a fresh series of puzzles. If Dante understands only a few words of that first nocturnal visit, repeated acquaintance leaves him little better off. In Chapter xii, for example, he asks his Lord why he is weeping.

> And he spoke these words to me: *Ego tanquam centrum circuli, cui simili modo se habent circumferentie partes; tu autem non sic* [I am as the center of a circle, to which the parts of the circumference have an equal relation; but thou art not so]. Then, thinking about his words, it seemed to me that he had spoken very obscurely, so that I gathered myself to speak, and said these words: "What is it, Lord, that you speak to me with such obscurity?" And he said this to me in vernacular words: "Do not ask more than is useful to you."
>
> [xii. 4–5]

The speech in Latin, one of the great cruxes in Dante studies, has perplexed later readers as much as the poet. Presumably Love reproaches Dante for his eccentricity as a lover; and it is possible that the god, seeing past and future as well as present (like that other, threefold Lord who lives within a circle), foresees and mourns the death of Beatrice, unknown to mortals. In context, however, the exchange seems almost comic with mystification: Dante knows so little, his Lord and the later Dante (author of the *Vita Nuova*) so much. The point is reinforced by the way that Love condescends to shift to Italian, a vulgar tongue for vulgar ears, instead of continuing in oracular Latin. At this stage the protagonist of the *Vita Nuova* can only grasp helplessly at meanings that elude him. But the time will come when the servant of Love will turn into a master and realize love's teachings in himself.

As the story proceeds, in fact, Dante grows progressively more skillful as an interpreter of love. His skill is recognized, within *La Vita Nuova,* by ladies who consult him with sophisticated questions about love and by men who commission poems from him. The famous *canzone* "Donne ch'avete intelletto d'amore" ("Ladies who have intelligence of love") displays his full mastery both as an expert and poet of love; if courage did not fail, he tells us, the strength of love in him would enable him to enamor everyone *(Farei parlando innamorar la gente).* Indeed, such knowledge is almost too great to bear—in his division of the poem, Dante fears that he has communicated its meaning to too many. Expertise like this can be achieved only by someone who has internalized Love, viewing him no longer as a strange and unintelligible god but as an emotion that lives in noble hearts. The *canzone* itself presents an extended play on these two notions of love. The ladies have "intelligence" (understanding or inner tidings) of love because their sensitive feelings hold him within. Therefore they are asked to listen to praise of Beatrice, in whose face a radiant Love is depicted, and to assist the poem, Dante's envoy, to reach its destination, where Love and Beatrice dwell. The unloving vulgar herd could never find the way. The personified god Love speaks at the beginning of stanza 4, but the question he asks—"Cosa mortale / come esser pò sì adorna e sì pura?" ("How can a mortal thing be capable of being so beautiful and so pure?")—ironically reveals her possession of love to be more pure than his. Issuing forth from her eyes and face, the insubstantial god falls under the sway of internal love, "an accident in a substance." And Dante's readers understood the distinction. When the *canzone* had circulated, we learn in Chapter xx, a friend "was moved to ask me to write what Love is, having perhaps, because of hearing my words, higher hopes of me than were my due." The sonnet with which Dante answered him puts love firmly in its place: "Amore e 'l cor gentil sono una cosa" ("Love and the gentle heart are but one thing").

The mastery displayed by Dante here, however, pertains above all to poetic style. In questions of love all true knowledge belongs to poets. The line that follows "Love and the gentle heart are but one thing" is "Just as the wise one puts it in his verse"; and "the wise one" *(il saggio)* refers to the poet Guinizelli, whose famous *canzone,* "Al cor gentil ripara sempre

Amore," helped to teach Dante the ways of love and verse at once. Possessed of a gentle, intelligent heart, the poet is transformed into a sage; his verses rule over scruples of love with all the finesse of a philosopher-king. Nor is Dante too modest to number himself among such wise ones. He too has mastered the sweet new style; he too has prisoned love within his heart. In a celebrated passage of the *Purgatorio*, Canto XXIV, Bonagiunta da Lucca, a versifier of an older school, greets Dante with fine professional respect. " 'Tell me if I see here him who brought forth the new rhyme, beginning "Ladies who have intelligence of love." ' And I to him: 'I indeed am one who, when Love inspires me [*mi spira*, breathes in me], takes note, and of that way he speaks within gives outward sign.' " And Bonagiunta realizes at once that he and his fellows fell short of the *dolce stil nuovo* because they had not learned this method, to draw love into themselves and let him speak through them. Not without pride, Dante marks here his own ascent to new poetic heights. Approaching the center of *La Vita Nuova*, in the *canzone* that made him famous, he demonstrates by precept and example that he has been initiated. At last he knows what it means to be a poet.

A poet does not reach such heights without the aid of friends. Just as Dante could not have scaled the Purgatorial mount but for his mentor Virgil, so the path to the *dolce stil nuovo* had been made smooth, in *La Vita Nuova*, by Guido Cavalcanti. It was Cavalcanti, in his own brilliant series of vernacular lyrics, who had perfected the new style, and his advice and counsel permeate the book of Dante's new life. Replying to the first sonnet that Dante had chosen to send abroad, he saw into it so deeply (perhaps more deeply, at that time, than the author) that he became the poet's best friend. Subsequently, we are told, he served Dante as teacher, confidant, and poetic crony. And we learn at last, in Chapter xxx of *La Vita Nuova*, that "my best friend, for whom I write this book, would have me write it for him solely in the vernacular." If Love and Beatrice inspire the spiritual substance of Dante's book, the only begetter of its poetic style is Cavalcanti.

Just as Virgil must be put aside before the summit of Purgatory, however, consigning Dante's further progress to his own strong will—"io te sovra te corona e mitrio" ("over thyself I crown and miter thee")—so Dante, in the course of *La Vita Nuova*, mounts beyond Guido's sphere. The break, though subtle, is sharp and dramatic. In Chapter xxiv Dante records some verses written, he says, for his best friend. The sonnet itself seems rather innocuous: an amorous spirit, Love, awakens in the poet's heart and heralds the approach of two ladies, Vanna and Bice—nicknames for Giovanna, presumably the lady who inspires Guido, and for Beatrice. One marvel comes after another! Love ends the poem with an appropriate compliment: "Quell'è Primavera, / E quell'ha nome Amor, sì mi somiglia" ("This one is Spring, / And this one has the name Love, resembling me"). The tone is jocular, and the point of the sonnet appears mainly its celebration of

pertinent question. " 'If you go through this blind prison through height of genius [*ingegno*], where is my son? why is he not with you?' And I to him: 'I do not come by myself: he who waits there [Virgil] leads me through here, perhaps to the one your Guido held in disdain.' " It is not by superior genius, Dante suggests, that he has surpassed Guido, in this present *Comedy;* it is by superior companions, and especially by virtue of that high lady to whom he aspires. From the lady Primavera one can learn a sweet new style, a style with some of the freshness and simplicity of spring. But the lady Beatrice, whom Guido disdained, is named Love. She dwells not on earth but in heaven; and from her one learns a higher style, a style that leads the poet toward the one True Light.

After Chapter xxiv the style of *La Vita Nuova* begins to change. Chapter xxv (as mentioned above) offers a long critical defense of Dante's way of personifying Love, which justifies His bodily attributes by claiming the same poetic license for vernacular verses as for the classics. Yet the poet's defensiveness should call attention to his resolve to reform. In the remainder of the book Love gradually ceases to be personified. He no longer appears to Dante in the guise of a young man or a lord of terrible aspect. Rather, he lives in Dante's heart and thoughts of Beatrice. At the same time the poet begins to inspect the conventions of love poetry that he had inherited and richly used: the delirious dreams, the thinly disguised sexual longings, the screen ladies. In Chapter xii, Love (a young man dressed in white) had told Dante, *"Fili mi, tempus est ut pretermictantur simulacra nostra"* ("My son, it is time to cast off our simulacra"). Simulacra, false images or phantoms, mean above all the screens through whom Dante had dissembled his love, guarding his devotion to his true lady by pretending to be in thrall to others. Yet by the end of *La Vita Nuova* Love has himself become a simulacrum. He too must be cast aside.

The casting-off of such false images does not come easily to Dante. From the beginning, as in the conundrum of sonnet 1, he had associated poetry itself with screens. The process of initiation requires a different view of poetry: no longer fabricating screens but seeing through them. Chapters xxxv–xxxviii of *La Vita Nuova,* the episode of the *donna gentile,* pose a remarkable test of how well he has learned his lesson. For the *donna gentile* is an epitome of simulacra. Her phantom charm is so sympathetic to the heart of the poet that she attracts to herself all the themes that most obsess him: Love, the tears of self-pity, poetry, and even Beatrice. Thus, on her first appearance, she vibrates so to Dante's grief that he concludes that Love—the capitalized *Amore*—must dwell with her. In the next section (xxxvi) his apostasy becomes still more astonishing, when the pale, compassionate face of the lady, the "color of love" according to his sonnet, reminds him of Beatrice's similar color. Here the *donna gentile* has indeed cast her shadow over the poet's eyes; though the prominence of the word "color," with its suggestion of mere rhetorical figures, may remind us that the lady and the love she represents are only phantoms of a greater love. The following chapter (xxxvii) confirms that Dante can no longer trust his eyes, which search out the gaze of the *donna gentile* when they should be weeping. Finally, in Chapter xxxviii, the desires of the heart wage a full debate against the reason of the soul. All Dante's love of simulacra asserts itself against his better knowledge that such false images are base.

Yet the charms of Love prove strong. Reason would not triumph over its adversary without an intervention from above. Indeed, the Dante whose thoughts have become obsessed with the *donna gentile* and all her shadow play can win no victory at all; he is too immersed in his own emotions, his sufferings *(martiri)*. Instead, the later Dante, coolly observing his younger self, must point us toward better reason. The last part of *La Vita Nuova* assumes that a knowing reader, having been educated by so many careful explanations, will see through the false images of the text. From Chapter xxxi, the author warns us, the divisions precede the poem, so that the poem may seem more widowed *(vedova)*; the reader is abandoned to his own devices. But no one open to grace is ever really abandoned, and every truly loving poem has a bride in heaven. The thought of Beatrice keeps our readings true. Thus the last word of Chapter xxxviii, *martiri,* which stands for the sufferings of heart and soul that the *donna gentile* has consoled, may also serve to recall another martyr: that blessed lady whose reappearance, in the following chapter, at once dispels all phantoms.

The medium of initiation, that is to say, is Beatrice, but a Beatrice, after Chapter xxviii, who has become a "citizen of eternal life" (*cittadini di vita eterna*, xxxiv. 1). Technically, Dante's most radical advance on the *dolce stil nuovo* consists of this new subject matter: praising a lady who is dead. But the new theme grows logically from the progress already made in putting aside conventions, desire, the body. When Dante is converted, in Chapter xviii, from dependence on his own feelings or Beatrice's smile to the joy that comes solely from words that praise his lady, he has already prepared himself for Beatrice's absence. Indeed, the most famous of all Dante's sonnets in praise of his lady, "Tanto gentile" (xxvi), anticipates her departure by recognizing whence she comes: "una cosa venuta / Da cielo in terra a miracol mostrare" (a thing come down / from heaven to earth to show a miracle). Thus fortified, the poet can assuage his grief as he had assuaged his pangs of love: by interpreting the miracle until it yields such truth as mortal men can know.

After the death of Beatrice, however, *La Vita Nuova* voyages into a different realm of poetry. Honoring his heavenly lady, Dante must leave behind the poetic exercises of his apprenticeship and try a new mode. That new mode is *La Vita Nuova* itself. Years later, in the *Convivio,* Dante tells how he had discovered what he must do, how he had gone in quest of silver and found gold.

> As the first delight of my soul was lost to me, . . . I remained fixed with such sadness that no comfort availed me. Nevertheless, after some time my mind, pursuing a cure, since neither I nor others could afford consolation, returned to a way [*modo*] that another disconsolate man had held consoling. And I set myself to read that book, not known to many, of Boethius, with which, prisoned and outcast, he had solaced himself. . . . And though it was hard for me at first to enter the meaning, finally I did enter it . . . through such genius as had, as in dreaming, already seen many things; as may be seen in the *Vita Nuova*.

Reading Boethius, Dante realized that his own poems—his "dreaming"—contained the potential meaning and solace of a book.

The significance of this discovery has often been overlooked because of the controversy that surrounds a related issue, the sensational reinterpretation of the *donna gentile:* is she really to be identified with the lady Philosophy, as Dante says in the *Convivio?* The answer, of course, is yes—yes *now,* in the *Convivio,* whatever she meant once. But this later interpretive finesse, so typical of Dante, should not blind us to his clear suggestion that Boethius had helped show him "the way": not only a means of consolation but a literary method. For *De consolatione Philosophiae,* like no vernacular work, anticipates the method of *La Vita Nuova:* the mixture of a narrative, poems, and commentaries; a progressive deepening of understanding, at first apparently secular, that finally manifests divine revelation; and an elaborate numerological arrangement of verses. Dante had met another companion. He had learned that his early dreams and verses, properly read and gathered together, composed a whole greater than its parts.

The point, though simple, bears repetition: *La Vita Nuova* is not a poetic and biographical miscellany (like troubadour collections with *veras* and *razos*) but a book. The mathematical proof of this assertion may be represented thus: 1-9-I-1-3-II-3-1-III-9-1 (one way of ordering the poems around the sacred sequence of one, three, nine). Whatever our arithmetic, however, it can only confirm the apparent unity we sense as readers. At some moment, surely—we shall never know just when—Dante must have apprehended that a great many of the poems of his youth obeyed a common principle: a principle that may be variously expressed as a tendency toward the number nine, praise for a divine lady, or an ontogeny recapitulating Christ's gift of grace. In that moment *La Vita Nuova* was conceived. Excising some poems from his canon, reinterpreting others to emphasize lines too faint for any other eye to have seen, Dante drew his life and verse into a perfect order—progressive, symmetrical, complete. In Chapter xxxix the book comes full circle when the poet, waking from the false consolation of the *donna gentile* at the ninth hour, has a vision of his lady just as she was: "I seemed to see the glorious Beatrice with those crimson garments in which she first appeared before my eyes; and she seemed young, the same age as when I first saw her." Dante returns to his starting point and experiences again his first conversion, the opening of his new life. Nothing has changed, and everything; he now knows what he sees.

In one respect, however, *La Vita Nuova* has no end: the process of reinterpretation can never reach a close. To be initiated confers a burden as well as a privilege; the effort at deeper understanding consumes one's life. This unfulfilled aspiration is beautifully signified, in the two penultimate chapters of the book, by the image of the pilgrim. All pilgrims search for Beatrice, their lost "bringer of blessing," Dante tells us in Chapter xl. They visit an empty city and journey beyond, never to reach their destination in this life. In the last poem of *La Vita Nuova,* Dante associates his own quest with those peregrine spirits.

> Oltre la spera che più larga gira
>   Passa 'l sospiro ch'esce del mio core;
>   Intelligenza nova, che l'Amore
>   Piangendo mette in lui, pur su lo tira.
>   Quand'elli è giunto là dove disira,
>   Vede una donna, che riceve onore
>   E luce sì, che per lo suo splendore
>   Le peregrino spirito la mira.
> Vedela tal, che quando 'l mi ridice
>   Io no lo intendo, sì parla sottile
>   Al cor dolente che lo fa parlare.
>   So io che parla di quella gentile,
>   Però che spesso ricorda Beatrice,
>   Sì ch'io lo 'ntendo ben, donne mie care.

> (Beyond the sphere that wheels the furthest way
>   Passes the sigh that issues from my heart;
>   A new intelligence, that Love
>   Weeping implants in it, draws it ever upward.
>   When it has reached the place for which it longs,
>   It sees a lady, who partakes of honor
>   And shines so, that by her own radiance
>   The pilgrim spirit descries her.
> Such sight is this, that when it gives report
>   I do not understand, so subtle are the words
>   To the sorrowing heart that makes it speak.
>   I know it speaks of that gentle one,

32

Because it oftens mentions Beatrice,
Thus far I understand it well, my dear ladies.)

Here many themes of *La Vita Nuova* pass again before our eyes: the inaccessible glorified lady, the guidance of Love, the difficulty of interpreting subtle words. Moreover, the prophecy of the first sonnet is now fulfilled: Love, once more "piangendo," at last communicates the reason for his tears, through the intermediary of Dante's sigh. But Love himself has changed. No longer a personified god or even an emotion in the poet's heart, he has become the bearer of "intelligenza nova," a new intellectual power that prefigures the greater love of the *Convivio* and the *Commedia*. Such love demands of its votaries not only a gentle heart but a mind able to master philosophy and cosmology. Aspiring to the Empyrean, Dante must be a pilgrim.

He sees, as yet, through a glass darkly. The mind can no more comprehend those blessed ones, the *ragione* tell us, than the eye can gaze into the sun. Indeed, the poet seems prey to cosmic irony, since the turn of his love has only exchanged one bewilderment for another. Yet instruction has begun: first, because Dante can recognize at least the name of Beatrice, who will lead him in the *Commedia* to the height of his pilgrimage; and second, because the very words he cannot comprehend are spoken by his sigh, the pilgrim spirit in him, his own poem. Intellectually, Dante has yet to anatomize the love that moves the stars; but poetically his words already record visions of the most high. As a poet he has beheld all value. Now, at the end of *La Vita Nuova,* the time has come to trace in the world the effects and meanings he has experienced in himself, and to apply his new intelligence to all the works of love.

He must write, that is to say, more worthily *(degnamente)*. The marvelous vision with which *La Vita Nuova* breaks off, harbinger of greater work to come, foretells a new kind of aspiration, more impersonal and self-possessed, in which Beatrice will cease to sow confusion and begin to expound theology. As at the end of the *Commedia,* moreover, the words that fail the poet also complete his pattern. Dante's leap of faith to his lady enables *La Vita Nuova;* his vision proves a new phase has begun. Suddenly, for the first time in the book, he refers to Beatrice in the present tense. Perceiving the secret order of his life, the poet has been chosen to interpret for others. Much, as yet, he does not understand. Yet the truth is there to find in the words he has written, in the words he has yet to write. The book of memory, like the book of human history, goes no further than the present instant, when all Dante's past gathers into a single insight envisioned as Beatrice. To understand that insight, however, the poet must see into the future. He glimpses that higher world explicated by a greater book. With the method learned in *La Vita Nuova,* and the inspiration breathed into him by so many companions, Dante dedicates his life to fulfilling his promise. He has performed, through grace, his ceremony of initiation. Now he must set himself to read.

The Marriage of Heaven and Hell

The Vision of Christ that thou dost see
Is my Visions Greatest Enemy
Thine has a great hook nose like thine
Mine has a snub nose like to mine
Thine is the friend of All Mankind
Mine speaks in parables to the Blind
Thine loves the same world that mine hates
Thy Heaven doors are my Hell Gates . . .
Both read the Bible day & night
But thou readst black where I read white
["The Everlasting Gospel"]

Behind *La Vita Nuova,* shrouded in images that conceal it from all but initiated eyes, the New Testament casts the shadow of its ideal form. Dante, like the Author he worships but dares not name, tells the story of a blessed one who visited earth to bring salvation and redemption from error; died; and (after three chapters) ascended to a home in Heaven. Innumerable details confirm this reading; a few of the most striking, like the interpretation of Guido's Vanna as John the Baptist and the transformation of Christ's pilgrims into Beatrice's, we have already glanced at. But Dante never makes his source explicit. A voice crying in the wilderness, he prepares the way of the Lord without pretending to understand more than a few of His words. Nor does he claim unusual powers. Rather, he suggests, all stories worth telling are the same. *La Vita Nuova* is Dante's Testament because it unfolds the meaning, at once personal and universal, that the one True Light has given to the life of every man.

William Blake, like Dante, writes a Testament; but Blake allows nothing tentative in his claim. For this poet all bibles are equal, all inspiration struck from the same fierce spark in the human breast. On the frontispiece of *All Religions are One,* Blake's early tablet of principles, the same familiar motto—"The Voice of one crying in the Wilderness"—underlies a youthful John the Baptist who points both arms left. Yet no Christ follows him. The priest-ridden England Blake preaches to may be indeed a wilderness of the spirit—the just man's vale of death—but none can restore Eden except the man with prophecy in his heart. The savior whose way Blake prepares is Blake himself, or each of us.

> The Religeons of all Nations are derived from each Nations different reception of the Poetic Genius which is every where call'd the Spirit of Prophecy.
>
> The Jewish & Christian Testaments are An original derivation from the Poetic Genius; this is necessary from the confined nature of bodily sensation
>
> As all men are alike (tho' infinitely various) So all Religions & as all similars have one source
>
> The true Man is the source he being the Poetic Genius

Since every man shares in the spirit of prophecy, it follows that every man is potentially capable of creating a Bible of his own. Nor does anything strike Blake as more blasphemous than the notion that one people, one text, could ever possess exclusive rights to the word of God. His notes to the Bishop of Landaff's *Apology for the Bible* hurl mockery upon such notions. "That the Jews assumed a right Exclusively to the benefits of God will be a lasting witness against them, & the same will it be against Christians. . . . If historical facts can be written by inspiration Miltons Paradise Lost is as true as Genesis or Exodus." The world of the imagination, Blake insists, is a democracy; the Bible belongs to every man's Genius, and its time is now.

The logic of this view permits only one conclusion: every true poet must spend his life making the Bible anew. Nor has any poet ever heeded this injunction more literally than Blake. From the very first, in the *Poetical Sketches* (1783), he had striven to reinterpret both Old Testament and New by his own light. But his own appropriate genius came into full flower only in his early thirties, when he invented the technique of illuminated printing that allowed him to present his vision whole. In a moment all that he had done and thought—the poems and sketches, the apprenticeship in engraving, the early prophecies, the sympathy for revolution, the embattled struggle for survival, above all the visions—suddenly came together. He knew why he had been born: to harrow Heaven with corrosive fire and make a book. And the importance of that discovery inspires the first and most literal of all Blake's bibles, *The Marriage of Heaven and Hell.*

The creation of the *Marriage,* like that of any work so rich, depends on many sources: the writings of Swedenborg (where Blake found not only memorable relations to parody but the amazing information that the Last Judgment had begun thirty-three years before, in 1757, the year of his own birth); the revolutionary fervor sweeping Europe in that year of 1790; the technical possibility, as it appeared to Blake, of a kind of book that would abolish the false dichotomy between form and content, the picture and the

Word. Yet knowledge of these sources will not initiate us into the secrets of the *Marriage* unless we perceive the spirit of prophecy that informs it. Here vision and interpretation wed. Poetic Genius, the same genius that inspired the Hebrew prophets, is at once Blake's subject and his object; he sets out to transmit not only the history of biblical inspiration but its nature. Nor will he accept a division between the human and the divine. The Bible contains all proper human history, since man reveals himself above all in his bibles. The *Marriage* aims at nothing less than renewing the partial testaments we inherit, converting them through fire to the present moment. Outrageously, with fearful energy, Blake grasps the Bible in his hand.

We open *The Marriage of Heaven and Hell*, in fact, to a page where all bibles are comprehended. "The Argument," in six brief stanzas, recapitulates and progresses upon the Old Testament and the New, summarizing them with a peculiar Blakean twist. Failing to see this, much intelligent and sensitive criticism of the poem has missed its essential point. Blake wastes no time on preliminaries; he starts, as all bibles start, at the Beginning.

> Rintrah roars & shakes his fires in the burdend air;
> Hungry clouds swag on the deep.

In the midst of primal chaos, a stew of elements where clouds lurch into and pillage the deep, and the air convulses with fire and earth, a Giant roars: Rintrah, "the Wrath of Prophecy." The moment is Genesis or immediately preceding; and Rintrah, a force either creative or destructive, here seems identified with Jehovah, "the Jehovah of the Bible," we shall be told on Plate 6, "being no other than he who dwells in flaming fire." Clearly Blake is retelling the myth of Creation. Yet this version, unlike the Hebrew Bible, pays little respect to Jehovah. Rintrah, Titanic wrath without reason, seems more a part of chaos than its master—cousin to those imprisoned Giants we see huddled and muddled together on Plate 16, "who formed this world into its sensual existence." The vision remains undefined. Though prophetic in its rhythms (that is, reminiscent of Hebraic poetry as described by Bishop Lowth), the very language is "burdend," clotted with multiple groups of consonants that retard the speed of the verse. Can such a jumble prepare the way for Genesis? Blake's answer, of course, is that it can—not because, at some past hour, a superior being spoke a word in the darkness, but because at every moment the human imagination bears the light of its own vision. For that reason Blake's parody of Genesis adopts the present tense. The moment of creation, he implies, is always at hand. It persists at every moment when the prophetic spirit within man sees primal chaos, the mere "withness" of matter or sensual existence, as an illusion. In Blake's own Bible, freed from illusions, Jehovah becomes Rintrah, and the Poetic Genius, no longer dependent on myths of nature, creates perpetual Genesis in its own image.

Historically, however, the first incarnation of prophecy belongs to a Chosen People and to their Book.

> Once meek, and in a perilous path,
> The just man kept his course along
> The vale of death.
> Roses are planted where thorns grow,
> And on the barren heath
> Sing the honey bees.

Here Blake summarizes, as he sees it, the essence of the Old Testament: "the fruit / Of that forbidden tree whose mortal taste / Brought death into the world, and all our woe, / With loss of Eden." The Jewish Bible, in this version, tells the story of mankind after the Fall: the way that Adam, Eve, and their descendants learned to take strength from their sentence and to build a world amid death and exile by the sweat of the brow. The theme of this story is justice. Man sinned, was rightly punished, and henceforth earned some stay of execution by hewing to the perilous mortal path of the straight and narrow. Nor does Blake underestimate the virtue of such straitened labor. The just man, though meek before his God, knows how to fight, to work; from thorns he makes roses and draws honey from the barren heath. Even Blake's language, simple and strong (some of it taken from Exodus and all of it biblical), reveals his admiration for the Jewish Testament and those men of law who built Jerusalem.

Moreover, the etching of the Argument offers remarkable pictorial support for labor. At the bottom of the plate a naked languid couple (presumably Adam and Eve) lie stretched at their ease—horizontal as worms on a leaf—in that repose of Eden where nothing ever happens. But the right margin bursts with an opposing version of Eden. An energetic figure, high in a tree, hands down something hidden—is it fruit?—to a woman who reaches upward. Verticality, the line of power and aspiration, pronounces this the Tree of Life. Is the scene a fortunate Fall? Not entirely, perhaps. The upward motion is arrested by the handing-down, the legs of the girl below are crossed, the action itself seems furtive. Yet the striving and energy at the right are surely preferable to the torpor below. The Tree of Life dominates a stunted little tree on the other side of the girl, a tree all loops and veerings from the upward path. The Tree of Knowledge, as Yeats maintained, belongs only to the unimaginative and idle. The couple at the right, on the other hand, need hardly fear their punishment. Their very act of sin exerts the energy they will require to make a life in exile; they will have force to plant a rose. Indeed, the moral vigor of the Old Testament can energize its readers still. The Hebrew people (we are told by the text) followed righteousness "Once," in that time consecrated by their Book; but their spirit of prophecy continues to live wherever men engage in mental fight. Roses are planted and honey bees sing in the present, the present tense. Jerusalem might yet be built again, in the twinkling of an eye, by modern prophets.

Nevertheless, the Old Testament is flawed, in Blake's eyes, by paying too much regard to death. The just man labors under an illusion: he thinks himself bound by mortal flesh. To awaken him from this dream, another Book is needed.

> Then the perilous path was planted:
> And a river, and a spring
> On every cliff and tomb;
> And on the bleached bones
> Red clay brought forth.

With the aid of conventional Christian typology, Blake rereads some episodes from the Old Testament—the creation of Adam and Ezekiel's vision of the valley of bones—in the light of the New. The classic of death makes way for the classic of resurrection; springs flow from the tomb. The final line of the stanza bears its thematic seed. In Hebrew, Adam means "red clay," the earth from which man was made. Yet the second Adam, who came to redeem the first, was Christ; and this Adam, though a man of flesh, was also the Creator. The peculiar grammar of "Red clay brought forth"—is clay the subject or object?—emphasizes that new life is generated, in the New Testament, not through an external agent but through humanity itself, the irrepressible flowering of Genius in man. Of itself clay brings forth life, Christ-Adam rises of himself. Prophetic spirits learned, from the new Book, that they need not wander in the wilderness of death. Wherever man has vision, Eden may yet be resurrected.

Unfortunately, once a bible gains authority vision may stagnate. The spirit of prophecy is kept alive in the human mind; by definition it cannot dwell in an established church, codified for unthinking, passive men.

> Till the villain left the paths of ease,
> To walk in perilous paths, and drive
> The just man into barren climes.

The great tragedy of history, Blake argues, is the theft of the Bible by men with no prophetic inspiration in themselves. After Christ, every charlatan with a memory can pretend to possess the Word. True Christianity, founded on Jesus who "acted from impulse, not from rules," knows no greater enemy than the Christian church. Within the mother church even perilous paths are shorn of terror and invite the villain to stroll without risk. Thus the just man, Blake's prophet, must enter exile once more. Forced to choose between the Bible and the Poetic Genius from which all bibles are derived, he must choose the latter, whatever the cost. Nor is the cost small: barren climes, heresy, willfulness, death—the catalogue of ills that Milton assigned to rebels in *Paradise Lost.* Such is postbiblical history, the nightmare from which Blake strives to wake.

What of the present?

> Now the sneaking serpent walks
> In mild humility.
> And the just man rages in the wilds
> Where lions roam.

Far from being alleviated, the tragic theft of the Bible by its enemies has set the world awry. The priesthood walks—as well as a snake can walk— the path of the straight and narrow, the prophet roars like Rintrah in a wilderness where justice comes from tooth and claw. The time, of course, is 1790, *now.* Revolution is in the air, and there can be no doubt where Blake's sympathies lie. Nor should one underestimate his indignation. With savage irony he travesties the "Eden" of today. *Now* the serpent, an upright parody of a human being, has usurped the place of man, while the true man rages in an exile he has not deserved. Woe to the false lords of the earth! Surely some Second Coming is at hand.

> Rintrah roars & shakes his fires in the burdend air;
> Hungry clouds swag on the deep.

No, no Second Coming; only a repetition of that primal moment before creation. "The Argument" comes full circle by restating its premise. Yet this time the refrain carries the burden of all human history. No longer identified with Jehovah, Rintrah now seems a harbinger of the wrath of modern life, all those sounds of rage that seek an outlet amid confusion: the cannons firing in America, the cries of France (a wounded Giant), the frustrated prophetic fire in Blake's own heart. Who can see a clear way through such turmoil? But the time of prophecy was not *then,* frozen in the past. Creation has not failed; rather, it has not yet been tried. The day when every man speaks the truth of his own Poetic Genius might dawn at any moment, for we all live at the dawn of creation. That is the argument of Blake's *Marriage.*

After so comprehensive an argument, however, embodying all human history and spiritual insight, what possibly can follow? The answer, of course, is that no parable immediately reveals all its meaning. As votaries, first we and Blake must learn to read. The greater part of *The Marriage of Heaven and Hell* is devoted to explaining its moment of revelation in the most explicit way Poetic Genius can find: not only by rational persuasion but by tangible acts of vision. Like a medieval illuminated manuscript, the book would strike even the illiterate as holy writ; but its shocking humor stings and taunts us into literacy. Blake makes a primer of prophecy. Every step of his little book is meant to be looked at, weighed in the hand, argued with, imagined. Layer upon layer it draws the orthodox reader into an abyss of the five senses where even the profession of faith conceals a serpent. On Plate 20, for instance, Blake redraws the terrors and torments of Leviathan—the biblical archenemy—into his own great looping line of knowledge. At length, learning to distrust his senses, the reader will learn to trust himself. The *Marriage* offers initiation into a great teacher's mode of vision; it shows us how to see with the eyes of Genius. (The deepest irony of Blake's career, perhaps, is that he was born to teach, though so few were born to study with him.)

The *Marriage* supplies a gloss, in fact, on most of the authentic sacred codes that Western poets have imagined. The pictures alone, without a text, would teach us new ways of reading. On Plate 5, for instance, Blake turns *Paradise Lost* upside down, correcting Milton's version of the Fall—"Those who restrain desire, do so because theirs is weak enough to be restrained"—by imagining it as a comic pratfall. Even Milton's habitual conflation of classical and Christian images is mocked: the figure who comes crashing down is not only Satan but Phaëthon, a poet who has lost his confidence and caused the sun and Pegasus to fall ("If the Sun & Moon should doubt / Theyd immediately Go out"). Standing on our heads, we could see the Devil's version of the story: another pilgrim, mounting with arms outstretched to Holy Fire.

Plate 11 repossesses and corrects a still more ancient bible: the animating stories of the ancient Poets, or Bards. Here objects quicken into life. A sun-god-sunflower, a bearded oak in which we see a bearded Druid's face, a naiad mother with a budlike infant joy, all proclaim a time when gods and geniuses dwelt in woods and in poetic tales. Yet man, as Plato knew, "has closed himself up, till he sees all things thro' narrow chinks of his cavern"; in later versions the whole scene is perceived through the opening in a cave. The cloistered vision of modern times has misconstrued the ancient poets. Their stories, Blake sees, are beautiful; but they must not lead us to forget that "All deities reside in the human breast." Abstraction will follow next— "thus began Priesthood"—and eventually the priesthood will issue forth the bibles of systematic reasoning. Not even a great poet like Dante is immune to such error. Commenting on his own designs for the *Commedia,* Blake was to accuse Dante of having relied on the poetry of the heathen. "Every thing in Dantes Comedia shows That for Tyrannical Purposes he has made This World the Foundation of All [;] the Goddess Nature Mystery is his Inspirer & not Imagination the Holy Ghost." Once again Blake sets matters straight by turning the picture upside down. Viewed from Hell's gate, he points out, the diagram of Hell is upside down, but from Purgatory it seems upright; "In Equivocal Worlds Up & Down are Equivocal." Thus Blake reinterprets Dante in terms of a Bible of Hell. God "could never have Built Dantes Hell nor the Hell of the Bible neither in the way our Parsons explain it. It must have been originally Formed by the devil Himself & So I understand it to have been." Within the vortex of the *Marriage,* all sacred codes revolve to Blake's perspective.

One sacred code above the rest needs to be redesigned. The form of the *Marriage* makes sense at once when we perceive how thoroughly it reenacts and contradicts the Bible. Like the Old Testament, Blake's book runs through an anthology of literary kinds: the parable on Plate 2; the series of propositions on Plate 4; the literary criticism of Plates 5 and 6; the proverbs on Plates 7 through 10; the historical analysis on Plate 11; the symposium with other prophets on Plates 12 and 13; and a host of "fancies," aphorisms, debates, and demonstrations. The logical culmination of this process occurs near the end, on Plates 23 and 24, when a Devil "proves" to an Angel that Jesus Christ broke every one of the Commandments: "I tell you, no virtue can exist without breaking these ten commandments: Jesus was all virtue, and acted from impulse, not from rules." Here the Devil's party finally breaks the most sacred of codes and wins its day. The Old Testament and the New, brought to violent confrontation, produce from their mutual destruction a fiery marriage: the new Bible before us.

Nor does the prophetic voice accept any authority but its own. In the symposium, for instance, Blake interviews Isaiah and Ezekiel, who confirm (as poets and prophets should) that imagination has dominion over the earth—a firm persuasion that a thing is so makes it so. The passage wittily proves its own point by abolishing time and space: two friendly prophets come to dine in Blake's imagination, where his firm persuasion of their presence makes them plainly manifest. The distance between Israel and England, between one prophetic age and another, disappears at once when the one Poetic Genius raises its voice. Indeed, even Diogenes the Greek and the North American Indians, congenial spirits, are welcomed in. Moreover, Blake turns the symposium form against itself. Ordinarily a symposium balances one speaker against another, creating a dialectic in which many sides of truth are exposed and perhaps reconciled; but all the speakers in Blake's interview sound just alike. All voices are one and all questions are answered when the true prophet speaks.

Yet a prophet may speak, as everyone knows, without being heard. The problem of the *Marriage* is not so much to explain itself—and many of its plates could not be more clear—as to persuade men to listen; to make vision answer to vision. Blake brings all his energy to the task of shocking the sleeping imagination awake. Even a lazy reader can be exercised into health. The Proverbs, certainly, provide such exercise.

> Drive your cart and your plow over the bones of the dead.
>
> The road of excess leads to the palace of wisdom.

> Prudence is a rich ugly old maid courted by Incapacity.
>
> He who desires but acts not, breeds pestilence.

Whatever they "mean," they sting and taunt the complacent mind so sharply that a dead body might be moved to respond. And so might a Christian. The apparent antinomianism of the *Marriage,* its advocacy of the Devil's side, challenges every belief that men accept without thinking: the evidence of the senses, the authority of the Bible, the reality of death. Blake demands not agreement—"Without Contraries is no progression"—but warfare. If men rise up in wrath against the *Marriage* and hurl their spirits against it, its purpose will have been served: every reader will find himself a prophet.

The rewards of such awakening, Blake promises, will be immense. For all its concern with violence and revolution, the *Marriage* is suffused with joy. As illusions disperse on every side and men begin to realize what flimsy manacles of law and organized religion have been suffered to impose on them, Blake swells with great good humor. Even the misguided angel of priesthood (Swedenborg; Plates 21–24), after being tutored by the devil (Blake), becomes his friend. Once we have been stunned and lose our senses, the *Marriage* affirms, a whole new world of vision opens.

> How do you know but ev'ry Bird that cuts the airy way,
> Is an immense world of delight, clos'd by your senses five?

The fear of death (which motivates the lines of Chatterton parodied here by Blake) yields to a delighted sense of the possibilities of life. Indeed, no aspect of the *Marriage* carries more energy than its repeated assertions that five senses are not enough. With confidence and imagination we might each take wing. "If the doors of perception were cleansed every thing would appear to man as it is, infinite" (Pl.14).

Remarkably, Blake thinks he can unlock those doors by means of the *Marriage* itself. The central image of the book is the book's own power, its leap beyond the senses. Blake proves his vision quite literally, he believes, by limning it before us. This mode of proof, the most convincing that he has to offer, will utterly escape us if we approach the *Marriage* solely as a literary text (or, worse yet, as one text within a larger book). It depends, instead, upon a marriage of text and picture—or, more precisely, vision and page—ordained by the new method of printing. Blake describes this "infernal method" on Plates 14 and 15. The latter, an extraordinary tour de force, represents "a Printing house in Hell," where each step of the process is translated into its visionary equivalent: the varnish a curling Viper, the acid bath Lions of flaming fire. Here Blake emblemizes the making of the plate itself, which involved building on copper a layer of varnish, later burned away by acid to reveal the design (a process opposite to ordinary etching). The excitement of the *Marriage* partly derives from the spiritual implications of this technique. Like a devil, the artist unleashes a terrible destructive energy that burns away all the crust of custom, exposing the true nature of things. (In aesthetic terms, he "defamiliarizes" nature, attacking our "stock responses.") This is the method of "corrosives, which in Hell are salutary and medicinal, melting apparent surfaces away, and displaying the infinite which was hid" (Pl. 14). Yet the material with which Blake works, clearly enough, is not only his copper plate but we ourselves: those bodies or caverns which mask our infinite, and which fire must consume.

Every particle of the *Marriage,* therefore, must be alive with vision; every pulsation of the artery beats with prophetic spirit. Indeed, the tiniest details of the book—the strokes that shape its letters, its "accidentals," the little tentacles and squiggles that flit among its lines—help signify its meaning. Blake can see the world in a grain of sand or a dot of ink. The most obvious of such signs, the serpentine curlicues or spirals found on almost every page, seem to be associated not only with the devil but with the transmission of knowledge. This association becomes specific on Plate 15, where the long curl that follows the first sentence, "I was in a Printing house in Hell & saw the method in which knowledge is transmitted from generation to generation," is reflected at the bottom of the page by a serpent grasped by an eagle. The spiral, which progresses (like "The Argument") by constantly coiling back and repeating itself, perfectly figures for Blake the progress of knowledge, in which each prophet adds another link to the constant chain of inspiration and none has priority over another. Plate 10, the last of the Proverbs of Hell, helps illustrate this process. Below, a devil unwinds a scroll of proverbs to be copied by a pair of scribes—the one at the right, alert and eager, suspiciously resembling the poet himself. Just above them, punctuating the appropriate proverb "Truth can never be told so as to be understood, and not be believ'd," a bird (winged like the devil) holds another kind of loop or scroll, presumably a serpent. Apostles of liberty like Blake, the bird and devil transmit their knowledge through a twisting line. And slightly higher on the plate another proverb tells us why such circuitous paths to the truth are necessary: "Improve[me]nt makes strait roads, but the crooked roads without Improvement, are roads of Genius."

To be initiated into the *Marriage,* then, one must walk a crooked road. Blake does not set out, like John the Baptist, to make a straight path for the Lord but to force his reader through a trial by vision. The *Marriage* is designed as an alphabet of hieroglyphics in which every mark fixed by the engraver's burin can test an independent spirit. But even if one resists those hieroglyphics, they carry on the work of prophecy. Two contrary persuasions, two opposing bibles, merely bring forth progression. The book does not destroy its enemies but regenerates them; and for all its hazards, it transports us to a happy end. The last two "memorable fancies" (Plates

17–24) both depict cosmic conflicts resolved in favor of the Devil's party. In the first, Blake opposes his vision to that of a scholastic Angel who would reduce the Bible to moral codes and "Analytics": "The man who never alters his opinion is like standing water, & breeds reptiles of the mind." At length the poet succeeds in imposing his fantasy upon that analytic reptile and makes Leviathan his own. The final "Memorable Fancy" records a still more decisive victory: a Devil and Angel confront each other on ultimate grounds—the Tablets of the Law or Ten Commandments—and the Devil's reading wins the last word.

A marriage of contraries ensues. On Plate 24 the Angel is converted; he leaves his cloud of mystery and joins the Devil in his flames. "I beheld the Angel who stretched out his arms embracing the flame of fire & he was consumed and arose as Elijah." Here Blake discloses the promised end for which the reader has been urged to risk initiation. Elijah, according to *A Vision of the Last Judgment,* "comprehends all the Prophetic Characters"; the reader who has committed himself to Blake's fire is now set free to read truth from his own prophetic spirit. The line following the conversion of the Angel portrays "a seminar of five prophets"—congenially interpreting a book—and all the rest of the text bursts with visual flourishes. Visibly and spiritually the prophet has won his day; initiation has been achieved. With the sweetness of that victory, soon to be celebrated in "A Song of Liberty," our instruction properly ends, except for two postscripts: Blake's promise to continue to read the Bible "in its infernal or diabolical sense," and the closing proverb that vanquishes the brutal image of Nebuchadnez-zar.

That proverb bears further inspection. "One Law for the Lion & Ox is Oppression," a rallying cry for revolution, clearly expresses Blake's hatred for all tyrannies, the "natural" laws that constrict most men—the unini-tiate—in bondage. Crouching on all fours like an ox, the tyrant Nebu-chadnezzar displays the essence of his kind: cramped boxes in a box; geometers whose rigid right angles, resisting the serpent's line of knowl-edge, reduce them to subhuman caricature. If the Angel embracing the flame of fire may be seen as an anticipation of Plate 84 of Blake's Dante designs—as a pilgrim who enters the fire not with reluctance but with con-fidence that he shall arise as Elijah—then Nebuchadnezzar may anticipate Plate 48, as a Vanni Fucci whose blood and rage have brought him to his knees, subjected to the mad sensual despair that trusts nothing but the senses.

The context of the proverb points also to another reading. If no one law has the right to constrain everyone, then everyone had best make a law for himself according to his own kind. "I must Create a System, or be enslav'd by another Mans." Thus Moses made a law in tablets, Christ by breaking the Commandments (on the previous page), the French by revolution—and

Blake by inverting the Book of Law with a Bible of Hell. The codicil of the *Marriage* fulfills the prophecy of its "Argument": another testament, a new law, has been created. Blake does not claim that his bible invalidates those of the past; any book touched by the Poetic Genius is infinitely persuasive. Indeed, if the creeping serpents of the establishment had seized control of Hell, he would doubtless have spoken for Heaven. Yet Oppression, the stultified and cautious interpretations of prophecy that insist on the letter of the text, has now been overthrown. Each man commands his own word. And Blake hopes that every reader will enter the Bible with him, like the Angel-Elijah embracing the flame of fire, and learn from him how to read it.

Our ability to read is immediately tested by "A Song of Liberty." Without a pause, the prophet launches into an apocalyptic story that anticipates all the major prophecies to come. An Eternal Female brings forth a son of fire, whom a starry king tries to stifle with war in heaven and commandments but who finally triumphs, stamping "the stony law to dust, . . . crying Empire is no more!" Thematically, the "Song" incorporates many ideas and images from the *Marriage;* formally, it draws the work full circle by returning to a poetic "argument," now appealing prophetically to the future rather than the past; and Blake bound them together as a single book. He needed the "Song," in fact, to complete his Bible; for "A Song of Liberty" constitutes nothing less than Blake's Book of Revelation. Just as the Bible itself ends in Revelation, a mode of pure prophecy that opens and reads the wonders of a book with seven seals, so the *Marriage* ends by rereading the wonders of John. Lest anyone should miss the point, Blake numbers his verses as in a biblical chapter. The "Song" draws all its narrative from Revelation, especially from its famous twelfth chapter, where there appear successively, as in Blake, the groaning woman who brings forth a wonderful son, the opposition of a jealous dragon-king, a war in heaven, the casting-out of the rebellious cohort to earth, and at last (Revelation 12:10) a triumphant founding of Christ's kingdom-to-be. Blake shares that triumph. He has read the Bible from first to last and shown anew how it must end.

The "Song," however, is Revelation interpreted with *liberty*. At his close, as so often throughout the *Marriage,* Blake turns the Bible on its head. Indeed, the upside-down versions of Hell we have already seen—reversals of Milton and Dante—might stand as emblems for much of the "Song." Plates 25 and 26 represent a motion of constant ungovernable falling.

> 5. Cast thy eyes O Rome into the deep
> down falling, even to eternity down falling. . . .
> 10. The speary hand . . . hurl'd the new born
> wonder thro' the starry night.
> 11. The fire, the fire, is falling! . . .

> 13. The fiery limbs, the flaming hair, shot
> like the sinking sun into the western sea. . . .
> 15. Down rushd beating his wings in vain
> the jealous king. . . .
> 16. Falling, rushing, ruining!

The starry, gloomy king who falls is not Satan but Jehovah (in the Devil's version), and with him fall the new-born sun god (both Christ and Phaëthon) and the keys of the Church of Rome. All mysteries, all constraints, must be cast into ruin before Blake's liberty can dawn.

The specific liberty Blake claims, Plate 27 makes plain, is liberty to read Revelation as he likes. Above all, he attacks a particular *mis*reading of the apocalypse, one given currency by the angel's proclamation in the ultimate chapter of Revelation:

> 14 Blessed are they that do his commandments, that they may have right to the tree of life, and may enter in through the gates into the city.
> 15 For without are dogs, and sorcerers, and whoremongers, and murderers, and idolaters, and whosoever loveth and maketh a lie.
> 16 I Jesus have sent mine angel to testify unto you these things in the churches.

Jesus, according to these lines, has come to enforce the commandments, strict rules interpreted by an established church; and the penalty for disobedience is exclusion from the heavenly city. The nineteenth verse supports this interpretation with a threat or curse: "if any man shall take away from the words of the book of this prophecy, God shall take away his part out of the book of life, and out of the holy city, and from the things which are written in this book." But all Blake's protestant heart rebels. *His* Jesus, we have seen, broke every rule. Though priestly eyes may view Him as a setting sun, He yet shall rise, "Spurning the clouds written with curses, stamps the stony law to dust." Against the Priests of the Raven of dawn, Blake raises the sons of joy; against the rules of the tyrant church, the impulse of the free; against exclusion, liberty. No one, no dog or lover, shall be barred from Blake's own heavenly city: "For every thing that lives is Holy." The final "y" of the "Song," curling up and outward from the page, affirms that no period can be set to Revelation. All things are married, and the book of life may yet be opened and renewed.

At the end of *The Marriage of Heaven and Hell* Blake's way is clear. At once the prophet of initiation and its votary, he will carry the light of his new understanding to every dark corner of contemporary life; he will build his holy city. The later prophecies fulfill that promise. "A Song of Liberty" holds the seeds of many harvests to come. Its "new born fire" would soon be christened Orc, its "starry king," ruined "on Urthonas dens," Urizen; its giant forms, Albion, France, Atlantis, would be given bodies to express their revolutionary throes. And at the center of revelation, making sense of his own life, would be the spiritual form of William Blake. After initiation, like Dante, Blake sets out to walk through the whole world of time and space, interpreting its secret history and meaning. Nor, since "every thing that lives is Holy," can any particle of life be excluded. Like the ideal cities of the *Commedia* and *A Vision,* the city of Jerusalem must make a place for every soul. It would be work enough for a lifetime.

Yet the way to Jerusalem proved more difficult, perhaps, than it had seemed at the time of the *Marriage.* For Blake, unlike Dante, has no master; he cannot follow others' ways. Nor can he assume that the Law he makes for himself—the Lion's way—can serve to guide the steps of other men. He is alone; and that aloneness, though a source of strength, fills the major prophecies with repeated moments of crisis and torment. Moreover, the search for meaning has no end. Blake cannot pass *through* the fire; corrosion, not purification, is his element. The *Marriage* burns away the Bible, but only to reveal that it is infinite. Blake's immense prophetic epic, that poem which includes as variants *The Four Zoas, Milton,* and *Jerusalem,* could never be fixed in a single pattern. After initiation Blake enters the refining flames of human life, where devils and angels perpetually converse. He had written his Bible. Now he must live it, sustained, like other prophets, only by faith in himself.

Per Amica Silentia Lunae

The friends that have it I do wrong
When ever I remake a song,
Should know what issue is at stake:
It is myself that I remake.

Young poets expect initiation. When Dante composed *La Vita Nuova* he was in his late twenties, ready in every way to come of age. He aspired to a new life, and reached it; and the very act of setting down a book called *Youth* proclaimed that his youth was over. When Blake began *The Marriage of Heaven and Hell* he was in his thirty-third year—no longer a young man, but a man whose age itself announced rebirth. The air was full of signs: revolution in France, the visions of Swedenborg, a crisis of empire and law, and the new discovery of "printing in the infernal method." Now was the time when "a new heaven is begun," enabling "the return of Adam into

47

Paradise." The world had grown young. At such moments initiation seems quite easy, perhaps inevitable. Instantly Blake knows himself a prophet.

> For in this Period the Poets Work is Done: and all the Great
> Events of Time start forth & are concievd in such a Period
> Within a Moment: a Pulsation of the Artery.

A young poet in such a state has no hesitation. He reads his early work with gratitude, perceiving that the spirit of a master—the poet he is yet to be—has guided his hand. He enters the ritual of his initiation as confidently as a young lord strides into his home.

Such confidence does not attend an aging poet. A poet whose faith in himself is troubled, who lacks the irresistible conviction that he is a prophet, must labor and labor to perform his initiation. Nor can he be certain that his early works, upon rereading, will not prove sterile. Time works against the aging poet; not many renew themselves. Is it possible that initiation happens only to the young? Will a new life dawn for the imagination simply because the imagination requires it? Asking such questions, we enter the mind of William Butler Yeats, a poet in his fifties, and the time of *Per Amica Silentia Lunae* (1918).

Yeats is a connoisseur of initiation. Again and again throughout his career he welcomes some version of a golden dawn, a sunburst of secret, newly disclosed meanings that will transform his future by connecting it to an earlier life. Such accessions of new light help account for his constant need to revise. Yet Yeats' conversions, however creative and persuasive, are never unconditional. Unlike the saint, the hero, the rhetorician, or the sentimentalist, he tells us in the beautiful fifth section of "Anima Hominis," we poets "sing amid our uncertainty." Nor can a poet afford to come to terms with his sources of dissatisfaction: "We must not make a false faith by hiding from our thoughts the causes of doubt. . . . The poet, because he may not stand within the sacred house but lives amid the whirlwinds that beset its threshold, may find his pardon." Yeats pauses on the threshold of initiation, perpetually converted, perpetually in vacillation.

Indeed, the question that haunts *Per Amica,* darkening all its hopes for spiritual certitude, is whether Yeats' poetic career can be renewed. Each of the two main sections, "Anima Hominis" and "Anima Mundi," ends with a vision of poetic sterility. In the first Yeats pictures himself grown beyond suffering, like "Wordsworth withering into eighty years, honoured and empty-witted" (342); in the second he thinks of putting his "barbarous words" aside forever, aging "to some kind of simple piety like that of an old woman" (366). Paradoxically, the very knowledge he seeks would, if attained, put an end to poetry. Creation, he argues, thrives not on piety and wisdom but on new bitterness, new disappointment—that "old man's frenzy," associated with Blake, he was to describe so brilliantly nineteen years later in "An Acre of Grass." The mysteries revealed by *Per Amica* lead Yeats to the edge of a precipice: a contentment too deep for poems to pierce it. Against this threat of creative impotence, he reasserts his own continuing frustration, his fascinated hunger for difficulties he cannot solve. *Per Amica* celebrates the form of an initiation without its consequences. It runs through a round, and leaves the poet the same yearning heart with which he began.

Yet the will to be initiated, always prevalent in Yeats, was never expressed more intensely than here. The book seems half a prayer or desperate plea for some outward sign of regeneration. Yeats needed such assurance. When he wrote *Per Amica,* in his early fifties, he was haunted by the fear that his creative life might have come to an end, dissipated forever by the heterogeneous whirl of activity—"theater business, management of men"—he had engaged in for many years. His world seemed to have passed. In many ways his best friends were the dead; always more eloquent in praising them than the living, he now spent much of his time conversing with them. Nor could he fail to see the ironies in his relation to his audience, that Irish race to which, in theory, he felt so close and with which, in practice, he was so often infuriated. Many poems of those years—for instance, "Lines Written in Dejection," "The Fisherman," "The People," "Easter 1916"—deal with his dread of flagging creative powers or with his ambiguous estrangement from his countrymen.

> "What have I earned for all that work," I said,
> "For all that I have done at my own charge?
> The daily spite of this unmannerly town,
> Where who has served the most is most defamed,
> The reputation of his lifetime lost
> Between the night and morning. . . ."

Perhaps he and Ireland were sinking together.

The doubts about his country were also doubts about himself. From the very beginning of his career Yeats had been supported by the belief that history was on his side and Ireland's. The apparent backwardness of the nation, properly considered, only meant that it had kept alive traditions forgotten by the rest of modern Europe and America. The Irish poet had inherited wisdom. Supported by scholars, he could

> begin to dig in Ireland the garden of the future, understanding that here in Ireland the spirit of man may be about to wed the soil of the world. . . . He himself would understand that more was expected of him than of others because he had greater possessions. The Irish race would have become a chosen race, one of the pillars that uphold the world.

Even the Anglo-Irish conflict in Yeats' own nature, the ancestry that kept Gaelic and the people foreign to him, might be seen as an advantage enabling him to translate the old world for the new. "I thought we might bring the halves together if we had a national literature that made Ireland beautiful in the memory, and yet had been freed from provincialism by an exacting criticism, an European pose." History had chosen Yeats. Yet it had also begun to forsake him. If the Irish people were indeed so resistant to their own best interests and best authors, if romance had died and "Modern Ireland has made up her mind, in our generation, to find her level as a willing inmate in our workaday Western world," then the Irish poet was nothing but a relic. Paudeen would fumble in a greasy till. Yeats had been robbed of his future.

Nor could he rely on poetry to save him. In the two decades between *The Wind among the Reeds* (1899) and *The Wild Swans at Coole* (1919), as Yeats strove to remake both himself and his style hard enough for the twentieth century, he could not overlook how many of the most talented young writers considered his work *passé*. "You are too old for me to help you," the twenty-year-old James Joyce told him (or might have told him) in 1902. And the help that the younger generation *did* give Yeats could be even more painful. In 1913 the brash young Ezra Pound wrote Harriet Monroe that "Yeats is already a sort of great dim figure with its associations set in the past." But that judgment did not discourage Pound from taking Yeats in hand: revising his poems, criticizing his diction, introducing him to new poetic voices and Noh plays, and even—for three winters beginning in 1913–14—serving as his literary secretary. Yeats profited from the advice. Pound's criticism "has given me new life," he wrote Lady Gregory. "To talk over a poem with him is like getting you to put a sentence into dialect. All becomes clear and natural." Yet insofar as Pound was right about what the age demanded, the poetry best suited to the age would not resemble Yeats'. "Ezra Pound, whose art is the opposite of mine, whose criticism commends what I most condemn, a man with whom I should quarrel more than anyone else if we were not united by affection," could only confirm what Yeats himself suspected: his verse was lost in the past.

Moreover, Yeats had personal reasons to perceive the faint absurdity that attends a man in his fifties—a successful public man—who still longs for an initiation. His interest in magic had placed him in strange, undignified company. Though scholars have rightly emphasized, of late, the depth and seriousness of Yeats' delving into the occult, a skeptical part of his mind also remained conscious that he looked ridiculous. And magic might well become a substitute for poetry, a rival rather than a friend for his muse. The artist W. T. Horton wrote Yeats in distress after having watched him scrabbling on the floor for a piece of automatic script: "I saw you as the man with the muck rake in 'The Pilgrim's Progress' while above you your

Beloved held the dazzling crown of your own Poetic Genius. But you would not look up & you went on with your grovelling." Nor could the poet find much meaning to his life except through magic. Beginning in 1914, with *Reveries over Childhood and Youth,* Yeats composed draft after draft of an autobiography, and confessed to himself how many follies he had committed and how much life lay behind him. The final paragraph of the *Reveries* sounds a recurrent note.

> For some months now I have lived with my own youth and child-hood, not always writing indeed but thinking of it almost every day, and I am sorrowful and disturbed. It is not that I have accomplished too few of my plans, for I am not ambitious; but when I think of all the books I have read, and of the wise words I have heard spoken, and of the anxiety I have given to parents and grandparents, and of the hopes that I have had, all life weighed in the scales of my own life seems to me a preparation for something that never happens.

By 1917, the year of *Per Amica,* Yeats had prepared for something else that did not happen. "Maurice," to whom the book is addressed through a Prologue and Epilogue, is a pseudonym for Maud Gonne's daughter Iseult. In this respect *Per Amica* performs a rite of courtship; for Yeats had proposed marriage to Iseult (some months after being turned down by Maud herself). Yet before the book was published Iseult rejected him. Another folly had been added to the list. Thus Yeats submits *Per Amica* more as a ceremony of leave-taking—a formal announcement that the poet is wedding spirits— than an engagement to new beginnings. Publically dissatisfied, artistically weary, privately wounded—was his life not over?

"Ego Dominus Tuus," the poem (completed two years earlier) that Yeats chose as an entrance to the mysteries of *Per Amica,* represents both that question and its answer. In retrospect, looking back as Yeats did from *A Vision* (1925), the poem clearly adumbrates the turn in his career, the first cycle of his visionary phase. The theory of the anti-self, the tracing of magical shapes beneath the moon, the supplication of an unknown image of reality would come to seem the poet's way out of despair into new life. Yet "Ego Dominus Tuus" itself displays less confidence. Yeats has not yet found the Master to whom he wishes to bow. Even the title contains an equivocation, since the "Ego," that completely formed, otherworldly "Lord of Terrible Aspect" who came down to Dante, does not appear to Yeats. Yeats merely *wishes* him to come. Unlike the poem that begins Dante's initiation, the poem that begins Yeats' records no vision. The title is a mysterious afterthought, an attempt to force interpretation onto the poem by making it speak another language (a language that Dante's Love spoke only in the commentary). All that Yeats knows for certain, at this point, is that the agent of his rebirth must be someone most unlike himself.

51

For the sake of that apparition, however, he is willing to give up every-thing. "Ego Dominus Tuus" is informed by a universal irritability, the restlessness of a man who walks in the moon, having "passed the best of life," and scorns everything but his own "unconquerable delusion." Modern art, self-deceiving because artists seek only to find themselves, has lost the "old nonchalance of the hand":

> We are but critics, or but half create,
> Timid, entangled, empty and abashed,
> Lacking the countenance of our friends.

Yeats needs a friend; not someone to approve his work but someone whose violent opposition will cause him to forget himself. For that forgetfulness he will surrender his personality, his ancestry, his reason, and even his book. The last is most daring of all. In the poem that had introduced *Responsibilities* (1914) Yeats had confessed to his ancestors that a book was all he could show.

> *Pardon that for a barren passion's sake,*
> *Although I have come close on forty-nine,*
> *I have no child, I have nothing but a book,*
> *Nothing but that to prove your blood and mine.*

But the poet of "Ego Dominus Tuus" abandons his open book to trace characters on the sands, "Because I seek an image, not a book." His blood and craft cannot sustain him. Nor can self-knowledge issue forth in wisdom.

> Those men that in their writings are most wise
> Own nothing but their blind, stupefied hearts.

Wisdom results paradoxically not from finding the self but from losing it in yearning. "Blind, stupefied hearts" pour themselves out in unselfcon-scious passion and sacrifice themselves to an image of whatever they do not possess. "For what mere book can grant a knowledge / With an im-passioned gravity / Appropriate to that beating breast . . .?" Yeats strives to blind himself, like Oedipus, and leave his book.

This point of view does not have matters all its own way in "Ego Do-minus Tuus," however. There are two speakers in the poem, Hic and Ille, and they do not agree. One is "Here," rooted to the things of the world and himself, the other "There," dreaming of his anti-self and spectral im-ages. Ezra Pound dubbed them "Hic" and "Willie"; and indeed Ille is given a more Yeatsian tone and the better of the argument. They might also be called "Ezra" and "Willie," logical extensions of the intense aesthetic debate that Pound and Yeats had been conducting, late into the night, for several years. Hic's distaste for otherworldliness, his recommendation of art like

52

Dante's that makes itself "plain to the mind's eye," culminates in two lines that might stand as a motto for much of Pound's early work:

> A style is found by sedentary toil
> And by the imitation of great masters.

Nor could Yeats deny that Pound's criticism had often left him timid and abashed about his art. Yet in the first draft of the poem those lines belong to Ille. Pound's cry for a harder, colder poetry had become part of the older poet's own second nature. Hic is no foreign presence but Yeats' bond, never absent for long, to the realities of a poet's life: his discipline and conscience.

Many other companions also inhabit "Ego Dominus Tuus." Properly speaking, the dialectic of the poem involves six figures: Hic and Ille, the rational and spiritual sides of Yeats; Dante and Keats, who represent two aspects of the discontent that motivates poets—the first at war with both the world and himself, the second able to sustain his happiness only by shutting out his life with a dream of luxury; and two versions of the Master or Daimon. One of these masters we may call Michael Robartes, whose book Ille leaves open when he walks on the sands. As early as *Rosa Alchemica* (1897) Yeats had invoked Robartes—"something between a debauchee, a saint, and a peasant"—as his instrument of initiation. Robartes, sometimes accompanied by Owen Aherne, constantly appears to the poet in his hour of need, bearing tidings of a mystery that, once solved, will open all the gates of wisdom. Yeats fears and quarrels with him. Yet eventually he proved the poet's true guide, Virgil and Beatrice in one. In "The Phases of the Moon" (1918), which stands to *A Vision* as "Ego Dominus Tuus" to *Per Amica,* Robartes would expound the cyclic visionary doctrine that Yeats came to accept as truth.

Nevertheless, to identify Robartes with the "Dominus" sought by the poet would be a mistake. Yeats felt embarrassed, on occasion, by the fictional "friend" or alter ego he had invented, and once even tried to kill him off. To make one's Beatrice out of oneself raises desperate problems—who is to guide the guide? In "Ego Dominus Tuus" Yeats walks away from the book that Robartes left. He yearns for another Master, one who will interpret the characters Robartes has scribbled on the sands.

> I call to the mysterious one who yet
> Shall walk the wet sands by the edge of the stream
> And look most like me, being indeed my double,
> And prove of all imaginable things
> The most unlike, being my anti-self,
> And, standing by these characters, disclose
> All that I seek. . . .

A shrewd reader of men, viewing these lines in 1917, might well have guessed that Yeats was looking for a wife. Indeed, *Per Amica* (dedicated to a lost love) proved his last fling at bachelorhood. A few months after the book was published he married Georgie Hyde-Lees, and was introduced by her to those spiritual communicators whose messages insured that he would never be lonely again. Told this way, however, the happy outcome of *Per Amica* (as Yeats himself told it in *A Vision*) sounds rather pat. "Ego Dominus Tuus" calls to a "he," not a "she," and Yeats' own later reading inveighs against easy solutions: "that only which comes easily can never be a portion of our being" (332). Another shrewd reader might have guessed that the mysterious one to whom the poet called, his only bride, was death. "I shall find the dark grow luminous, the void fruitful when I understand I have nothing, that the ringers in the tower have appointed for the hymen of the soul a passing bell" (332). Yet that solution also seems too easy. Yeats invites death only on condition that its dark be luminous, fertile with spirits who will respond to him. Though death has no dread for him, more than anything he dreads a failure of imagination. He needs a vital image to wed. If his happiness as a husband depended partly on the dowry of spirits that George brought with her, his happiness with the spirits was achieved only when they spoke through George. Her traces led away from death. Yeats wants a Master both familiar and strange, equally mysterious and intelligible—at once his double and his anti-self. The "rich, dark nothing" enchants him like a female principle, hinting that it contains all he holds dear. And the mysterious interpreter to whom he calls is named not only Robartes but Legion.

Per Amica Silentia Lunae is intoxicated, in fact, with ambiguous acts of interpretation. Like a medium, Yeats divines hidden meanings in his poem; his dreams; a chance remark; a bit of hawthorn; the movements of a cat. The poet sets out to read events from his past life as if they were messages sent him by some fraternity of the dead. The form of the book, perhaps the most subtle ever devised by Yeats, is predicated on a deliberate calling-forth of such messages. In Chapter ii of "Anima Mundi" Yeats records the method of evocation that Goethe had prescribed against literary sterility: the critical faculty, intellect, and desire must be suspended until images take shape of their own will. Having no natural gift for evocation, Yeats explains, he invented a new process, inducing

> dreams during sleep, or rather visions, for they had none of the confusion of dreams, by laying upon my pillow or beside my bed certain flowers or leaves. Even to-day, after twenty years, the exaltations and the messages that came to me from some bits of hawthorn or some other plant seem, of all moments of my life, the happiest and the wisest.
>
> [345]

Per Amica contrives a similar ritual. But now Yeats evokes visions not with a flower but with a poem. Suspending his critical faculty, he reads "Ego Dominus Tuus" as if it had been not a beseeching of the anti-self but an emanation from it—an object of worship.

Like the Dante of *La Vita Nuova,* moreover, Yeats finds a significance in his poem that no uninitiated reader could hope to uncover. The first part of *Per Amica,* "Anima Hominis," pursues the images of "Ego Dominus Tuus" to their origins, literary and psychological, in the poet's own thought. Above all we learn the sources of Ille's dissatisfaction. "Anima Hominis" opens with Yeats' description of his own mood when writing a poem. He begins with a mistake: the common modern error of believing that, in art, "I have found myself." Coming home from a dinner party, troubled by having "lost his head," having dispelled himself in nervous reactions to the company, he invites "a marmorean Muse, an art where no thought or emotion has come to mind because another man has thought or felt something different, for now there must be no reaction, action only, and the world must move my heart but to the heart's discovery of itself" (325). But the sense of self-discovery is an illusion. He has found not himself but his anti-self or Daimon: everything he desires and cannot attain. The images of his poem, already complete and elaborated without his own volition, "must come from above me and beyond me" (326). They are as willful and miraculous as Love in *La Vita Nuova* or the dream woman in Rossetti's "Hand and Soul," who informs the abashed artist that "I am an image, Chiaro, of thine own soul within thee." The poem has a life of its own. In creation Yeats gives himself up to the Other.

What is the nature of that Other? Unlike Keats, who had suggested that a true poet "has no Identity—he is continually in for—and filling some other Body," Yeats refuses to acknowledge the world at large—other identities, concrete reality and living people—as his Master. His distress when other people press and impinge on his identity specifically contradicts Keats' account of the annihilation of his identity by a room full of people. Such annihilation would demonstrate a negative capability, the generous openness to experience that marks Keats a poet. But Yeats, by contrast, finds people "crude allegories," unrefined images of that more perfect world where poetry has its being. A notorious passage of "Ego Dominus Tuus" (glossed by "Anima Hominis") reinterprets Keats' "love of the world" as an illusion fostered by poverty. Thirsting for luxury and unable to slake his thirst with beautiful objects, the young poet was driven to imaginary delights, luxuriating in a world fashioned by his own need. Keats' Other, according to Yeats, is psychological necessity: the grasping of the mind for everything beyond its reach. "Anima Hominis" meditates on this possibility. Yeats goes so far as to concede the Freudian definition of dreams—"certain" dreams, "for I do not grant them all" (341)—as the day's unfulfilled desire. Yet he distinguishes such dreams from vision, which "prolongs its power by rhythm and pattern, the wheel where the world is butterfly" (341).

Vision persists long after we know that the desires that call it forth can never be fulfilled. Hence the creative process, from the artist's point of view, consists of putting aside the personality that inhabits the day and submitting oneself to the "boundless and the unforeseen": the dark side of the mind.

The images that give birth to poems, therefore, must harbor in the soul of man—"Anima Hominis." Yeats hopes to renew his poetic career by tracing once more the lineaments of his unsatisfied desire. But *Per Amica* also entertains another possibility. "Whether it is we or the vision that create the pattern, who set the wheel turning, it is hard to say" (341). If poems visit us in our sleep, perhaps they master us because they maintain a powerful existence independent of our will. The second part of the book suggests that the source of all creation may be Henry More's "Anima Mundi" ("the soul of the world"). Drawing upon his research in occult science, Yeats plays with the notion that poems are inspired by the spirits of the dead: "it is the dream martens that, all unknowing, are master-masons to the living martens building about church windows their elaborate nests" (359). As usual in this mood, he hedges his supernatural claims with more rational alternatives. If, as Blake would argue, all men share the Poetic Genius— Daimon, spirit of prophecy—then Anima Mundi itself may be projected by the individual imagination. *The Marriage of Heaven and Hell* furnishes a proper authority: "God only acts or is in existing beings or men" (352). Yet Yeats clearly wants a poetic renewal that does not depend quite so uncompromisingly on his own personal initiative. He reads his work, his life, asking for a sign: "an impulse from some Daimon that gives to our vague, unsatisfied desire, beauty, a meaning, and a form all can accept" (362). The poems of his future live in that Great Memory. He hovers on the shore of the Anima Mundi, praying that it may break over him and take him in.

Even the title of *Per Amica Silentia Lunae* testifies to Yeats' effort to immerse his mind in the general mind. His own explanation, at the beginning of "Anima Mundi," characteristically obscures as much as it clarifies. The secret must be whispered as in an initiation rite. Liberating his mind from modern thought, he suggests,

> that I might so believe I have murmured evocations and frequented mediums, delighted in all that displayed great problems through sensuous images or exciting phrases, accepting from abstract schools but a few technical words that are so old they seem but broken architraves fallen amid bramble and grass, and have put myself to school where all things are seen: *A Tenedo tacitae per amica silentia lunae.*

[343]

The Latin ("From Tenedos through the friendly silence of the quiet moon") derives from the *Aeneid* (II. 255). The Greek fleet, which has been concealed on the island of Tenedos, stealthily moves toward Troy, where it will join the forces unloosed from the Trojan horse. But Yeats probably associates his phrase with less direct sources. Victor Hugo had used "Per amica silentia lunae" as an epigraph for "Clair de Lune" in *Les Orientales;* and Verlaine, whose own "Clair de Lune" epitomizes the Symbolist movement, wrote another night-piece called *"Per Amica Silentia."* These rich associations evidently stir Yeats to the same excitement, "in which one discovers something supernatural, a stirring as it were of the roots of the hair," that Arthur Symons had once induced in him by reading from Verlaine and Mallarmé. Indeed, Yeats' account of such moments, in *The Trembling of the Veil* (1922), specifically brings together the Symbolist poets, the moon, classicism, his own rereading of his first poems, supernatural meanings, and the effort to find a lucid pattern in them all: "I am certain that there was something in myself compelling me to attempt creation of an art as separate from everything heterogeneous and casual, from all character and circumstance, as some Herodiade of our theatre, dancing seemingly alone in her narrow moving luminous circle." The phrase from Virgil, rubbed to mysterious smoothness by its passage through many hands, purchases an entrance to the ancient "general mind."

The line also conveys another meaning. The silence of the moon befriends a sacrilegious human breach of faith. Both Hugo and Verlaine emphasize, in their poems, the violence that underlies the quiet. Hugo's soft night-sounds turn out to emanate from the sobbing of heavy sacks that hold "something like a human form"—slave girls murdered by drowning; and Verlaine's pastel lesbian lovers are touched by the stigmata. Yeats associated both poets with such effects of beauty and savagery mixed. A single paragraph in *The Trembling of the Veil* quotes Verlaine on Hugo as "a supreme poet, but a volcano of mud as well as of flame," and comments that to read Verlaine's "sacred poems is to remember perhaps that the Holy Infant shared His first home with the beasts." Hence the tranquillity of the Latin motto sheathes a beastly reality. The Greeks, on their murderous errand, represent the world of activity, heroic distraction; yet they succeed thanks to the moon, their eternally passive fate, which supplies the phase they need for triumph. Yeats asks for a similar fate. Despite his involvement in chaos and war, and the muddle of his heart about that woman who for him was a second Helen, he comes home to Anima Mundi by submitting to the dictates of the moon. Henceforward his destiny alone will control him. *Per Amica Silentia Lunae* announces with its title the poet's intention: to mask his face with moonlight and steer his course by the moon.

It does not signify, however, an end to struggle. Like the Greeks before Troy or Dante before entering the flame, Yeats knows that his trials will not soon be over. The Daimon is a deceiving spirit who does not bring peace. "When I think of life as a struggle with the Daimon who would ever set us to the hardest work among those not impossible, I understand why there is a deep enmity between a man and his destiny, and why a man loves nothing but his destiny" (336). Yeats' initiation merely substitutes one kind of mortal combat for another. In "Ego Dominus Tuus," adapting a memorable phrase from Verlaine, he had spoken of the work of men of action as "The struggle of the fly in marmalade"; and Yeats was also thinking of himself. *Per Amica* defines both his own work and that of "any great poetical writer" in a different light. "I comprehend, if I know the lineaments of his life, that the work is the man's flight from his entire horoscope, his blind struggle in the network of the stars" (328). The man of action struggles in the thick of business, the poet in the network of the stars; but both struggle, and both are blind. Yeats puts aside the quarrel with others in order to quarrel with himself. His destiny will prove as recalcitrant as the woman he has loved.

Formally, to insure the continuance of that struggle, *Per Amica* divides everything into two. Like the poet himself, parceled into Hic and Ille, the words of the book are designed to register opposite meanings. The unknown writer of *A Vision* took his theme from *Per Amica*'s "distinction between the perfection that is from a man's combat with himself and that which is from a combat with circumstance," but he might equally as well have begun with subjective/objective, self/anti-self, Hominis/Mundi, or terrestrial condition/condition of fire. Considering how much Yeats owed to Blake, one of the most interesting of these oppositions, described in Chapter xi of "Anima Hominis" and Chapters xv–xvi of "Anima Mundi," contrasts the winding movement of nature (the Path of the Serpent) with the straight line of the saint or sage (emblemized by a woman shooting an arrow into the air). Yeats associates the former, "those heaving circles, those winding arcs," with mathematical cycles of history, clearly anticipating the gyres of *A Vision*. On the contrary, those who take the straight path renounce nature and time for intellect and faith; they shoot beyond the tangible. "In so far as a man is like all other men, the inflow finds him upon the winding path, and in so far as he is a saint or sage, upon the straight path" (361). Viewed in these terms, the possibilities of life seem discriminated as perfectly as the two halves of a couplet.

The poet, however, follows neither path. "I think that we who are poets and artists . . . live but for the moment when vision comes to our weariness like terrible lightning" (340). The power of the Daimon, we are told, descends in "neither the winding nor the straight line but zigzag, illuminating the passive and active properties, the tree's two sorts of fruit" (361). Creation, for Yeats as for Blake, occurs in the pulsation of an artery, in lightning. When all the subtleties and ceremonies of interpretation are done, the poet must put them aside and seize his moment: "never progress as we understand it, never the straight line, always a necessity to break away and destroy, or to sink in and forget." Thus Yeats renews himself not by completing his initiation but by recapturing his sense that in a moment it is about to begin. His human impulse breaks the dialectic, and its shattered images inspire the poem. Again and again Yeats' later works repeat this process. Standing amidst a gathering storm, an apocalypse, a widening gyre, he flashes out with a single question "like terrible lightning." Neither an ordinary man nor a sage, he mediates between them; the poem is not the answer of the mysterious one but his call to it.

Per Amica ends in questions too. For Yeats does not resolve his own uncertainties. He finishes his initiation without knowing whether its images have come from Hominis or Mundi, his personal need or unseen benefactors. "I am full of uncertainty, not knowing when I am the finger, when the clay." Nor does he know whether his questioning will bloom in poetry. "As I go up and down my stair and pass the gilded Moorish wedding-chest where I keep my 'barbarous words,' I wonder will I take to them once more" (366). Above all he must fear a total identification with the dead. So much of "Anima Mundi" concerns the secrets of the dead that Yeats himself, like any reader, must pause to wonder whether his writing will come back to life. He is specially tempted by the notion of cycles. Perhaps time endlessly repeats itself, and individual efforts like those of the poet are doomed to futility. In that case poetry must yield to Yeats' other mistress or profession: magic.

The final words of *Per Amica* address that situation. In the "Epilogue" dedicated to "Maurice," Yeats superimposes his worship of French poets, twenty years earlier, on Iseult's interest in the new generation of French poets. Only the preoccupation with religion remains the same; and the poets of today submit everything not to the Soul and the Image but to Mother France and Mother Church. Then Yeats realizes that he has been describing himself. "Have not my thoughts run through a like round, though I have not found my tradition in the Catholic Church, which was not the Church of my childhood, but where the tradition is, as I believe, more universal and more ancient?" (368–69). The question is repetitious in more ways than one. In the draft of an autobiography that Yeats had just finished, he had reminisced about a faith that obsessed him in 1895: "I was convinced that all lonely and lovely places were crowded with invisible beings and that it would be possible to communicate with them. I meant to initiate young men and women in this worship, which would unite the radical truths of Christianity to those of a more ancient world." His thoughts have indeed run through a round; he is still harping on the same old string. Yet in one respect everything has changed. The tradition established by *Per Amica*, however eccentric, has given the poet a new way of reading; new keys; an *alphabet*. That was what he claimed for his system. "I find the setting it all in order has helped my verse, has given me a new framework and new patterns. One goes on year after year gradually getting the disorder of one's mind in order and this is the real impulse to create." Yeats had sent himself to school and learned to read. It was time to apply the lesson.

Nor was it only the dead who had taught Yeats his lesson. In some ways he could be a very stubborn and reluctant pupil, for there was only one message he was willing to hear: that he could live again. Emblems of initiation and rebirth, always his preoccupation, swell into flood tide in *Per Amica*. In that respect also the book makes a circle. To regenerate himself, Yeats had studied a religion. But that religion had a single cardinal point of doctrine: regeneration. Everything that he came to believe—the reincarnation of souls, the returning cycles of time, the presence of the dead, the power of art to make God "fill the cradles right"—confirmed that, within his old poems, new poems struggled to be born. *Per Amica* instructs Yeats to wait quietly for his nativity. "The purpose of most religious teaching, of the insistence upon the submission to God's will above all, is to make certain of the passivity of the vehicle where it is most pure and most tenuous" (362). Having accomplished this emptying of himself into innocence—"A condition of complete simplicity / (Costing not less than everything)"—the poet is ready for his second coming. Chapter xix of "Anima Mundi" calls up Spenser's image of the rebirth of souls,

> sent into the chaungeful world agayne,
> Till thither they retourn where first they grew:
> So, like a wheele, around they ronne from old to new.

Chapter xx, citing the innocence of Blake, aspires toward another birth: "Within ourselves Reason and Will, who are the man and woman, hold out towards a hidden altar a laughing or crying child." And in the following chapter, thirsting for wholeness, Yeats begins "to study the only self that I can know, myself," and opens a book of verse, and reads it as if reborn.

That passage supplies the climax of *Per Amica*. Emerging from its ordeal of thought, the book crosses the threshold into a state of innocence. Yeats pictures himself blessed like a child (he would recount the experience again, poetically, in the fourth section of "Vacillation"). Once again, as in "Ego Dominus Tuus," a book lies open before him. Once again, as at the beginning of *Per Amica*, his solitary creative mood is juxtaposed with the presence of other people. Yet now, rather than depressing him, they add to his exaltation.

> At certain moments, always unforeseen, I become happy, most commonly when at hazard I have opened some book of verse. Sometimes it is my own verse when, instead of discovering new technical flaws, I read with all the excitement of the first writing. Perhaps I am sitting in some crowded restaurant, the open book beside me, or closed, my

excitement having overbrimmed the page. I look at the strangers near as if I had known them all my life, and it seems strange that I cannot speak to them: everything fills me with affection, I have no longer any fears or any needs; I do not even remember that this happy mood must come to an end. It seems as if the vehicle had suddenly grown pure and far extended and so luminous that the images from *Anima Mundi,* embodied there and drunk with that sweetness, would, like a country drunkard who has thrown a wisp into his own thatch, burn up time.

[364–65]

United with the soul of the world, the poet momentarily draws no distinction between his own high calling and the life of ordinary people. Strangers seem closer than his friends; indeed, the very notion of a stranger "seems strange." The democratic feeling extends even to the prose, where the humble simile of the country drunkard (like one of Dante's "homely" images) expresses the apocalypse. Significantly, in this state of mind Yeats does not even distinguish his own book of verse from someone else's: either can flood him with excitement. Every soul, whether dead or living, has its place within the sheltering arc of Anima Mundi. Creatively, the eternal presence of the world-soul offers Yeats a well of images never to be exhausted. Personally, it offers relief from the loneliness, the solipsistic obsession with one's own daimonic pain, that had often seemed to him inseparable from creative labor. *Here* the body is not bruised to pleasure soul. Anima Mundi, where the poet's own Daimon lives, also bestows on him a full society of souls, the blessed knowledge that he is not alone.

Yeats' initiation was complete. Time stopped for him, and he began to write with all the energy of a young man or a convert. Almost every paragraph of *Per Amica,* on rereading, turned out to contain material for a new poem. He would never again exhaust his stock. Nor would he ever again lose faith in his power to renew creation. Against all the odds, weary, aging, self-doubting, confused, the poet actually did begin another life. And poems began to come. Not withering like Wordsworth, not mute like a pious old woman, Yeats shook himself into a growing self-possession. Like Dante and Blake he made good his promise that his greatest effort still lay before him.

Initiation is possible for an aging poet; the example of Yeats confirms it. Yet the same example shows how much dedication an older poet may need. As if performing a ritual, Yeats carefully repeated each of the steps that his mentors Dante and Blake had taught him. He mixed together verse and prose. He made a sacred book. He called on a master to interpret it. He invented a history to put himself back in phase and a method of reading that would cast new light on poems that had once seemed dead. And he prophesied the greater work that would culminate his vision. *Per Amica*

61

Silentia Lunae is a blueprint for initiation—a model that worked. Even its faith is calculated to bring some order to the life of the poet, by making a religion of his own rebirth.

To make a religion of his own rebirth—that was why Yeats had undergone initiation. But can so private a religion lead to anything but solipsism: eccentric poetry intent on worshiping itself? T. S. Eliot, thinking about the later Yeats, was haunted by such questions. At an earlier time Eliot had supposed he knew the answer. Yeats, above all other major poets of his time, had hearkened after strange gods, and his work had been vitiated by the same crankiness that infected his teacher. "And about Blake's supernatural territories, as about the supposed ideas that dwell there, we cannot help commenting on a certain meanness of culture." Yet by the time that Eliot himself had entered his early fifties, he had begun to appreciate the necessity of self-renewal by whatever means. His interest both in Yeats and in initiation reached a peak in the years just before and after the older poet's death. Consider, for instance, the way that "An Acre of Grass" (1938)—

> Grant me an old man's frenzy,
> Myself must I remake
> Till I am Timon and Lear
> Or that William Blake
> Who beat upon the wall
> Till Truth obeyed his call

—reappears in *East Coker* (1937–40):

> Do not let me hear
> Of the wisdom of old men, but rather of their folly,
> Their fear of fear and frenzy, their fear of possession,
> Of belonging to another, or to others, or to God.

And the last section of *East Coker* specifically endorses Yeats' position: "Old men ought to be explorers."

Indeed, the *Four Quartets* return again and again to initiation. Eliot broods throughout on the need for going back to origins, discovering the end in the beginning: "And approach to the meaning restores the experience / In a different form." Formally, he repeats many of the procedures we have noticed: the alternation of lyric verse with harsher, often prosy explanations; the self-conscious attempt to read, and teach us to read, his own past work in a different way; the labor to create a single coherent book encompassing many sorts of poem; the vision of history as "a pattern / Of timeless moments"; the constant aspiration toward new beginnings. Spiritually, he casts himself into refining fire. A memorial lecture on Yeats, delivered at the Abbey Theatre in 1940, reveals the direction of Eliot's thought.

Now, in theory, there is no reason why a poet's inspiration or material should fail, in middle age or at any time before senility. For a man who is capable of experience finds himself in a different world in every decade of his life; as he sees it with different eyes, the material of his art is continually renewed. But in fact, very few poets have shown this capacity of adaptation to the years. It requires, indeed, an exceptional honesty and courage to face the change.

Yeats had shown that courage. Would Eliot be equal to the task? The question is asked, the answer given, above all in *Little Gidding* (1942). The season of the poem is midwinter spring, a suspended time when an aging poet may feel that "The soul's sap quivers"—if faith can be renewed. In the second section the poet walks a "dead patrol" (in the dawn after an air raid) with "a familiar compound ghost." Many of the illustrious dead join in that "spirit unappeased and peregrine," a whole procession of ancestors. But Dante and Yeats are foremost. From Dante, his first poetic master, Eliot had learned what a poet could be; from Yeats, he had taken the challenge to renew his career. Now they return—not with consolation but with prophecy of the gifts reserved for a poet's age: "And last, the rending pain of re-enactment / Of all that you have done, and been." The destructions wrought by war, by life, cannot be diverted merely by mastery of words. Rather, the familiar ghost offers nothing but a new ordeal: the ordeal of initiation.

> From wrong to wrong the exasperated spirit
> Proceeds, unless restored by that refining fire
> Where you must move in measure, like a dancer.

Dante and Yeats bring Eliot their fire, their dance. They ask him to hazard everything for the sake of being reborn; and they join in his prayer.

> We shall not cease from exploration
> And the end of all our exploring
> Will be to arrive where we started
> And know the place for the first time.

"See, they return." Dante, in *La Vita Nuova,* redeems his youth by finding that it holds a number he had not previously counted on; Blake, in *The Marriage of Heaven and Hell,* restores the primal moment of creation by seeing that now, as ever, he holds the Bible in his hands; Yeats, in *Per Amica Silentia Lunae,* puts himself back in phase by coupling his spirit and the spirit of the world within a single book. Each of them, as in the transparency of fire, sees through himself as if for the first time. And at the end of *Four Quartets* Eliot moves in their company. Like every poet who wishes to start again, he returns to the pages where his new life is already written and learns what his words have meant. He opens the book with us. He begins to read.

II

HARMONIUM

The Tradition of One
and *Four Quartets*

As a poet grows old, the way that he reads his earlier work often changes. Poems that once seemed full of meaning now retreat into the background, perhaps to be absorbed by anthologies where their fragile unselfconscious life freezes into the classic. Other poems—the ugly ducklings, which have always seemed to belong to someone else—suddenly emerge into the mainstream. And something even stranger can happen. Very often a great old poet begins to regard his poems as possessing no individual interest (at least for him). Even his masterpieces, taken one by one, appear partial, transitory, splintered—as the aging Goethe notoriously declared that all his works were "only fragments of a great confession" ("nur Bruchstücke einer grossen Konfession"). Another logic determines such reading: the logic of the whole. Old masters who refer to "the work" frequently intend no specific piece of art but rather everything they have done, everything they still hope to do. And an artist devoted to "the work" can easily become impatient with its mere particular examples. Old poems are hard to read; their concern with themselves tends to embarrass an author who has passed to larger concerns. One by one they go into the dark. Or, if the poet is very great or very lucky, they join together in another pattern.

Indeed, the existence of such a pattern has seemed, to many critics, the essential test of a poet's greatness. As Eliot grew old, he became preoccupied with this criterion. The questions raised by two essays of 1944—"What is Minor Poetry?" and "What is a Classic?"—respond to the question posed so insistently, over and over again, by *Four Quartets:* "Why should my work be saved?" Nor has he any illusions about the standard he must meet.

> The difference between major and minor poets has nothing to do with whether they wrote long poems, or only short poems—though the *very*

65

greatest poets, who are few in number, have all had something to say which could only be said in a long poem. The important difference is whether a knowledge of the whole, or at least of a very large part, of a poet's work, makes one enjoy more, because it makes one understand better, any one of his poems. That implies a significant unity in his whole work.

Eliot tries his own work by the same hard measure. Why should the agèd eagle stretch its wings? Only to show how much its wings have spanned.

Focusing on the pattern of the whole, an aging poet may find that he needs new glasses. Myopia often afflicts the middle-aged; but many people become farsighted as they grow old. Books must be held at a distance. And the change in vision can result in some curious methods of reading. First of all (as I have said), certain pages begin to fade, while others stand out in sharp relief. In the work of a master a trivial verse that fills a necessary link in the pattern may count for more than a great anthology piece that repeats an earlier success. (Eliot's little "Landscapes" acquired a new significance in the wake of *Four Quartets;* "The Hollow Men," with considerable stretching and groaning, had to be converted into a harbinger of Christian faith.) Every time a really new work of art arrives, Eliot said in a famous passage of "Tradition and the Individual Talent" (1919), "the *whole* existing order must be, if ever so slightly, altered; and so the relations, proportions, values of each work of art toward the whole are readjusted." But thirty years later, praising Joyce, he shifted the principle of order from tradition to the individual master. A great writer must be read as a tradition of one, his own continuum.

> Joyce's writings form a whole; we can neither reject the early work as stages, of no intrinsic interest, of his progress towards the latter, nor reject the later work as the outcome of decline. As with Shakespeare, his later work must be understood through the earlier, and the first through the last; it is the whole journey, not any one stage of it, that assures him his place among the great.

The word "journey," reminiscent of Dante and the epic, marks Joyce as an author of destiny, whose every writing points to a single end. Now he joins the company of the immortals and makes one with them. And the relative success or failure of any individual work, within the pattern made by the whole, ceases to matter.

Indeed, even "The poetry does not matter." As Eliot reads his earlier poems, like the "periphrastic study in a worn-out poetical fashion" that introduces the second part of "East Coker," he seems oppressed by their virtuosity, their self-conscious verbal tricks and gestures, their constantly failing "raid on the inarticulate." All that is "poetry," an ephemeral accomplishment in the here and now, and "Love is most nearly itself / When here and now cease to matter." An old poet has no time for poetry. He wants to go beyond his craft of verse, his peculiar power over words; he wants a reading that will never change; he wants to redeem the time.

A final result of such farsighted reading, therefore, is likely to be a new sense of pressure, perhaps even fear. The aging poet is haunted by the ghost of his past. With every poem he writes, the pattern alters and the whole meaning of his work is rearranged. For a poet as self-conscious as Eliot, agonizingly aware that every poem is an epitaph, the disparity between his reputation and his private life can induce acute schizophrenia. My earlier discussion of the manifold "familiar compound ghost" in "Little Gidding" omitted one crucial member: the poet himself.

> So I assumed a double part, and cried
> And heard another's voice cry: 'What! are *you* here?'
> Although we were not. I was still the same,
> Knowing myself yet being someone other—
> And he a face still forming.

Ventriloquism, in short. The point, I think, is that the aging Eliot is two people. One of them, a somewhat frail and provisional person, lives in the present. He cares a great deal about cheese and ancestors, writes letters to the editor and verses about cats, and worries incessantly, in this time of war, about extinction. At the moment he looks rather comical. A fire-watcher's hat perches oddly on his head, and bystanders might notice that he is talking to himself. Yet another Eliot walks with him: a master poet. The ghost perceives the design of the whole, "the gifts reserved for age / To set a crown upon your lifetime's effort." And though the gifts are bitter, the crown ironic, the sense of the passage is somehow consoling. The master lays many fears to rest. His perception of eternity removes the poet from his captivity in time and fits his loneliness into a pattern. "In the disfigured street / He left me, with a kind of valediction." Even a tragic career, when conceived as a whole, takes on a tragic dignity. Here Eliot literally realizes his detachment from self—a condition which, according to the next section of "Little Gidding," can liberate one from the future as well as the past.

Many aging poets require that form of liberation. Before they take leave of their ghosts, they must put their affairs in order. Above all a book is needed: the *Aeneid; Faust; Four Quartets; The Complete Poems; The Deathbed Edition*. Only a last full effort can compensate for the insufficiency and partiality of everything that has gone before. Last works, like last words, have a special aura of authenticity.

> O, but they say the tongues of dying men
> Inforce attention like deep harmony.

> Where words are scarce, they are seldom spent in vain,
> For they breathe truth that breathe their words in pain.

There is no time for ornament or deception: only a vast silence into which every word reverberates. Small wonder that poets should take such care to end on a proper note. The work will abide. "I *must* make a perfect edition of my works," said Alexander Pope, who had labored so hard to instruct posterity to view him right; "and then I shall have nothing to do but to die."

The summing-up can take many different forms. At one time the prestige of the epic led many poets and critics to believe that nothing but an epic could conclude a career. Thus the history of poetry is strewn with the wreckage of failed careers—poets whose epics were never finished. But the criterion itself is obviously faulty. After the apocalypse of *The New Dunciad*, where Pope calls down a personal last judgment on the whole of his civilization, are we really to consider his lifework incomplete because he did not finish *Brutus?* Does the *Christiad* really establish Vida as a more entire poet than Petrarch? In the presence of *Un coup de dés*, do we really regret the absence of Mallarmé's *Grand Oeuvre?* And who cares what Blackmore finished? The epic does not exhaust the possibilities for closing a career. Instead it provides a way—and only one way—for a poet to end.

The essential question for the poet, however, is whether he has accomplished everything of which he is capable. That is why the epic acquired its prestige. It challenges the poet to sing, to plot, to stretch, to suffer; it drains him of all his abilities. "By the general consent of criticks," according to Samuel Johnson, "the first praise of genius is due to the writer of an epick poem, as it requires an assemblage of all the powers which are singly sufficient for other compositions." From the standpoint of the poet, then (as opposed to the standpoint of his civilization, his audience, or those who police the conventions), the epic can be defined as a work that draws on all his powers. It is in this sense—and probably no other—that Pound's *Cantos*, for instance, belong to the epic tradition. The hero of modern epics, or shards of epics, is always the poet. Yet older epics are not altogether different. There too the poet often associates himself with his hero, intrudes into the action, or establishes a personal narrative voice for us to recognize. Perhaps the most valid distinction between epic modes (a version of the distinction between oral and written narrative) would set the anonymous poem—one whose author seems collective or indistinguishable from the action itself—apart from the poem that bears a signature. The composers of *Gilgamesh* or the Eddas blend into their culture; Milton stands alone. Similarly, the hero of the *Iliad* seems unconscious of the bard who tells his story, but the hero of the *Aeneid* never quite manages to dissociate himself from his author. In signature-epics the grounds of the story always lie in the poet's own career.

How does the *Aeneid* begin, for instance? "Arma virumque cano . . . ," we learned in school—the origin of the Latin race, the lords of Alba, and the outworks of towering Rome. But an alternative beginning also survives from antiquity, a version that great poets have always preferred and imitated, and that textual scholars as well as critics have often considered authentic.

> Ille ego, qui quondam gracili modulatus avena
> carmen, et egressus silvis vicina coegi
> ut quamvis avido parerent arva colono,
> gratum opus agricolis; at nunc horrentia Martis
>
> (I am the one who once measured his song by a simple
> reed; then, leaving the woods, compelled the neighboring
> fields to obey those who till them, however greedy,
> a work pleasing to farmers; but now of Mars' bristling
> arms and the man I sing. . . .)

Whatever the provenance of these lines, they follow a logic that runs through Virgil's work: self-conscious recapitulation of his progress as a poet. Woods, fields, battlegrounds; a shepherd's pipe, a commanding lyre, a martial trumpet; pastoral, georgic, epic; *Eclogues, Georgics, Aeneid*. The Sixth Eclogue emphasizes that Virgil has chosen pastoral over epic, for the moment, only as a matter of policy ("I do not sing unbidden"); the last line of the *Georgics* echoes the first of the *Eclogues*, drawing the poet's journey through woods and fields into a perfect round; the *Aeneid* constantly reminds the reader of eclogues and georgics. The measures may change, but the poet remains the same. And he claims our attention. Behind the story of arms and the man, another insistently makes itself felt, the Virgilian story that begins with *Ille ego*—"I am the one."

That story, in fact, survived the death of the epic form itself. It is possible to quarrel with the notion that either *The Faerie Queene* or *Paradise Regained* is an epic but not with the epic signature that opens each poem: "Lo! I, the man whose Muse whylome did maske, / As time her taught, in lowly Shephards weeds" and "I who erewhile the happy garden sung." Spenser and Milton take precedence, at least for a few lines, over the arguments they are about to rehearse. The career of the poet comes first. Similarly, Virgil's best student begins with himself, not only in Canto I of the *Commedia* but in the formal invocation of the *Inferno,* Canto II, where even Virgil's presence does not keep Dante from noting that he goes this way alone ("io sol uno"), like any poet, and that he must rely above all on his own high genius and memory ("O Muse, o alto ingegno, . . . / o mente che scrivesti ciò ch'io vidi"). Everything happened to *him*. And the lesson was not lost on other ambitious poets, like the one who based an epic action on his own brain and his own left foot, where Milton had descended, or the one who made the growth of his own mind as a poet the subject of his longest poem. Blake and Wordsworth are the ones; they tell their own stories. Most subsequent poets, in their time of summing-up, have chosen the very same focus. The modern "epic" is dominated by one story and one story only: the life of the poet.

If the final subject of a poet consists of nothing less than his whole career, however, why should anything be excluded? The longest poem a poet makes is the ensemble of all his poems together. Thus many modern poets (Cavafy and Yeats are striking examples) seem to regard the ultimate fruit of all their work as a poetic autobiography in the shape of a single book. No poem can be separated from the others or from its place in the poet's life. And every poem is one poem. Thus Collected Poems may be considered, in many cases, the modern equivalent of the epic: "an assemblage of all the powers" a poet can muster. The book, for such poets, regains some of the aura that books possessed when they were still thought to be symbols of the unity of the world. To make such a book is to redeem individual poems from their solitude and the poet's life from time. One hope is left to the poet: to see his fragments, retrospectively, as a single great confession.

When Wallace Stevens published his first book, for instance, the act of gathering the poems together seems to have modified his view of them. At first he was depressed. "All my earlier things seem like horrid cocoons from which later abortive insects have sprung." But the notion of a book, while intimidating, could also serve to bring out links among the poems. Perhaps they might join into one. That is the implication, at any rate, of a title he later discarded:

THE GRAND POEM:
PRELIMINARY MINUTIAE

His next and better suggestion, sent by telegram, was still more to the point:

USE HARMONIUM

And more than thirty years later, when the time had come for Stevens to sum up his work in one last volume, he still liked the sound of that word. The title he wanted to end with, in fact, was this:

THE WHOLE OF HARMONIUM
COLLECTED POEMS
OF
W. S.

He was not allowed to use it. But perhaps we can.

Why was Stevens so fond of the word "harmonium"? He must have been attracted, first, by its literal sense: "a keyboard wind instrument, or reed organ." Like Peter Quince's clavier or the blue guitar, a harmonium furnishes the poet with a rare distinctive instrument on which to play his tunes. Poets are performers. They make their verses, more or less whimsically, from a patchwork medium that consists of words, themselves, the imagination, or whatever reality the wind can catch. Thus Stevens thinks of his book as a recital: a collection of improvised pieces. But "harmonium" also suggests deeper strains, the harmony in which a poet hopes the pieces of his book will join. Poets are not only performers but creators.

> Hi! The creator too is blind
> Struggling toward his harmonious whole,
> Rejecting intermediate parts,
> Horrors and falsities and wrongs
>   ["Negation"]

"The creator," in these lines, is God as a soldier might see Him (the poem was originally one of the "Lettres d'un Soldat"), a principle of order that might explain, if not justify, the suffering and disconnectedness of war. Stevens, like Keats, regards the world as a vale of soul-making. But the poet can also rival creation. Though blind and clumsy, not ready as yet to make the parts of his world into a single book, he struggles toward a more cohesive whole—his own *Harmonium.*

At its furthest reach, indeed, the notion of the harmonium seems to border on *harmonia mundi,* the music that binds the world. The later Stevens becomes obsessed with composing or transcribing such music. Hence *The Whole of Harmonium* no longer refers to a specific musical instrument; the final word lacks an article like "a" or "the." Evidently *Harmonium* must be abstract in its essence, synoptic as a supreme fiction or a book that completes another book. And the problems of the Canon Aspirin, in conceiving that fiction, seem identical with the poet's own, in planning his collected poems.

> He had to choose. But it was not a choice
> Between excluding things. It was not a choice
>
> Between, but of. He chose to include the things
> That in each other are included, the whole,
> The complicate, the amassing harmony
>   ["Notes toward a Supreme Fiction"]

Stevens' final book would achieve the whole harmonium at last, not by leaving anything out but by creating the whole poem of which all the earlier books had been only pieces or notes.

Does such a harmony exist as anything but a fiction? The question has tormented many poets. In works intended to close a career, music often serves as a metaphor—"hark, I have dared and done, for my resting-place is found, / The C Major of this life: so, now I will try to sleep"—but it does not resolve all conflicts. Is the poet a composer or only a musician? Even the word *harmonium,* we have seen, harbors a double meaning. It can signify a glorious consummation, in which the poet orders the world he has created like a god. Yet it can also represent a peculiar, inflated instrument, whose notes remind us that even the sublimest composition depends in performance on the way that one eccentric person happens to hit the keys— "Such tink and tank and tunk-a-tunk-tunk." An aging poet may try to persuade himself that the two meanings are one, like a fire and the rose it consumes, or "music heard so deeply / That it is not heard at all, but you are the music / While the music lasts." But music dies away. The poet is left, in the end, with himself; with the disparity between the instrument he plays and the ever-receding harmonium toward which he aspires.

*   *   *

Few poems have ever stated the disparity more movingly than *Four Quartets.* Even their music sounds broken. The awkwardness and dissonance of many parts, the tension in which "Words strain, / Crack and sometimes break, under the burden," testify to the poet's difficulty in finding a significant unity in his work. He struggles to begin. So much was expected of Eliot— and he produced so little. Eventually he cured his writer's block, like many other authors, by writing about it. But he never became quite comfortable with his role as master. A sense of the ridiculous hovers, often, just out of sight—the ridiculousness of trying to redeem the "waste sad time."

The first section of "Burnt Norton," for instance, enters a world of speculation where the poet, following the logic of *Alice in Wonderland,* re-visits a place he has never seen before, gazes into a drained pool full of water, and is laughed at by children who are not there. The scene owes much to Kipling's "They," a story about an estate haunted by ghosts of children. Kipling, who had recently lost his own daughter, stresses parental affliction, the need for a last fading communication with those who have gone. But Eliot's position seems closer to that of the blind woman who owns the estate, privileged to be visited by ghostly children because she never had children of her own. It is the unborn—the might-have-been children who never were, the poems that have never been written, the Christian society that never happened, the serene and masterly old age that never arrived—who come to Eliot's haunting. See, they return. All the missed opportunities of life assemble in *Four Quartets.* Now that life is almost past, the time that was wasted reproaches the poet with all that he has not done.

Nor can he be content with what he *has* done. In that essay of 1940 where Eliot so obviously reviews his own problems through the medium of Yeats (whose mantle as the greatest living poet he had just inherited), he refers to the worst temptation that faces aging poets: "that of becoming dignified, of becoming public figures with only a public existence—coat-racks hung with decorations and distinctions, doing, saying, and even thinking and feeling only what they believe the public expects of them. Yeats was not that kind of poet." But perhaps Eliot was. Yeats' terrifying repeated image of the aged man as a coat upon a coat hanger applies only too well to Eliot in his later public guise, Old Possum—discreet, dapper, desiccated, dignified; most of all, deathly. The image of the coatrack stands for death, unless "soul clap its hands and sing." Behind the stately public façade of Eliot in late middle age a genuine terror often sounds its note. The words "survive" and "perish" recur in his writings with odd insistency. In the little pamphlet *Reunion by Destruction,* for example, whose title and date connect it to "Little Gidding," the question of church organization in South India becomes a matter of life and death: "it is the question whether the Church of England shall survive or perish." Nor could the survival of England in the early 1940s be taken for granted. For Eliot, as for Pope in the Fourth Book of *The Dunciad,* the destruction of civilization and his own personal extinction join in a single horror: fear of the dark.

Four Quartets often descend to the darkness. Wherever the poet goes, the same crossroads await him—not only the intersection of the timeless with time but the meeting of a younger with an older self. The places he visits, like the poetic idioms he uses, remind him that nothing lasts. And a question confronts him at every turning: survive or perish? Insofar as the *Quartets* represent Eliot's epic journey, the chapter they reenact most often is the visit to the underworld. Its particular moment occurs, as in the *Aeneid,* just before the middle—at the opening of section three. The image of an underground train, carrying its disaffected passengers into a circle of darkness, recurs in that section of "Burnt Norton," "East Coker," and "The Dry Salvages." The corresponding moment of "Little Gidding," which follows the most extended of all the poet's otherworldly visits, offers a final way out: those who vanish will "become renewed, transfigured, in another pattern," since only the indifferent are truly dead. Survive or perish? A hero descends to the underworld, traditionally, for prophetic reassurance and a lesson in reincarnation. Thus Aeneas learns that the dead will return and learns of the future race that will bear his name. Eliot goes there for a similar reason. He wants to be reassured that the life of his poetry, the life of his civilization, will be born again. So many things have ended. Are *Four Quartets* a beginning or an end?

From beginning to end the poems debate the question, and again and again, more and more insistently, they return to the same conclusion: "In my end is my beginning." Eliot declares himself ready for initiation, willing, even eager, to give up everything for "A condition of complete simplicity." He renounces his factions and parties, he renounces his desire to have been other than he was, in order to demonstrate that time and death can be redeemed and even the weariest poet can start again. The waste sad time is purged by refining fire. Biographically, he searches the faces and places of his past to discover that "Home is where one starts from" and "We are born with the dead." Poetically, he redeems a series of old phrases, images, ideas, motifs—the stock-in-trade of his poetic career—by arranging them into a new creation. In a coda that consists entirely of quotations, the broken fragments of his life and civilization are shored by an act of faith renewed not in any single part but in the transfiguring pattern of the whole. Historically, religiously, philosophically, the pattern is the same—timeless moments redeeming time. The transitory and the permanent, Eliot the private person and Eliot the master, the destructive fire of war and the ever-blooming rose of love, resolve alike into one perfect symbol, "And the fire and the rose are one."

Yet such consolation is not achieved without a cost. By finding a place for everything—even his despair—in the pattern, Eliot had used up all the resources of his poetry. The rhetoric of exploration cannot conceal that he knows where he will arrive; technically, the coda of "Little Gidding" repeats the brilliant patchwork that ends *The Waste Land.* Nor did Eliot really believe, as Yeats had believed, in reincarnation. During the twenty years he was still to live he would write no more major poems. Later poets have taken the point. Unlike *The Waste Land,* the *Quartets* were not a place to start from. They founded no idiom, they fathered no school. Instead they represent the poet's last testament—timeless, the work of a master. *Four Quartets* leave nothing unfinished. "Quick now, here, now, always"—they come to an end.

But why should they need to end? The business of a poet, after all, is to make poems, not to shape a career. Would not his best last words be something unfinished—the new poem he was writing, like a soldier in the field, when death interrupted him? Eliot did not think so. In a remarkable poetic "Note on War Poetry" that dates from the same year as "Little Gidding," he denies (like Yeats before him) the very premise of war poetry.

> It seems just possible that a poem might happen
> To a very young man: but a poem is not poetry—
> That is a life.

War poetry, of course, is not a life. It is an accident that happens to very young men. And their poems tend to be moving not because any weight of life or craft lies behind them but because they clutch a world in the presence of death. The best war poems, like the best war poets, will never grow old. Yet Eliot has a different notion of poetry, just as "Little Gidding" is a different kind of war poem. He requires a poetry that consists of something more than poems, a poetry in which even "The poetry does not matter." He wants nothing less than a *life:*

> the abstract conception
> Of private experience at its greatest intensity
> Becoming universal, which we call "poetry."

An aging poet in this state of mind has no time for incidents or interruptions; he needs to arrive at his destination.

Yet the cost of ending is high. It demands many sacrifices, the sealing of many passages. "In the perfection of any style it can be observed, as in the maturing of an individual, that some potentialities have been brought to fruition only by the surrender of others." *Four Quartets* acquiesce to that surrender. Their relentless drive toward finality leaves no room, for example, for the humor and spontaneity of the younger poet. Moreover, they deliberately withdraw from many of the concerns of life. Eliot's careful distinction between detachment and indifference, in the middle section of "Little Gidding," responds to a powerful unspoken accusation: what gives a man the right to say that poetry is not for the young, that here and now cease to matter? The time of war makes such accusations all the more forceful. Eliot retreats into his timeless musing, the perfect circle where destruction leads to reunion, just at the moment when England faces a real and agonizing fire.

With characteristic subtlety of allusion, he even incorporates the situation into his poem. The end of "The Dry Salvages," with its emphasis on "prayer, observance, discipline, thought and action"—"The life of significant soil"—strongly recalls Virgil's *Georgics,* which Eliot was later to claim had first affirmed "the importance of good cultivation of the soil for the well-being of the state both materially and spiritually. . . . the principle that action and contemplation, labour and prayer, are both essential to the life of the complete man." Like Eliot, Virgil had retreated to the soil in a time of war. The famous conclusion of the *Georgics* specifically invokes the contrast:

> Thus of agriculture and the care of flocks I sang
> And forestry, while great Caesar fired his lightnings.

No doubt the same contrast induced C. Day Lewis to translate the *Georgics* in 1940—a translation that Eliot later recommended over the original. In "Dedicatory Stanzas" to Stephen Spender, Day Lewis squarely faces the implication of his retreat. "Where are the war poets? the fools inquire." They have gone to "search for a right soil / Where words may settle, marry, and conceive an / Imagined truth."

Now when war's long midwinter seems to freeze us
And numb our living sources once for all,
That veteran of Virgil's I recall. . . .

Eliot begins "Little Gidding" in the same midwinter. But his mind travels to another season, "not in time's covenant": midwinter spring. Here, in his own time of war, Nicholas Ferrar had retreated to search for a right soil of labor and contemplation; here Eliot will kneel in prayer. The way to liberation is not indifference, the poem tells us, but detachment; not war poems of anger and incident but a poetry of peace made blinding through frost and fire. "Little Gidding" claims its spring, its living sources, in spite of the midwinter that surrounds it. Precisely because of the war, the poet must sacrifice every external consideration to the integrity of his work, "A symbol perfected in death." Only by accepting death will he complete his life. "And yet," Eliot wrote of Virgil, "it may be the man who affirms the apparently incompatible who is right."

The life of a poet, in short, is more than a career, more even than a vocation; it is a destiny. Or so Eliot believed. How had he come to such a conclusion? One earlier poet above all had guided him there, the poet who could be named through many ages merely by mentioning *the* Poet. Virgil, Eliot thought, has "the centrality of the unique classic; he is at the centre of European civilization. . . . the poet in whom that Empire and that language came to consciousness and expression is a poet of unique destiny." It was he who had taught Eliot, as he had taught so many others, the ultimate refinement of poetic method: a pure poetry, *la poésie pure,* of pattern and music; a layer of quotations that connect the individual talent with tradition. And it was he who had invented the *harmonium.* The poet's sense of destiny can be traced to Virgil. In Eliot's mind the journey of Aeneas, "the prototype of a Christian hero," is transformed into a pilgrimage to the world's end. And "Aeneas' end is only a new beginning."

The *Aeneid*

The idea that poets share a peculiar destiny was not invented, perhaps, by Virgil. But no other poet has ever done more to define it. Right from the start Virgil has been famous for knowing above all others how to cultivate his gifts. Content to lick a few verses into shape each day, willing to destroy his masterpiece rather than allow it to escape unperfected before the world, he represents his own ideal: "labor omnia vicit / improbus" ("unremitting labor conquered the world"). However uneasy such a view of poetry makes modern readers—*labor* and *prudentia* seem stingy virtues for a poet!—Virgil's example continues to reproach all those who have wasted their talents. Nor was his husbandry restricted to individual poems. What he created, at last, was something larger than poems, larger even than the books within which those poems were arranged. His master creation was the sense of an inevitable destiny: his life as a poet.

Creation on this scale has been so rare in Western poetry (though many poets have modeled their own careers on Virgil's) that it deserves a closer look. What is involved in husbanding a career? First of all, the management of a canon. A poet who keeps the total effect of his work always in view will not publish anything he does not consider a finished masterpiece. *Eclogues, Georgics, Aeneid*—these three works, and these only, belong to the *cursus honorum* that Virgil pursued (even the *Aeneid* may qualify against its author's will). Together they complete a "wheel" or pattern. Even the famous epitaph harps on the self-same theme.

> Mantua me genuit, Calabri rapuere, tenet nunc
> Parthenope; cecini pascua rura duces.

> (Mantua bore me, Calabria snatched me away, now Parthenope
> holds me; I have sung pastures, the country, leaders.)

The three sites responsible for the poet's moments of passage are balanced by the three stages of his work: the high grounds of pastoral, the homesteads of georgic, the military outposts of epic. No other verses count. Whether or not we accept the authenticity of the *Appendix Vergiliana*—and the manuscripts that preserve it date from many centuries later than the codices of the three main works—the poet himself cannot have meant to publish such trifles. The epilogue to the collection, ascribed to Varius, confesses that it deals in goods of a lower order.

> Vate Syracosio qui dulcior Hesiodque
> maior, Homereo non minor ore fuit,
> illius haec quoque sunt divini elementa poetae
> et rudis in vario carmine Calliope.

> (He who was sweeter than the Syracusan bard and Hesiod's
> better, nor less than Homer in his speech—
> these beginnings also belong to that divine poet,
> and to his rough Calliope these diverse songs.)

Theocritus, Hesiod, Homer—bucolic, didactic, epic. Whatever the antiquarian interest of Virgil's first raw muse, his canon rests on surer grounds: *Eclogues, Georgics, Aeneid.*

The names of the Greek poets should remind us of a second way that a poet husbands his destiny: by making use of other poets. During Virgil's own lifetime critics had already assembled lists of his "thefts" ("Why don't they attempt the same thefts themselves?" he is said to have replied. "Then they might really understand that it would be easier to rob Hercules of his club than Homer of a line"). But Virgil goes far beyond borrowing from his predecessors; he farms them. Every passage of the *Aeneid,* perhaps every line, ploughs over the ground of earlier poetry. Virgil is a poet who will allow nothing to go to waste. While a sense of competition undoubtedly enters into the challenge that he poses to each of the Greek masters in turn— the Roman poet will improve and correct the Greeks even in their own arena—a sense of reverence or piety enters into it too. The *Aeneid* preserves the older epics by incorporating them within its fabric, as a great empire must aim not so much to conquer and destroy other nations as to colonize them into part of itself. Virgil's epic, as critics have noted from ancient times, contains both an *Odyssey* (the first six books) and an *Iliad* (the last six books). Reverence for Homer requires both. Similarly, the poet includes a wide variety of gods—ancient and modern, Greek and Roman, animistic and anthropomorphic, local and cosmic—without disavowing any. Curtius speaks of "the fundamental law of life that applied throughout Antiquity; the law, according to which the sanction for all new creations was in the traditional works from which they derived and to which they had to refer." Whether or not *all* poetry obeys such a law (as some modern critics believe), Virgil's poetry certainly does. It is made of allusions, not occasionally and adventitiously but regularly and fundamentally. It springs from roots in the past.

"Pius," however, also means "responsible." Farming the classics, a poet assumes a pressing obligation: in some way to surpass them. A destiny, when husbanded, must also bear fruit. That is a third criterion of poetic cultivation: progress, successive improvement. In each new work, most of all, the poet must surpass himself. The model for which Virgil is responsible offers a clear line of succession. In his youth the poet sings sweetly and passionately about a pastoral landscape that exists only in his budding imagination; in middle age, without losing his earlier inspiration, he demonstrates in addition how much he knows about the world as it is; as old age comes on, he gathers all his powers for a mighty effort that epitomizes the collective wisdom of his civilization, the world as it has been and should be. Three years for the *Eclogues,* seven for the *Georgics,* eleven—or infinity— for the *Aeneid.* That is a poet's *curriculum vitae.*

The passing years accumulate an enormous pressure of expectation, a pressure that only the fittest poet can withstand. Augustus himself commissioned the *Aeneid.* Scarcely had it been begun when Propertius announced in verse that "Something greater than the *Iliad* is born." Meanwhile the emperor, away on campaign, demanded to see excerpts or a first draft, in such letters as only a Caesar can write, "threatening in jest." The Empire waited. No wonder that the *Aeneid,* like so many other works intended to crown the efforts of great poets—Chaucer, Petrarch, Ronsard, Spenser, Wordsworth, Ezra Pound—appeared posthumously and unfinished. Rome's poem would not rise in a day. A great career, carefully husbanded, builds slowly toward its final moment of truth, its ultimate reaping: immortality or death.

The poet who lives with such a responsibility has only one way to meet it: planning ahead. To husband a destiny, finally, one must be able to think in terms of decades, perhaps generations. The plot, structure, characters, themes of an epic project will precede its concrete realization by a span of years. Virgil spent his life preparing the *Aeneid.* And according to many later Virgilians, that was what made him a poet; the plan counts for more than its execution. Thus Alexander Pope, a year before he died, discussed his projected *Brutus.* "Though there is none of it writ as yet, what I look upon as more than half the work is already done, for 'tis all exactly planned." On his death he left an outline, a few scraps, and just eight finished lines of verse. Is *Brutus* really more than half done? Despite the pathetic insufficiency of the fragment from a reader's point of view, from the poet's point of view his claim was not exaggerated. An epic, like a pear tree, requires a good deal of tending before it blossoms, and Pope had already planted his epic—though unfortunately it went to seed. The husbandman-poet cannot afford to watch the clock. He measures out his life in master plans, and waits for a stretch of time to fill them in.

Obvious as it is, the need for a poet to plan his work thoroughly before carrying it out may be the most difficult of all conditions for a modern author to grasp. Few poets now have such confidence in the future, such a luxurious sense of time, or such understanding patrons. In a rapidly changing world, moreover, a project that requires decades may well become quaintly anachronistic long before it is finished. Nor does such delay seem psychologically healthy. Elaborate planning can inhibit the fresh starts in unexpected directions, the ever-quickening sense of discovery, that many writers live for. As recently as Yeats, poets commonly began long poems by outlining them in prose; but the practice no longer is common. Indeed, it may even appear radically antipoetic. Poetry depends—does it not?—on spontaneity and lack of forethought, on its utter opposition to prose. At one time poets did not think so. They based their work on prose; they planned ahead. Perhaps such habits lead to different attitudes toward poetry, a different poetic state of mind.

Consider, for instance, Suetonius' fascinating description of Virgil's method.

> After first preparing the draft of a prose *Aeneid* and dividing it into
> twelve books, he commenced to compose it bit by bit, just as he pleased,

and taking nothing in order. And lest he should retard an impulse, he left some parts unfinished, and propped up others with very light words, as it were, which he said in jest were inserted as scaffolding to sustain the work until solid columns should arrive.

It is exactly by keeping the design of the whole so firm that Virgil preserves his impulse (*impetus,* that characteristically dynamic Latin word which stands at once for attack and passion, impetus and impetuosity). The author of the *Aeneid* can afford to interrupt his journey at any moment; he knows so well where he is going. And the internal evidence, most scholars would agree, tends to corroborate this account. Virgil did not compose the verse *Aeneid* in sequence but in bits, jumping forward and backward from part to part. Thus some books, especially the even-numbered, seem far more finished than others (Virgil is supposed to have read Augustus three books, the second, fourth, and sixth). There was no need to hurry. The master plan, like scaffolding, holds everything in place.

Moreover, the architectural metaphor probably points to another aspect of structure: its basis in mathematics. Roman architects planned the proportions of their works by counting numbers, and so did Virgil. The *Aeneid,* some scholars have argued, follows a precise arithmetic. The famous ratio of the Golden Section, the division of a length so that the lesser part is to the greater as the greater to the whole (the fraction works out to .618), controls the patterning of many lines and verse paragraphs. In the first book, for example, the invocation is followed by 26 lines (12–37) recounting the causes of Juno's wrath, then 42 lines (38–79) in which her fury mounts until she asks Aeolus to destroy the Trojan ships. Mathematically, 26/42 equals .619 (to the nearest decimal point), and 42/68 (the whole passage on Juno's wrath) equals .618. Figures like these seem unlikely to have resulted from chance. Yet it would not be wise to exaggerate their importance. The *Aeneid* was not planned by Pythagoras. The Golden Section may well supply it with structural divisions yet hardly with its content or beauty. Nevertheless, the use of mathematics does suggest that the poet was willing to accommodate his work to a preexisting abstract grid, a frame or loom of numbers. Every line must be calculated according to the master plan. Virgil, after all, was the poet who taught Dante to count.

The larger architecture of the *Aeneid,* more significantly, also follows a blueprint. Each of the first six books (the *Odyssey* half) closely corresponds to its opposite number in the second, or *Iliad,* half (Book I with Book VII, II with VIII, etc.). Sometimes these correspondences involve a direct parallel, sometimes an ingenious reversal. At the beginning of Book I, for instance, the Trojan sails are blown away from Italy; at the beginning of Book VII they reach Italy with the help of a favoring wind. More subtly, the poet contracts much of the theme of his work into a mirror image that concludes Books II and VIII. At the end of Book II Troy has fallen, an era is over; in the last line Aeneas takes his father on his shoulders ("cessi et sublato montis genitore petivi"). Commentators ancient and modern agree on the symbolism: Aeneas now carries the burden of the past, the Trojan race. At the end of Book VIII the shield contrived by Vulcan depicts the future glory of Rome; in the last line Aeneas takes the shield, "his parent's gift," on his shoulder. This time the text makes its symbolism explicit: he is "lifting on his shoulder the fame and fate of the sons of his sons" ("attollens umero famamque et fata nepotum"). He carries the Roman race. Aeneas' relation to the past is a son's to his father; it reminds him of his mortality. His relation to the future is a father's to his sons; it reminds him of his immortality (the gift comes from Venus, his immortal parent). Troy will be reincarnated in Rome. Virgil's contrast of the two sides of Aeneas' mission could scarcely be more elegant. Similarly, at the close of Book VI Aeneas ascends from the underworld, a sign of rebirth, while at the close of Book XII Turnus descends to the underworld, never to be reborn. The *Aeneid* is built on such contrasts. Like the columns of a building, its passages balance each other with opposing stresses; they do not stand alone.

The *Aeneid*, therefore, is not only a planned but a haunted work. Every scene reminds us of something else, in Homer or Virgil himself. And whenever the poet invented a scene, apparently he had to invent another, in the corresponding part of the other half, to balance it. The method induces a sort of double vision. Two consequences in particular may be noted. First, the texture of the poem is largely determined by a sense that at every moment at least two distinct possibilities, events, or meanings are simultaneously present. Just as *Absalom and Achitophel* depends on the simultaneous presence of the biblical and modern stories, or *The Rape of the Lock* on the simultaneous presence of epic and petty affairs, so the *Aeneid* depends on the relationship between the immediate occasion and its distant companion. (When Dryden and Pope alluded to Virgil, they were imitating him in more ways than one.) Thus neither Celaeno's prophecy that the Trojans will eat their tables (III. 247–57) nor the actual eating of the "fateful circles of crust" (VII. 114–15) would signify much unless they reflected each other. During the former scene we cast our minds forward; during the latter we cast them back. The significance inheres in neither part but in the relation between them: their simultaneous presence in the mind. That is one reason why the *Aeneid* relies so much on prophecy as well as memory; the earlier moment draws the later into itself.

A second consequence follows. If every moment of the poem looks forward to the future or backward to the past, then what is the status of the present? It can no longer be seen as independent; its materiality inevitably begins to diminish. Virgil's sense of destiny imposes tremendous constraints on the moment-to-moment life of his epic. The *Aeneid* tends to lack immediacy. Nor can one ignore the constraints placed on the hero. As Aeneas gazes at the scenes of Roman triumph,

> talia per clipeum Volcani, dona parentis,
> miratur rerumque ignarus imagine gaudet

> (he admires these things on Vulcan's shield, his parent's gift,
> and though ignorant of the events rejoices at their images)
> [VIII. 729–30]

and assumes them as his own burden. Despite the glory and heroism of the passage, it is also pathetic. Aeneas marvels at a future he will never know or understand and smiles at images without a substance. His ancestors once rode on his shoulders, and now his descendants ride; but when will Aeneas' own time come? Not in this life. He has left his home, his wife, left Dido too, in order to fulfill an alien destiny; he must fight a war he does not want, for the prize of a woman he does not love. The melancholy inherent in this perpetual sacrifice of the present has seemed, to many modern critics, the essential element of Virgil's poem. No imaginary empire can compensate for the loss of a real Dido. And however exaggerated this modern reaction may be—surely it reflects some disillusionment about our own imperialisms—it does respond to emotions in the text. The *Aeneid* is a melancholy epic, whose most famous lines return to tears, silence, and deprivation. Destiny prevails; but destiny does not consult the feelings of the hero.

Indeed, the powerful control exerted by a master plan even determines the hero's nature. A prisoner of the past and future, involved with plots anticipated by his maker years before they are realized, he has no choice but to submit. That is what Virgil requires. Aeneas—by no means popular with those who like their heroes to be spunky, impetuous, quick-witted and bad-tempered, like city people—has some of the virtues of a farmer. He fits his enterprises to the seasons; he follows the ancient ceremonial customs; when the gods speak and the weather changes (however little he likes it), he does what he is told. In another, quieter incarnation he might have written georgics. Moreover, he also has some of the virtues of a poet: above all patience, the willingness to sacrifice anything he owns for the sake of fathering something that will last. What he lacks, however, is an independent existence. All his assignments are commissioned, all his emotions predictable and predicted (Dido's love required a visit from Cupid, but Aeneas' response could be taken for granted). He obeys the plot. Nor does he ever become quite separate from the needs of his maker.

Aeneas, in short, is neither more nor less than a product of the *Aeneid*. Even his size, his looks, his age can change as the story decrees. Appearing before Dido he takes on a youthful luster, long hair, and glowing eyes (I. 588–93); prepared for battle he swells into a giant, huge as father Appenninus himself, lifting his snowy head to the sky (XII. 701–3). Gentle and brutal by turns, he adapts himself to the occasion. No wonder that critics have charged him with inconsistency! But his malleability itself is consistent, just as "piety" consists of worshiping whatever gods are germane to the case. Like a poet who writes in various genres, he suits his style to the context. Nor does he make his own decisions. Even his refusal to spare Turnus, in his very last words of the poem, belongs to someone else.

> . . . Pallas te hoc volnere, Pallas
> immolat et poenam scelerato ex sanguine sumit.

> (. . . It is Pallas who strikes, Pallas
> sacrifices you and exacts a penalty from your guilty blood)
> [XII 948–49]

Aeneas is only the executioner, not the author, of his action. Pallas demands the sacrifice; and Virgil; and the poem.

What the poem demands of Aeneas at last, in fact, is that he vanish. In the final books of the *Aeneid* Turnus claims so much of our attention that the other characters seem reduced to instruments of his destiny. The shape of Aeneas wavers; he fulfills his duty and disappears into his fate. Virgil cannot allow the fortunes of his hero to interfere with the destiny of the poem. We tend to lose interest in Aeneas. The greater question, from the poet's point of view, is how his poem—the work of his life—will end.

Yet the *Aeneid,* according to tradition, was never finished. What does that mean? Not, as some readers have supposed, that the poem was planned to go on beyond the death of Turnus; for that ending, I hope to suggest, carries the full weight of the poem behind it. Rather, the ancient report that Virgil, "in his last extremity, continually called for his manuscript [*scrinia,* book boxes] that he might burn it himself," stands for something more profound: the tremendous importance, at the moment of death, of leaving no unfinished business that might hinder the soul in its passing—no lack of change for Charon, no cock forgotten for Aesculapius. No fate was worse, the ancients thought, than being suspended in Limbo. The word for "burning," in Suetonius' account of Virgil's end, is *crematurus.* Cremation was usually reserved, then as now, for the bodies of the dead. But Virgil uses it for the *Aeneid*: the work of his life, forever imperfect, "unless restored by that refining fire." A magnificent legacy! always to serve as a reproach to poets. For no poem is *more* finished than the *Aeneid.* Yet Virgil demands a perfection that allows no revisions, no afterthoughts. He leaves a standard still higher than the work he accomplished: the idea of the work as it might have been.

The importance of leaving nothing unfinished, indeed, is a key to the way the *Aeneid* ends. Why did Virgil choose to conclude as he did? Not with the Trojan triumph; not with the marriage of Aeneas and Lavinia, which would so naturally follow the reconciliation between Jupiter and Juno a hundred lines before; but with a scene of almost unparalleled brutality. Turnus, aware that the gods are against him, suddenly loses his force. His body will not obey him, as in a dream, he does not know himself. Then the spear of Aeneas rips into his thigh. He falls, he begs for mercy—not for life so much as that his lifeless body be returned to his kin. And Aeneas listens, at least for a moment. Then his eye falls on the trophy that Turnus wears on his shoulder: the belt of Pallas, monstrously engraved with a frieze of murdered bridegrooms. And in the name of Pallas the pious Aeneas strikes.

> . . . ferrum adverso sub pectore condit
> fervidus. ast illi solvuntur frigore membra
> vitaque cum gemitu fugit indignata sub umbras.

> (. . . he buries the iron in the front of his breast,
> burning. But the limbs of the other shivered with cold,
> and life, with a moan, fled bitterly below to the shades)
> [XII. 950–52]

Such is Virgil's valediction—and the heritage of Rome.

In the last few decades a good many critics have come to view this scene as absolutely crucial to the *Aeneid* as a whole. For some it represents Virgil's ultimate condemnation of his hero; for others it serves to condemn Virgil himself. But the consensus, subscribed to by almost all the parties, is that the scene completes a theme that has been building through the last six books: the theme, as a recent book labels it, of "the victimization of Turnus." To a surprising extent, scholars now agree that the second half of the *Aeneid*, so long neglected, tells the poem's essential story and that that story is, far from the triumph of Rome, the triumph of darkness—suffering without purpose, force imposed by the strong on the weak, losses that cannot be retrieved. Rome's greatness, like that of her poem, depends on a heap of broken human beings. And the last word in Virgilian criticism, as in the poem itself, is *umbras*—shadows.

Doubtless this reading contains a part of the truth. No one knows better than Virgil that destiny can be a cruel master. But another part of the truth, I think, is suggested by an ancient tradition: that the *Aeneid* concludes in such a way as to avoid a sequel. No other hand could be permitted to take up the story after Virgil's death (the lesson, unfortunately, was lost on many successors); the end of Turnus is too brutal, too decisive, to allow another word. This is a curious argument, quite foreign to modern criticism. Yet perhaps it deserves some attention. For it leads us away from our own reactions, our justified revulsion at acts of blood, and toward the rather different problems that the poet faced. To read the *Aeneid* like Virgil, we must also be prepared to learn his methods of reading, to go to the texts where he went and see what he saw. We can hardly understand the end of Book XII, that is to say, without understanding how Virgil read its companion passages: the end of Book VI and the end of the *Iliad*.

As soon as we apply this principle in earnest, a peculiar line of interpretation leaps out at us. The theme of the *Iliad*, as Virgil read it, is not so much the anger of Achilles as the return of a body. That, of course, is how the *Iliad* concludes—with the ransom of Hector by his kin and with his funeral rites. To a Roman the importance of this ending can scarcely be overstated. Rome had been built, after all, by Trojan souls. Most prominent citizens liked to point to a legendary Trojan ancestor, often mated, like Anchises, to a god (thus Augustus derived his stature not only from Julius Caesar but from a truer, heavenly father: Apollo). And the claim that Augustus, for instance, reincarnated Aeneas was no mere figure of speech; Romans believed in reincarnation. Yet the soul could not return unless properly laid to rest; otherwise it must wander in Limbo. When Achilles returned the body of Hector, therefore, he made it possible for the glory of Troy also to be reborn—not in the same generation, but after due purification in the underworld. Hector had been buried; he would live again, in Rome. That, for Virgil, was the final meaning of the *Iliad*.

The evidence for this reading is abundantly spelled out by Virgil and Anchises in the other companion passage: the end of Book VI of the *Aeneid*. Before Aeneas can visit the underworld, he must perform funeral rites for Misenus (according to the commentaries, this Trojan trumpeter of battle stands for his city's cursed past, which must be buried before the survivors can be reborn and inherit their new land). Later the shade of Palinurus pathetically begs Aeneas for a funeral, without which no spirit can enter the lower world. These ghostly encounters, so learnedly glossed by Eduard Norden in his classic edition of Book VI, prepare the discourse that many scholars have thought the climax of the book, if not of the whole *Aeneid*: Anchises' teachings on reincarnation and the Roman future. Why should souls want to return? Aeneas asks. "Why this mad longing for the light?" ("quae lucis miseris tam dira cupido"; VI. 721). And Anchises replies by showing him the future, "and fired his soul with love of the fame that would come" ("incenditque animum famae venientis amore"; VI. 889). Spirits, like poems, must undergo progressive revisions, new trials in the world, until they reach perfection. One can always begin again. And Book VI ends soon after, with Aeneas' ascent to the world.

But Turnus goes down. His plea has been rejected, his body will not be buried. He has cause to groan with indignation, since now he must languish forever without hope of reincarnation (the word *indignata*, related to "indignities" as well as "indignation," suggests that his spirit has been dishonored). Turnus will not return. And that, I believe, is the point. The

Roman future is vested in Latins, Trojans, and friendly races like the Arcadians (Pallas' people). A successful empire depends on weddings as well as treaties. Thus Jupiter and Juno conclude their long matrimonial squabble by pledging a bargain: the Trojans will achieve their triumph only at the price of merging their blood with the Latins and adopting their language. But history allows no place for Turnus or his Rutulian heroism: an undisciplined individualism that breaks all bounds and boasts of spoils and personal glory. He is doomed by the trophy he wears, evoking the slaughter of the sons of Aegyptus (X. 495–50)—emblem of shattered covenants. Rome has no room for his ego.

But why should Virgil be so hard on Turnus? The answer, of course, is that destiny demands it. A few earlier lines may serve to show the compelling force exerted by destiny, not only on the large movements of history but on the texture of the verse. In the scene that precipitates the end Turnus, disarmed, remains defiant.

> nec plura effatus saxum circumspicit ingens,
> saxum antiquum, ingens, campo quod forte iacebat,
> limes agro positus, litem ut discerneret arvis
>
> (Saying no more, he looked around and saw a mighty stone,
> an ancient stone, mighty, which lay by chance on the plain,
> set on the land as a boundary, to sever strife from the fields)
> [XII. 896–98]

With enormous strength he lifts and throws it, but the stone falls short; a sense of faintness and powerlessness overcomes him; he meets his end. One reason for his failure, perhaps, is that Virgil has weighted the stone with so much history. It holds its appointed place; it will not be moved. The repetition of *saxum* and *ingens,* dragging against the flow of the verse, emphasizes this heavy resistance. Turnus is trapped in his fate like a mammoth in ice.

He is also opposed by the weight of epic tradition. Several heroes in the *Iliad* had raised up a similar stone; indeed, Aeneas himself had lifted one against Achilles in Book XX. Nor does Virgil conceal his borrowings. He even calls attention to modern degeneracy, since Homer conventionally says that two strong men, "as men are now," could hardly lift such a stone, while Turnus heaves a weight that would daunt *twice six* "men of such bodies as earth now produces" (XII. 900). Virgil knows that he is not living in an age of giants. The world has become more civilized since Homer's days, when gods fought and bragged like angry children and Athena knocked down Ares, impiously enough, with a boundary stone (*Iliad* XXI. 403). But the crucial allusion, for Virgil's purposes, is to *Iliad* V. 303 ff. There the great Diomedes, tossing a mighty boulder, had crushed the hip of his antagonist—Aeneas himself. The Trojan-Roman epic replays the scene of the Greek. And Turnus, who likes to think of himself as a Grecian hero, Achilles or Menelaus born anew, is given his chance to crush the same opponent. But this time the stone falls short. It carries, in its recirculation, too huge a burden. For in the previous book of the *Aeneid,* Diomedes himself had refused to come to the aid of the Latins and had regretted his own impiety in violating the fields of Ilium and opposing the gods of Aeneas. Nothing but evil can come from warring against piety and fate. "Join hands in treaty, / as best you may; but beware of clashing arms against arms" ("coeant in foedera dextrae, / qua datur; ast armis concurrant arma cavete"; XI. 292–93). Diomedes warns the Latins what will happen if they use him as a model: the parallel will break down. And so it does. This time the Trojan version wins the day—the epic that knows its limits.

History is loaded against Turnus in still another respect. In Virgil's description of the stone, the final clause has no precedent in Homer. The notion itself is Roman: literally, "so that it might separate quarrels from the tilled lands" (*lis* suggests lawsuits, as in its English derivative "litigation"). When Turnus seizes the stone, therefore, he converts a primary instrument of peace to a tool of war. Indeed, he is trying to reverse the whole course of civilization, since, according to a famous passage in the First Georgic, the invention of boundaries enabled all the other arts.

> ante Iovem nulli subigebant arva coloni;
> ne signare quidem aut partiri limite campum
> fas erat: in medium quaerebant. . .
>
> (Before Jove came no settlers subdued the field;
> nor was it lawful even to mark the plain or divide it
> with boundaries: men prospered in common . . .)
> [*Georgics* I. 125–27]

No milestones existed in the Golden Age—no calendar or seasons, no private property, and hence no farmers. But Jove the Father, by placing stones, introduced the art of agriculture, and the other arts came after. The accomplishments of humanity began with a sense of limits. And Virgil, like W. H. Auden, worships the god who gave us "games and grammar and metres."

> Venus and Mars are powers too natural
> to temper our outlandish extravagance:
> You alone, Terminus the Mentor,
> can teach us how to alter our gestures.

But Turnus in his fury recognizes no limits. Plucking up the boundary, he turns the clock back to the age of Saturn and reduces the land to primal unmarked wilderness. Jove will not smile on such efforts. Even in an epic poem, according to Virgil, he prefers the arts of peace to war. Nor does the poet himself, whose own property rights were once so strongly threatened by a soldier, want to revert to the Golden Age. His labor would count for nothing; he would be thrown back on eclogues. Symbolically, then, Turnus stands revealed as what Aeneas has always called him: a breaker of treaties. Poor hero! A stone-age savage who obeys no law but strength, a headstrong, old-fashioned epic warrior, he cannot survive in the Roman world, where piety is due even to the stones. The boundaries abide in Virgil. The battlefields of the *Aeneid* were farms once, and one day will be Rome— the place of law.

Knowledge like this can inhibit action. When every line sustains a burden of time and history, each line weighs as heavy as Turnus' stone, and for the same reason: it must adjudicate among conflicting claims. At every moment Virgil must check his impulse against the master plan, the epic tradition, the laws of piety, his own past work. A poet who taxes himself this way can barely manage to lift a few lines into place each day. And no poem deals more thoroughly than the *Aeneid* with the constraints that piety puts on action. Virgil's poetic decisions, like Aeneas' quest for a nation, are ringed round by the politics of the gods. The past and future demand their tribute, their sacrifice. Augustus asks for his poem. "And any action / Is a step to the block, to the fire, down the sea's throat / Or to an illegible stone: and that is where we start."

The most powerful gods that a poet must obey, however, are the gods of poetry. Virgil offers his sacrifices to them above all. Nor is this way of speaking only a metaphor. The connection of poetry with prophecy and the poet with the *vates,* in the ancient world, descended from Greece to Rome in the figure of Apollo: inspirer of the Sibylline oracles, master of poets—and, according to Augustus, a type of himself. Virgil is a priest of Apollo. He tends the mysteries, which include such articles of faith as the structure of the underworld and the divine origins of prominent Romans. Hence Virgil's enduring reputation as The Poet, an amazing double tradition: both the most careful of all craftsmen and the most inspired of seers. Both sides of the tradition seem to have existed already in The Poet's own lifetime. Virgil's husbanding of his talents did not preclude him from testifying, most famously in the Fourth Eclogue, that he was renewing the scattered songs of Cumae and spelling out the future. He accepts his destiny as a poet and speaks the words that the god has put in his mouth.

Those words do not make his speaking any easier. Apollo is a demanding god who insists that his votaries be not only inspired but correct. And Virgil knows that even his most prophetic utterances must fit the plan. One method for insuring that this will happen consists of what one might call the mode of preauthenticated prophecy—a mode of which Virgil, if not the inventor, is certainly the master. The poet fills his work with prophecies, and all of them come true. That is hardly surprising, since the story of Rome, which lay in Aeneas' future, had already reached its climax in the age of Augustus. The *Aeneid* unfailingly predicts the past. Wherever Aeneas goes he asks the gods what lies in store, and they frequently tell him: Latins and Trojans will join, Romulus will found Rome, Augustus Caesar will defeat Antony and Cleopatra and bring about a new Golden Age. Indeed, Aeneas' hunger for such reassurance might almost seem childish, were it not that the future contains his only source of gratification. Moreover, it runs in his family. We discover the shade of Anchises in a green underworld valley, lost in his favorite occupation: reviewing the line of his beloved descendants (VI. 679–83). Nor is this project so idle as it may appear to rootless moderns. A belief in reincarnation suggests that the future is rooted in the past, that history will repeat itself even to the persons. Thus preauthenticated prophecy can join, in the cycle of time, with genuine inspiration. In Latin *prudentia* means "foresight." Virgil moves deftly from one mode to the other, a historian and prophet in one.

Foreknowledge like this, nonetheless, can also constrain the poet. The *Aeneid* has been ordained; it lacks suspense. Even Virgil himself must have chafed at times as the wheels of destiny slowly ground to their objective. What happened when his impulse, his *impetus,* contradicted the master plan? Suetonius does not tell us. It may well be that the original prose *Aeneid* had a firmer architecture than the poem eventually left us and that, the closer Virgil came to finishing, the more he ignored his earlier calculations. The poem itself, in any case, reveals the tension between human impulses and the designs of the gods.

Consider, for instance, that archetypal prophet–poet, the Sibyl of Cumae. Before she can vent the oracles, Apollo must make her his own.

>. . . "deus, ecce, deus!" cui talia fanti
>ante fores subito non voltus, non color unus,
>non comptae mansere comae, sed pectus anhelum,
>et rabie fera corda tument, maiorque videri
>nec mortale sonans, adflata est numine quando
>iam propiore dei. . . .
>   At Phoebi nondum patiens, immanis in antro
>bacchatur vates, magnum si pectore possit
>excussisse deum; tanto magis ille fatigat
>os rabidum, fera corda domans, fingitque premendo.

>(. . . "The god is here, the god!" As she speaks this
>before the doors, suddenly neither face nor color is the same,
>nor does her hair stay tied, but her breast heaves,

89

and madly her wild heart swells, and she looks taller
nor does she sound mortal, the sway of the god is
already breathing nearer. . . .
    But not yet yielding to Phoebus, monstrous in the cave
the prophetess rages, as if she could shake the great
god from her breast; so much the more he exhausts her
maddened mouth, tames the wild heart, and presses her to the mold)
[VI. 46–51; 77–80]

Eventually the Sibyl becomes Apollo's perfect instrument and later, returned to herself, the hero's trusty guide. Yet neither of these aspects is so vivid as her torment when divine and human forces tear her between them, contending for her being. The Sibyl endures a horrible parody of labor pains—labor in reverse, since the god compels an entrance. Her fate is to lose herself. An aged virgin, whom Apollo granted immortality but not perpetual youth, she is filled by a genius both hysterical and fruitless. Nor does she own her own soul; her very name, according to Virgil, is Deiphobe, derived from the mastering god. To be a *vates* under such circumstances— a worn-out puppet in the hands of a divine ventriloquist—may be more than flesh can bear.

A poet is more than a prophet. At best he serves not merely as the instrument of the god but as his interpreter. (If Virgil had lived to finish the *Aeneid,* the ancients tell us, he intended to spend the rest of his life studying philosophy.) Divine and human at once, the poet can mediate between two worlds. Just as Beatrice succeeds Virgil as a guide in the *Divine Comedy,* so the Sibyl in the *Aeneid* is succeeded by father Anchises; prophecy must yield to truth. Yet Virgil never forgets the Sibyl's predicament. To be immortal yet wholly vulnerable, to swell with the breath of the god yet fight for control at every gasp—these are the ways of the poet. Moreover, passion at its deepest is always bound on a similar rack. The most highly charged moments of the *Aeneid,* the moments in which the poet enters the feelings of his characters most fully, return again and again to the same situation: a desperate losing struggle against a god. Dido's fatal divine infection, caught from Cupid, wars against her savage human pride, which eventually fires a hatred as strong as her love. Turnus, driven mad by Allecto, seethes with an anger that seems directed against his own demon as much as the enemy. They shake with the god like poets.

Such fury can come only from within. But we would be mistaken to interpret these invasions of passion merely as metaphors for natural psychological states. Dido's love and Turnus' anger go far beyond the natural and human; they prey on life and will survive the grave. When Turnus throws the stone, in his final stand, he vanishes into a dream where even the greatest effort has no effect. His knees falter, his blood freezes, *he does not know himself.* A modern author might diagnose a burst blood vessel. But Virgil subscribes to a different truth. The dream that Turnus enters is more real than his life; it is his fate, where nothing that he does or is can make the slightest difference. Those whom the gods possess are condemned, in their storms of passion, not to know themselves. That is why Dido keeps her silence in the underworld, cutting Aeneas dead and responding to his apology no more than "hard flint or rough Marpesian rock" (VI. 471); she refuses to know the woman who loved Aeneas. So long as her humanity does not die she will not be reconciled to her fate, even though robbed of breath.

Virgil, in such passages, writes like a god. He participates in the inmost feelings of these mortals, knows all their secrets, exposes them with tenderness and compassion, but never ceases to mold them to his will. They follow a higher destiny: the destiny of the poem. Even the gods in the *Aeneid* are subject to fate. From the poet's point of view, that fate must be described as the consummation of the poem itself, which will not allow even immortals to tamper with the success of Aeneas' mission. Indeed, the momentum of the *Aeneid* proved still more decisive than its author, whose death it was able to survive. Virgil had forged his career so powerfully that at the last it did not require him for its fulfillment. Nor was this a matter of chance. As Rome draws Aeneas on, choosing him for its hero and founder no matter how great his personal reluctance or inadequacy to the task, so the *Aeneid* drew Virgil. The future must have its poem; Western civilization itself (according to such critics as Sainte-Beuve and Theodor Haecker) hung in the balance. How could one frail human being resist such a destiny?

He did not resist it. He surrendered to the god. Yet the *Aeneid* leaves a record of its poet's struggle. The harmony that Virgil builds into every element of his poem, the will to perfection he never relaxes, are shot through with profound recognitions of human limits. The city of Rome is pitched over the ruins of battlefields and farms; Turnus must pay for breaking the bounds, Aeneas for staying within them. And Virgil understands the laws that govern both. He glorifies the victors while giving the victims the better speeches. The *Aeneid* faces two ways. It mourns the passing of time, the death of the old civilization where men stood taller and parleyed face to face with familiar gods; it looks forward to the future, to strange new worlds where smaller men—men more on our scale—worship new gods they never quite catch sight of, settle but never quite feel at home. The two halves of the poem, the Trojan story and the Italian, balance each other perfectly, and we, like the characters, are caught between. Rome would have her epic, on one condition: the glory of her destiny would always be mixed with retrospective sadness.

When the poet read the *Aeneid* to his emperor at last, one scene affected the audience more than any other. It was the description of Marcellus,

Augustus' chosen successor, the hope of Rome. But now he was dead, dead at nineteen. In a curious reversal of his usual preauthenticated prophecy, father Anchises wishes for a future that he knows will not come to pass.

> heu! miserande puer, si qua fata aspera rumpas,
> tu Marcellus eris!

> (Alas! lamented boy, if only you could break harsh fate,
> you will be Marcellus!)
>
> [VI. 882–83]

Even the grammar falters, since Anchises' conditional wishful thinking, in the first verb, immediately lapses into a hopeless future tense. And then he scatters ghostly flowers on the ghostly grave—promising Marcellus, in advance, those rites and that honored place in the Roman future which will be denied Turnus at the corresponding moment of Book XII. But consolations like these are weak. Fate had been stronger than Marcellus; a poet's wish could not bring him back; his glory was not to be. The empress, his mother, fainted. Instead of laurels,

> nox atra caput tristi circumvolat umbra

> (black night with its gloomy shadow hovers round his head)
>
> [VI. 866]

Though Virgil could not have planned the scene at first (the death of the heir occurred in 23 B.C., six years after the plotting of the epic), Marcellus joins Turnus in the shade.

The *Aeneid* casts its own shadow on the future. The model of epics, as Virgil of poets, it shows how intimately triumph must live with failure, how closely success is tied to a sense of limits. And it does not encourage a sequel. Trying to emulate Virgil, thousands of would-be epic poets learned to live with failure. In a way their deficiencies even exemplify his great theme—the curbs that piety puts on action—since piety to Virgil proved fatal to epic action. The *Thebaid, Africa,* the *Franciade, Brutus,* the *Achilleis,* even *Amelia*—such was the destiny of ambitious disciples. The *Aeneid* does not lend itself to improvement. Yet the triumph of Virgil's career, finally, was that he made a work much larger than its parts, a harmonium much greater than himself. The poem would live when Rome had died. For all its limits, it seems to define what an epic can do, what a poet can do. It holds its place. It seems to be made of stone.

*   *   *

The question remains: did Virgil sacrifice too much for his dream of perfection? And other questions follow. Can a poet make a harmonium that depends on plenitude rather than refinement, on abundance rather than sacrifice? Can the sense of destiny be accommodated to a process of continual change, and the sense of unity to infinite variety? Must the poet's career always describe a closed circle, a faithful rounding-off of obligations, or might it stay open at every point to unexpected directions and new beginnings? (In a freer poetic world, could an *Aeneid* be written sometime in which Aeneas chose to stay with Dido?) Does harmony always require a kind of death, a barrier of stones to trouble the living stream? Or might one define a poem as something that obeys no constraints, that has no end, that lives in action alone? No poet asks such questions more insistently than Goethe; no poem more than *Faust.*

Faust

By all rights, certainly, *Faust* is a poem that should never have ended. There is nothing quite like it in literary history. A poet in his late seventies resumes a project that he had planned more than half a century earlier, before coming of age. Working with astounding energy he completes a second part that resembles nothing ever seen before, more than 7,000 lines of verse, and seals it on his eighty-second birthday (August 28, 1831) for posthumous publication. And the finished work stands like a polygenetic cathedral in its mixture of historical styles: begun in *Sturm und Drang;* famous, at the turn of the century, as the key to German Romanticism; and at last revealed as a post-Romantic or modern fusion of classicism and surrealism. How did Goethe learn to think on such a scale; not years, not decades, but centuries? Where did he find the strength? He must have sold his soul to the Devil.

But what could his bargain have been? There is another reason why *Faust* should never have ended: its own internal structure of ideas. Right from the start Goethe conceived his play as an attack on the very possibility of ending. Endless activity, courage to face change, perpetual striving upward constitute his vision for humanity. Nor does Faust, in his bargain with Mephistopheles, set any definite period to his striving: no number of years, no one achievement. Rather, he will end, he agrees—if he ends.

> Werd ich zum Augenblicke sagen:
> Verweile doch! du bist so schön!
> Dann magst du mich in Fesseln schlagen,
> Dann will ich gern zugrunde gehn!
> Dann mag die Totenglocke schallen,
> Dann bist du deines Dienstes frei,
> Die Uhr mag stehn, der Zeiger fallen,

Es sei die Zeit für mich vorbei!

(If to the moment I should say:
Linger awhile! you are so fair!
Then bind the shackles on to me,
Then I shall gladly be no more!
Then let them toll the passing-bell,
Then quit your service and be free,
The hand may fall, the hour stand still,
And time be over then for me!)
                    [1699–1706]

If the moment should stay, that is, then let the moment stay; the punishment of timelessness will perfectly fit the crime. Faust's pact, in Goethe's version, is intended to have its comic side, like a vaudeville turn in which two con men swindle each other. Faust cannot conceive of a hell that consists of anything but inactivity; and neither can Goethe. So poor Mephistopheles will inevitably lose. He has made the mistake of agreeing to an orthodox Christian bargain in the work and the world of a very unorthodox author.

When Goethe subverted the terms of the traditional Faustian bargain, however, he also rendered null and void the usual structure of the Faustian play. Ordinarily, not only in Marlowe but in puppet drama, such plays have a powerful obligatory opening—the pact scene—and an overwhelming obligatory ending—the damnation of Faust. In between they are often in trouble. What doth it profit a man to gobble strawberries in January if he must pay with his soul? The middle seems no more than an interlude. But Goethe's play follows a different logic. Action, not overreaching, is its subject, and action is what it consists of—one act after another. Goethe's *Faust,* unlike its predecessors, is almost all middle. No damnation awaits the protagonist; he lives to the age of a hundred, performing his acts, and the play still continues after 12,000 lines. How could it reach an end?

The problem troubled Goethe through most of his life. For *Faust,* like a vow or a *daimon,* was the soul of that life. Periodically, about once a decade, he would return to the manuscript and incorporate in it everything he had learned. *Faust* contained the essence of his experience and his wisdom; it had grown with him through all the years and would carry him on. Indeed, his immortality literally depended on it, since those who had fulfilled their destiny in this life, Goethe believed, would be granted another. His greatest work could not be allowed to die. And to leave it unfinished would deny it that organic unity which, according to his own scientific studies, all living things possessed. (The reason why Faust is 100 at the end of the play, I believe, is that he matches *with his life* the divine numerology of Dante's *Commedia;* Goethe substitutes a living principle for Dante's formal

94

and anagogical causes.) The work must have an end. Yet ending did not come easily to Goethe. Even after he sealed the manuscript, as a matter of fact, he broke the seal to make one last addition. And his penultimate last words, the line that set *In Memoriam* in motion— "Von Änderungen zu höheren Änderungen" (From changes to higher changes)—might well be translated "from revisions to better revisions." If all things change, if even men (as Goethe thought) do not die but only start again, how can a poem stop?

To find the answer took a lifetime. Much of Goethe's career, through all the variety of its phases and interests, may be considered a heroic effort to discover a principle of unity that binds together the multiplicity of appearances. As a scientist, he consistently seeks out the *Urphänomen* lurking behind the restless phenomenal world of metamorphoses: the *Urpflanze* or primal plant toward which all plants tend; the *Urbild* or primal anatomy that provides a scaffold for every body; the magnet or primal power of attraction that corresponds to a physical *harmonia mundi;* the *Urlicht* or indivisible light that resisted all Newton's attempts to break it into a spectrum of colors. And there is also an *Urfaust* (1775), a primal manuscript whose germ of an idea persisted through so many changes. Yet Goethe's search for unity did not protect him from a natural inclination toward its opposite. The primal force in his world and in his own character was metamorphosis, the principle of motion that eventually dissolves all other principles. At the end of the second act of *Faust* Part II, the "Classical Walpurgis Night," the tiny spiritual Homunculus at last finds the secret of life: he is carried off to sea by Proteus.

Goethe constantly found the same secret: the way to unity was *through* metamorphosis. Confronted by a Heraclitean nature where flux and transformation rule the rhythms of life, swept along by a Heraclitean self, the poet submits to the stream, trusting that something imperishable will survive. What is that something? The final stanza of "Dauer im Wechsel" ("Permanence in Change," 1804) gives an explicit reply.

> Lass den Anfang mit dem Ende
> Sich in eins zusammenziehn!
> Schneller als die Gegenstände
> Selber dich vorüberfliehn.
> Danke, dass die Gunst der Musen
> Unvergängliches verheisst,
> Den Gehalt in deinem Busen
> Und die Form in deinem Geist.

> (Let the beginning and the end
> Draw together into one!

Swifter than the world of objects
Let yourself be hurried on!
Thankful, that the kindly muses
Promise they will leave behind
Immortal substance in your feelings
And the form within your mind.)

Substance and form will abide, just as the poem itself, a "favor of the muses," has a meaning and shape that incorporate both its restless beginning and serene conclusion. Yet permanence does not contradict change; it lives within it. The final couplet gives thanks not for form alone but for the dynamic form and content, ever changing but enduring, that are ceaselessly modified by the human feelings and spirit in which they dwell. Goethe celebrates a marriage between inner and outer nature.

The unity of *Faust,* therefore, could not be imposed from without. Goethe did not admire Virgil. Perhaps no two poets have ever shared a stronger sense of destiny; yet destiny has a different meaning for Goethe. It does not stand for orderly progress, a pattern engraved on life, but for a triumphant intuitive fusion with the process of growing and aging. Goethe refuses to acknowledge the separation of his own will from the will of nature. An instinctive pantheist, he thinks of his mind and feelings as microcosms of the universe, not transcending but immanent in objective reality. "Divinity [*die Gottheit*] is active in the living, not in the dead; it is in the becoming and the transforming, not in the become and the congealed." Thus his piety, as a man and a poet, is owed to no other divinity than his own indwelling creative principle—world without end. The destiny of Faust and his creator does not depend, like that of Aeneas and Virgil, on reaching a goal, but on remaining endlessly open to a state of becoming.

The difference may be seen as a matter of perspective. Aging poets, I have said, often need new glasses; but Goethe refused to wear them. Even when his sight grew dim he followed his own favorite *Theory of Colors* (*Farbenlehre,* 1810), which had insisted that colors reside in the observer as much as in the thing observed. What one sees, he believed, results literally as well as figuratively from a creative identity of the seer with the seen. Hence the cure for farsightedness was a deliberate adjustment of the vision, keeping an organic, not mechanical, consonance with the world (Goethe, it should be noted, often astonished friends with his ability to describe things in accurate detail, even with his eyes closed). Newton's optics, like Virgil's, had been wrong. Believing form and matter to obey mechanical principles, they both assumed a separation between the living person and the forces that drove him: a transcendent fate. But Goethe had been born to demonstrate their error. His own example would show the power of an individual to build his fate at any moment, to see things nature's way.

The difference may also be seen as a matter of form. Throughout Goethe's career he resisted prescribed notions of how to shape a work of art. The theme is stated in a review as early as 1772: "It is no great sin to say that a poet who is correct has no great poetic genius. When one reads Homer, then one cannot (without being Scaliger) refrain from saying that even about Virgil." Goethe was true to his own counsel. Indeed, it is possible to argue that the central thread of his poetry consists of a repudiation of artificial forms (Barker Fairley, for example, defines Goethe's main poetic principle as "the defeat of convention," and Erich Heller locates the center of *Faust* in "the avoidance of tragedy"). He does not follow the way of Virgil or anyone else's way. Dividing his work according to the Virgilian triad—pastoral, didactic, epic—we notice at once that *Hermann und Dorothea,* his bourgeois "epic" in the style of Homer, belongs to the classical period of his mid-career (1796) and is dressed in a pastoral mode. All stages are mixed together; Goethe writes what he likes when he wants to.

Nor does he create his forms as most poets do, by observing the terms of a genre. Is *Faust* a play? a "tragedy," as its subtitle maintains? Certainly much of it is designed with great imagination for the stage, and Part I has often proved stageworthy. Even Part II, in the hands of a gifted director, can provide theatrical sensations; and a successful production can be imagined, though I never expect to see one. Yet *Faust* seems too large, too diffuse, to occupy any space smaller than the mind. Whole operas have been built from small chips of it, and not even Berlioz—the composer who thought he could set the *Aeneid!*—could fulfill Goethe's hope of music on a scale grand enough for Part II. Still less does *Faust* resemble a tragedy. Though the last line of the Prelude speaks of a journey that would satisfy at least Dante's definition of a tragedy—"From heaven through the world to hell!"—the poem itself never descends nearer to hell than an open grave, and it ends with a movement upward. Nor does Faust suffer the catastrophe or the inexorable grip of fate that tragedy and the traditional Faust legend require. Scene by scene, with all its brilliance, Part II progresses in a series of leaps and diversions in which, for long stretches of time, the hero himself disappears. Nothing is predictable or inevitable. Hence at every point the sequence of events seems determined not by the laws of drama or by previous works of literature but by something in Goethe's "nature."

The genre of *Faust* is probably best understood, in fact, as a clash between tragedy and epic. Goethe's return to the work in 1797 immediately followed his searching correspondence with Schiller on the distinction between the two genres. Their joint essay "On Epic and Dramatic Poetry" summarizes their conclusions: "the epic poem presents man doing things outside himself: battles, journeys, every kind of undertaking, which requires a certain breadth of treatment. Tragedy presents man guided by something within, and therefore the plot of a true tragedy needs only a little space." Because of the difference in scope, the direction (or *motive*) of a tragedy tended to be progressive *(vorwärtsschreitend)*, while epic tended to be retrogressive *(rückwärtsschreitend)*, seeking out means of retarding the action. Drama lived in the present moment, epic in the past. But *Faust* would be both—inner and outer, forward and back, direct and meandering, present and past, tragic and epic. Goethe's interest in distinguishing epic from tragedy seems to have prepared him above all to violate the distinction. He would protect himself from static Virgilian correctness by resorting to a form beyond all reason: epico-tragedy, tragedo-epic.

A similar clash of element against element accounts for much of the energy of *Faust*. As the Lord himself comments in the Prologue (340–43), human activity depends on polarities; the Devil is necessary to shake a man from his repose. Colors, Goethe believed, result from the opposition of light and shade. And dramatic coloring could hardly exist without the same polarity, the irresolvable tension of one purpose working against another. Thus Faust's most explicit statement of principles, the "Prelude in the Theater," offers a debate among three figures—Director, Poet, Clown—whose conflicting notions about drama are not reconciled so much as projected forward into action. In its form as in its theme, the poem is fueled by antagonism: Devil against God, active versus passive, male against female, Part II against Part I.

More subtly, however, the polarities of *Faust* create its form not through simple opposition but through mutual reflection. "Opposition is true friendship"; contraries mirror each other. Goethe's own phrase for this effect, *Wiederholte Spiegelungen* (repeated reflections), emphasizes the way that images and experiences keep recurring, both in art and life, as in a magical looking glass. And at the center of his art he places an inexhaustible symbol. "Since many of our experiences do not let themselves be expressed plainly and imparted directly, long ago I chose the means of revealing the hidden sense to the attentive by setting images against each other, reflecting themselves, as it were, within one another." Meaning resides in the play of image against image, as facing mirrors multiply their forms without end. In a similar way the return of *Faust* to ideas, images, themes from previous scenes extends the range of meaning to infinity: the earlier scene comments on the later, which in turn changes the significance of the earlier, which then alters its relation to the later, which in turn. . . . The process has no end. Goethe draws his reader into a limitless series of reflections, as impossible to define or solve as experience itself.

In most of Goethe's major writings, in fact, the principle of *Wiederspiegelung* is embodied in a characteristic form—a doubling or reprise of the past. Each of his novels falls into two parts, the second half retracing the movement of the first, sometimes very schematically. Thus Werther, in the second part of the book that made Goethe famous, returns to the scene of his love, undergoes a winter version of his summer of happiness, revisits people and places whose former healthy life has cruelly wasted away, substitutes Ossian for Homer, repeats himself to the point of nausea, and dies only after Lotte has said that she will not see him again. *Die Wahlverwandtschaften* not only describes but exemplifies a series of complementary "Elective Affinities"; the eighteen chapters of Part II neatly mirror the eighteen chapters of Part I, often recapitulating the subject matter (architecture, for instance, in Chapter 1) as well as the attendant emotions. Even *Wilhelm Meister*, for all its disjointedness, reviews the *Lehrjahre* in the *Wanderjahre*, as when Wilhelm, on his pilgrimage to Mignon's birthplace, encounters each of the scenes she had evoked in "Kennst du das Land." Goethe is the poet of returning—of second love.

Faust, above all, embodies the mixed emotions of returning. Part by part, act by act, it seems always to begin again, progressing, if at all, not by a steady movement forward but by retracing its steps. Even the first words of the work, the *Zueignung* (Dedication) composed on June 24, 1797, sound oddly unlike a beginning. They plunge immediately into reminiscence, a confused reliving of experiences and feelings that had long seemed past.

> Ihr naht euch wieder, schwankende Gestalten,
> Die früh sich einst dem trüben Blick gezeigt.
> Versuch' ich wohl, euch diesmal festzuhalten?
> Fühl' ich mein Herz noch jenem Wahn geneigt?
> Ihr drängt euch zu! nun gut, so mögt ihr walten,
> Wie ihr aus Dunst und Nebel um mich steigt;
> Mein Busen fühlt sich jugendlich erschüttert
> Vom Zauberhauch, der euren Zug umwittert.
>
> (Once more, unquiet figures, you draw near,
> Who early passed before my clouded sight.
> And shall I try this time to hold you here?
> Does my heart feel its frenzy even yet?
> You press me close! ah well then, be the master,
> Rising to me through fog and misty light.
> My breast, as though a boy's again, is shaken
> By currents of the magic breath you waken.)
>
> [1-8]

The poet is haunted. The "wavering shapes"—at once the half-formed characters of *Faust*, the manuscript pages whose drift he now seeks to recover, and the friends for whose sake he once wrote—reduce him to a passive instrument of their own determination to exist. Song sweeps over him like wind on an Aeolian harp. Though retaining the stanza *(ottava rima)* of the epic he had been planning to write, he abandons its clarities for the misty realm of visions and fairy tales.

> Was ich besitze, seh' ich wie im Weiten,
> Und was verschwand, wird mir zu Wirklichkeiten.

> (What I possess, I see from far away,
> And what is lost becomes reality.)

[31–32]

At the moment of starting, Goethe looks back.

More than one critic has complained about this opening. In the crucial first lines, the lines that traditionally state the plan, the theme, the intention, the plot, the poet muses instead about his own dispossession and surrenders to the spirits. Goethe takes us into his unconscious. *Faust* has grown through all the years, not like a work of art but like a painful unplumbed memory that will no longer be repressed. Yet the opening also symbolizes, in Goethe's fashion, the work as a whole: its eternal return. No feeling is more dominant throughout than *déjà vu*—or *Wiedersehen*. The famous development of Part II, Act II, where the work goes back to Faust's chamber, parodies his temptation, and then provides a "Classical Walpurgis Night" as a counterpart to the "Walpurgis Night" of Part I, is only the most conspicuous of many another *Wiedersehen*. *Faust* is a structure built on its own ruins. But Goethe is less interested in simple repetition than in the development or unfolding of hidden potential. "What is lost becomes reality" only on its reappearance; to return is to become conscious of what has changed. If Goethe had written the *Aeneid,* Aeneas would have found himself, in the second part, back on the shores of Troy—and the experience would have made him a different man. Only by reliving the past do we gain the courage to go on.

Indeed, the emotions generated by *Faust* often seem related to the poet's own sensations as he picks up his manuscript again, propelled by new ideas that nevertheless must harmonize with those that have gone before. "Eleusis servat quod ostendat revisentibus" (Eleusis keeps things to display to those who return), Goethe wrote to C. J. L. Iken, impressing him with the need for coming back and back to *Faust,* each time to discover something different. The poet had followed the same advice. The text of *Faust,* like a palimpsest, preserves the marks of successive reworkings over many decades, of remembered intentions and abandoned transitions. Goethe was forced continually to reconstruct his earlier thought. It would be surprising if such a process of composition did not lead at times to contradictions or afterthoughts. (With mischievous relish, Goethe told Eckermann that the masked Boy Charioteer who appears in the Carnival of Part II, Act I, was "really" Euphorion, who would not be born until Act III.) While Goethe sometimes insisted that the "idea" of the whole *Faust* had been present from the beginning, he also admitted that his carrying-out of that idea had gone through many diversions. And critics of the work, like its author, may choose to emphasize either its frequent changes of direction or its abiding unity.

The vast body of Faustian criticism divides, in fact, into roughly two camps: followers of process or product. One party tries to unravel the work by sorting out the various stages of its composition, each with its own autonomous logic. The other accepts the final text as a definitive end result, a single whole whose apparent contradictions can be resolved by understanding its principles. Yet Goethe himself was untroubled. The vitality of the work, he saw, depended on its adaptation to both states of mind: process and product, metamorphosis and the One. For the reader as for the author, *Faust* would be a single work—endlessly reinterpreted.

It would also recapitulate the history of literature. In the looking-glass world of *Faust*, an immense anthology of literary languages, forms, and styles is reflected by Goethe's German. The "Prologue in Heaven" challenges comparison with the Book of Job, the final scene with Dante's *Paradiso*; the Intermezzo of Part I is titled "Walpurgis Night's Dream, or Oberon's and Titania's Golden Wedding." Goethe exemplifies his own theory of an emerging world literature by drawing classics from all languages—not only Greek and English but Persian and Norse—into his own sinewy way of speaking. Stylistically, the "plot" of *Faust* consists of demonstrating the adequacy of German to reproduce all varieties of poetry. Faust's effort to translate the "holy original" of the Gospel of John into "my beloved German" culminates with his insight that *Logos* may be rendered by *Tat*, Word into Deed (1220–37). Goethe finds a similar solution: the verbal acts of his poem translate the spirit of dead languages into a modern reality. Daringly, he even builds his poetic line out of the crudest materials, the *Knittelvers* of Hans Sachs and puppet plays, to show that native stock can take a graft from the highest vines in Parnassus. Thus Faust's opening monologue, beginning with doggerel, eventually modulates into a free-flowing Romantic verse shaped by the rhythm of his feelings. The progress of civilization is summarized in the language of *Faust;* the Muses of Greek and Hebrew return, to find themselves speaking German.

When Goethe himself returned to *Faust* in 1825, in fact, it was with this effect that he began. To remember his greatest poem he would also have to remember the universal history of poetry. That is the function of Part II, Act III, the *Helena,* which Goethe published separately in 1827 as a "classic-romantic phantasmagoria. Interlude to *Faust.*" He had had it in mind from the beginning ("The *Helena* is one of my oldest conceptions, simultaneous with *Faust,* always tending toward one meaning, but always shaped this way and that") but had long been baffled by the sheer incongruity of the two lovers, antique Helen and barbarous Faust. Schiller had seen that the point was crucial: "If you bring off this synthesis of the noble with the barbaric, as I do not doubt, then you will also have found the key to the remaining part of the whole." Yet Goethe did not find a solution until he realized that it lay in representing the problem itself: the marriage of beauty to coarseness, dream and reality, Greek and German.

Helena embodies this mixed marriage in its own succession of styles. The first scene, in the palace of Menelaus, concocts a facsimile of Greek tragedy, with meters and sentiments drawn from Aeschylus and Euripides, in which Helen learns that she can escape her fate only by taking refuge in another mode of verse/life. Next, in a Gothic castle, a variety of medieval and Renaissance verse forms is climaxed by the pretty exchange in which Faust teaches Helen how to rhyme.

> HELENA. So sage denn, wie sprech' ich auch so schön?
> FAUST. Das ist gar leicht, es muss von Herzen gehn.
> Und wenn die Brust von Sehnsucht überfliesst,
> Man sieht sich um und fragt—
> HELENA.   wer mitgeniesst.

> (HELEN. Tell me how I can speak that lovely part.
> FAUST. That's easy, it must issue from the heart.
> And when the spirit's rising aspiration
> Flows over, it looks round for—
> HELEN.   consummation.)
>   [9377–80]

The consummation or mutual enjoyment, not only a poetic but a sexual climax, is blessed with an offspring: Euphorion or Byron, the modern spirit of poetry. "As representative of modern poetic times," Goethe told Eckermann, "I could not use anyone but him, who without question must be considered the greatest talent of the century. Also, Byron is not antique and not romantic; rather, he is like the present day itself." Euphorion's meteoric career, like Byron's, ends with his early death. But the final note of the *Helena* is a triumphant poetry of nature—perhaps, in Goethe's view, the poetry of the future. Greek and German have wedded and brought forth. Goethe's interlude, like the larger drama it epitomizes, shows that seemingly dead languages, like seemingly dead manuscripts and emotions, can be made to live again.

Nevertheless, a trace of strangeness always lingers around this *tour de force* of versification. We are never allowed to forget its theatrical aspect. Under the mask and veil of Phorkyas, Mephistopheles stands ready to prompt the action and wake us (like Faust and Helen) from our dream of harmony. Moreover, the sense of *déjà vu* invades the reality of the characters, their emotions, their language, making them seem strange—somehow *unoriginal*—to themselves. Thus Helen is forced to remember her legendary betrothal to Achilles, a simulacrum copulating with a shade.

> Ich als Idol, ihm dem Idol verband ich mich.
> Es war ein Traum, so sagen ja die Worte selbst.
> Ich Schwinde hin und werde selbst mir ein Idol.
>
> (I as a phantom bound myself to phantom him.
> It was a dream, the words themselves say so.
> I disappear, becoming to myself a phantom.)
>
> [8879–81]

Idol retains the sense of *eidolon,* an image as well as ghost; and the reason for Helen's fainting spell at this point is that her memories of what happened only in legend remind her of how much she herself is such a memory, a fiction, the ghost of a ghost. Even the word *Idol,* transplanted into German, reverberates with a strangely hollow ring. A German Helen, no matter how beautifully imagined, is still not Helen of Troy. Faust will marry a shade: not Greece as it was but Greece as conjured up by Goethe. And Faust himself is another shade: the romanticized folk theme in whose image Goethe's own poetry was born. For all its virtuosity of style, the *Helena* does not pretend to restore the past. That would be impossible; nothing returns as it was. Rather, Goethe sets out to capture the mystery of a past that lives within the present, a past made out of images. Helen is right to doubt herself. A reflection in a mirror, she is not real.

Yet human beings are not *more* real. The final wisdom of the poet, as he gathered his powers to complete the work of his life, envisioned a world created from images: "Alles Vergängliche / Ist nur ein Gleichnis" (Everything transient / Is only an image). Hence the curious status of the *Helena,* a pastiche of styles that reconciles classic to romantic only at the cost of mutual alienation and loss of identity, does not separate it from the concerns of "life"; for life itself, according to the poet, is characterized by a sense of displacement. We live as creatures of memory, like Faust and Helen—forever meeting and parting. That is our reality. The might-have-been, the what-should-have-been, accompany us everywhere, just as the wavering shapes of an imperfect *Faust* had so long haunted Goethe himself. Nor does anyone live in the present. When Faust reaches his climax of ecstasy, rhyming with Helen, he momentarily asks time to stop.

FAUST. Nun schaut der Geist nicht vorwärts nicht zurück,
  Die Gegenwart allein—
HELENA.   ist unser Glück.

(FAUST. The mind does not look forward now, nor back,
  The present moment only—
HELEN.   is our luck.)

[9381–82]

But a genuine (rather than dreamlike) acceptance of this mood would violate not only the terms of his wager but the principle of his character: the perpetual discontent that makes him not likable, not satisfying, but human.

Indeed, the rhyme of *zurück* and *Glück* emblemizes, for Goethe, much of the human predicament. *Glück,* the word for "fate" and "happiness" as well as "luck," suggests the fatal pull of the future, the expectation or hunger of imagination that reduces life to a game of chance and keeps men from ever giving themselves wholly to the present. Significantly, it is only the timeless "idol" Helen who can pronounce it as a decisive note of resolution. But the rhyme word *zurück* shows where the spirit usually turns its gaze. Even at the moment when Faust denies a backward glance (at his love for Gretchen, for instance?), the object of his worship is more an antique image than a living woman. The love scenes of Faust and Helen, never entirely free from a tinge of irony, reflect the precarious balance of love: a lucky rhyme between two opposing forces. And their wedding does furnish, as Schiller had hoped, a key to the whole. The consummation of the lovers cannot stop time or the play. At best they can only pause for a moment at that height imagined by Hart Crane "For the Marriage of Faustus and Helen," the height

> The imagination spans beyond despair,
> Outpacing bargain, vocable and prayer.

Yet the dependence of beauty on time, of the most nearly perfect illusion on the coarse rumblings of stage machinery and action, cannot be denied; it enables the work to go on. As Greek clashes against German, so the world itself is renewed by unresolved polarities. Faust and Helen join in forgetfulness, in a lovely instant of stasis; but the business of Goethe and life is to make them remember.

If stasis is not permitted, however—if *Faust* is always condemned to visit its own past or look to a future haunted in turn by *déjà vu*—how is the work ever to reach a conclusion? Does the restlessness of Faust really carry him forward, or is all the sense of progress merely an illusion? Goethe posed these questions again and again, in practice as well as theory. And his first, preliminary answer, the conclusion of *Faust* Part I, was hardly encouraging.

In abandoning Gretchen, Faust stumbles like a sleepwalker through a dark parody of his need always to be moving on. Her whole presence rebukes him. Imprisoned by the past and her own consciousness of guilt rather than by the actual dungeon walls, Gretchen cannot move. She is at one with herself, ready for death, ready to be judged. In contrast, Faust wants desperately to take her away "ins Freie"—a freedom that she interprets as the grave. She cannot leave; he cannot stay. And on this one occasion, at least, his compulsive restlessness seems equated with damnation. Mephistopheles drags him off the stage, at the curtain of Part I, for all the world like a conventional devil claiming a conventional victim. The dynamic tension of the scene—an irresistible masculine force confronted by an immovable feminine object—is symbolically as well as dramatically shattering. Does all Faust's activity, his refusal to linger, amount to no more than this: flying from the consequences of what he has done? We in the audience are also torn. Our anxieties link us to Faust—the executioner comes, it is time to be going—but our hearts remain with Gretchen.

Goethe could not stay satisfied with that conclusion. Despite its theatrical power, the "Damnation of Faust" reduces its hero's ardor for life to a nervous disorder and exalts a fatalistic inner peace that resembles a death wish. Philosophically, one might argue, Goethe's dramatic instinct has subverted the theme of his work. If human salvation requires unceasing activity, if the one unforgivable error is standing still, then why do we sympathize so much more with Gretchen than with Faust? Does Gretchen represent (as Nietzsche charged) the conscience that makes cowards of us all, the conventional morality that prevents Faust from realizing his superhuman potential? Has Goethe sacrificed his soul for the sake of ending? The end of *Faust* Part II provides a kind of answer. Goethe reviews the play as a whole and strives for a larger harmony. Indeed, the last part of *Faust* may be considered an extended meditation on the nature of ending. An ultimate *Wiederspiegelung,* it holds up a mirror to the work.

Once more an unquenchable hungry restlessness confronts a static vision of perfection; Gretchen comes back. Merging into the company of the *Mater Gloriosa* as *Una Poenitentium,* she prays for Faust's salvation. Characteristically, her words enact a return on a return, since they adapt her own prayer of Part I (3587–3619), which was itself a version of the *Stabat Mater.* But now they serve another purpose.

> Neige, neige,
> Du Ohnegleiche,
> Du Strahlenreiche,
> Dein Antlitz gnädig meinem Glück!
> Der früh Geliebte,

Nicht mehr Getrübte,
Er kommt zurück.

(Incline, incline,
Thou without likeness,
Thou rich in radiance,
Thy gracious countenance on my good fortune!
The once belovéd,
No longer troubled,
Comes back again.)

[12069–76]

Once more the rhyme of *Glück* and *zurück* stands at the center. Yet now its meaning has been transformed, partly by the heavenly context, which lends *Glück* its Christian sense of "bliss," and partly by the pressure of the ending, which releases *zurück* from its regressive yearnings into direct fulfillment. Faust has come home; the past and future draw together; the words are reconciled. And Gretchen is also transformed. "Nestling" against the heavenly host, she has become "A Penitent, formerly called Gretchen"; once and for all her luck has changed. A Beatrice to Faust's Dante, she welcomes him to a realm where the past no longer holds him, where he performs no action, where his mortal part does not appear and his name is not mentioned (on stage he might be represented, like the Homunculus earlier, merely by an effect of light). Only Faust's *Unsterbliches* remains—the undying part that the Devil cannot claim. Now he is ready for birth.

What such a birth might involve is clarified by Gretchen's next speech, her second and last in Part II. In this play and this scene so dominated by Mothers, only a mother who has lost her child can understand the problems of a life as it struggles upward.

Vom edlen Geisterchor umgeben,
Wird sich der Neue kaum gewahr,
Er ahnet kaum das frische Leben,
So gleicht er schon der heiligen Schar.
Sieh, wie er jedem Erdenbande
Der alten Hülle sich entrafft
Und aus ätherischem Gewande
Hervortritt erste Jugendkraft.
Vergönne mir, ihn zu belehren,
Noch blendet ihn der neue Tag.

(Wrapped round by soulful choruses,
Himself the new one scarcely knows,
The dawning life he scarcely guesses,

Already like the holy host.
See there, how every ancient veil
Of earthly swaddling he shakes off
And through that dress, ethereal,
The primal youthful strength steps forth.
Permit me to enlighten him,
As yet he is blinded by the dawn.)

[12084–93]

And permission is granted; she will ascend to higher spheres, and he will follow. If Faust has become a child again, at the close of the play, he no longer lacks direction. Goethe exquisitely combines two possible associations of the "Eternal Feminine": the sexual attraction that leads men to aspire to glory, and the mothering protectiveness that saves even the most restless soul from suffering the consequences of its actions. Faust will be drawn upward, by Gretchen's anti-gravity, as a babe comes out of the womb into light, as a young man pursues his love, as a pilgrim mounts to the Holy Mother, as an unappeasable spirit seeks behind every appearance a higher symbol. Is this heaven? or a return to the world?

Something of both. For despite all the mystic rapture of this final scene, its "higher things" remain tied to Goethe's concern with the things of this world—his work and his life. The Christian machinery, he acknowledged to Eckermann, was devised mainly to give "to my poetic intention a salutary limited form and solidity." Like his own creature Faust, Goethe uses the terms of Christianity to strike a secular bargain.

"Wer immer strebend sich bemüht,
Der können wir erlösen."
(Whoever struggles, always striving,
That one we can redeem.)

[11936–37]

Goethe himself added the quotation marks to point the moral of Faust's salvation. "In Faust himself there is a continually higher and purer activity until the end, and from above eternal love comes to his aid." These remarks strikingly resemble Goethe's argument for his own immortality: "My conviction of our permanence springs from the notion of activity; for if I work without rest until my end, then nature is obliged to direct me to another form of existence, when the present one is no longer able to sustain my spirit." An active soul that realizes its imaginings makes a covenant with the future. And so does an active poem. Faust's transcendence does not depend on a single religious framework so much as on a set of eternal images, images whose shifting interplay defines the complexity of the natural world as well as the supernatural realms that art can reach. Goethe builds his scene from the most elementary oppositions—youth and age, male and female, life and death, the actual and the potential—and tries to imagine their reconciliation. It is a final great return, a return on his whole life's work.

In the end of *Faust* is its beginning. Thus the epilogue in heaven clearly reflects the "Prologue in Heaven," and the "new day" that blinds Faust during his final ascent repeats the glory of the first day, perpetually renewed, as the archangels sing, in God's creation. Once again, at the end of the play, we view a heavenly hierarchy contemplating the nature of man. Yet heaven has changed. In place of the authoritarian dispensation of that first celestial locker room, so entirely masculine that no Eve had to be included in Faust's temptation, we turn to a heaven of women. Here the *Mater Gloriosa* rules, not by edict but through the power of her example. And instead of the reliance on human will—

> Ein guter Mensch in seinem dunklen Drange
> Ist sich des rechten Weges wohl bewusst

> (A good man in his darkling stress
> Is surely conscious still of the right way)
> [328–29]

—we are told that salvation depends on gracious intercession, a leading from above,

> Und hat an ihm die Liebe gar
> Von oben teilgenommen

> (If love on high be ready
> To take his part).
> [11938–39]

Unconditional activity yields to the need for a higher guidance. The two heavens do not contradict each other (if women are the objects of worship at the end, men are the worshipers), but they do embody complementary values: activity and mercy. The end contains the beginning but also something more, a harmony that brooks no disputation.

Before *Faust* achieves such harmony, however, it must prove its right to end. Nor could that right be taken for granted. The series of anticlimaxes or false endings that precede the conclusion manifests the author's own inner debate. Virgil wished to destroy the *Aeneid* because he did not consider it finished; Goethe sealed *Faust* because he feared he would start it again. "I went on so long that at last I thought it advisable to cry out: Shut the irrigation ditch, the meadows have drunk enough." The metaphor echoes Faust's own last grandiose scheme, reclaiming lands from the sea, and

108

Goethe shows that he does not think the ambition absurd (an enthusiast for such projects, he regretted that he would not live to see the Panama and Suez canals or the linking of the Danube with the Rhine). He preserves until the very last moment the freedom to change his mind. *Faust* could not be complete unless it represented, in one of its aspects, the superficiality and impossibility of ending.

Part II incorporates three endings, in fact. The first occurs, naturally enough, at the moment of the hero's death. Faust dies in a vision of activity, expressing the wisdom of his life:

> Nur der verdient sich Freiheit wie das Leben,
> Der täglich sie erobern muss.

> (They only merit freedom and their lives
> Who daily must reconquer them.)
>
> [11575–76]

Stirred by this dream of a vigorous and fruitful society, he pronounces the magic words—conditionally.

> Zum Augenblicke dürft ich sagen:
> Verweile doch, du bist so schön!

> (Then to the moment I would say:
> Linger awhile, you are so fair!)
>
> [11581–82]

In the hope of a better future he enjoys his highest moment—and dies. But Mephistopheles understandably chooses to take these last words as the ful- fillment of the bargain.

> MEPH: Die Uhr steht still—
> CHOR: Steht still! Sie schweigt wie Mitternacht.
>   Der Zeiger fällt.
> MEPH: Er fällt, es ist vollbracht.

> (MEPH: The hour stands still—
> CHOR: Like midnight it is stilled.
>   The clock hand falls.
> MEPH: It falls, it is fulfilled.)
>
> [11593–94]

It is fulfilled—for Faust as for Christ, the mortal bond has been consummated. But the Chorus of Lemures knows better. Immediately it corrects Meph- istopheles' wording to the more neutral *es ist vorbei* (it is over). The cer- tainties of the *Faustbuch,* the Protestant ethic which insists that every bargain must be paid for, have no place here. And the revision of the story provokes the Devil to a definitive statement of his essentially negative outlook.

> Vorbei! ein dummes Wort.
> Warum vorbei?
> Vorbei und reines Nicht, vollkommnes Einerlei!
> Was soll uns denn das ew'ge Schaffen!
> Geschaffenes zu nichts hinwegzuraffen!
> "Da ist's vorbei!" Was ist daran zu lesen?
> Es ist so gut, als wär' es nicht gewesen,
> Und treibt sich doch im Kreis, als wenn es wäre.
> Ich liebte mir dafür das Ewig-Leere.
>
> (Over! a stupid word.
> Why over, why?
> Over and purely Not, the same thing perfectly!
> What use is all this limitless creation!
> Creating only brings annihilation!
> "It's over!" What is that supposed to mean?
> As good as saying it had never been,
> Yet it still runs around as if it had.
> I like, myself, the Ever-Void instead.)
>
> [11595–603]

Faust's activity, in this view, has meant literally nothing; all effort, human and divine, turns out to be equally futile (we must remember that Mephistopheles himself has put in a lot of work for nothing). With prophetic parody, the Devil also mocks—or will be mocked by—the penultimate lines of the poem: *Hier ist's getan* (Here it is done, as opposed to It is over) and *Das Ewig-Weibliche* (the Eternal Feminine, as opposed to *das Ewig-Leere,* the Eternal Emptiness). Something done, even more than something over, implies the possibility of achievement; an Eternal Feminine, rather than an Eternal Emptiness, implies a prolific life-force. Mephistopheles is right to object. The end of Faust is supposed to belong to him, but Goethe's play on words has taken it away.

What Goethe reclaims, still more, is the right of his poem to salvation. For Mephistopheles' speech disputes the ability of the author himself to come to an end. The usual conclusion of a Faust drama, the Devil knows, will no longer do. Audiences are too sophisticated now to believe in the closed forms of moralities, where the whole of a life can be boiled down to one word of judgment: "fulfilled" or "over." Life is no longer like that—and neither are plays. Mephistopheles wittily describes the open form of *Faust* itself: endless creation, ceaselessly running around in circles (or circling back), and never quite managing to reach a logical stopping place. If *Faust* resembles life, then what is its purpose? The echo on *vorbei* (an effect repeated

110

at the climax of *Der Rosenkavalier)* suggests a last diabolical revenge: the triumph of non-existence. Not without seriousness, Goethe looks into the Void—not a satisfying abyss of hell but a space as empty as an unfilled page.

Mephistopheles pays for his cynicism. The following "burial" scene, the second ending of *Faust,* by rights should enact his victory. Here is the moment when, by every convention, the stage yawns open into hellfire and the Devil drives. But something else happens: a farcical resurrection. Not only is Mephistopheles robbed of Faust's soul, he is converted into an ironic analogue of Faust. A choir of angels distracts him sexually, drawing his attention upwards through "love" just as Faust will be drawn up by Gretchen. Instead of burning he is burned, by holy fire, and afflicted by boils like Job's (another inversion of the usual story). Poor devil! Even the suggestion of pederasty—the angelic boys have such sweet bottoms!—comments on his inability to reach a proper end. In a world without a female principle there can be no issue, the beginning and ending are truly the same. All over and purely Not, in Mephistopheles' version of the plot, have come together. He is exactly what he has imagined Faust to be, a perpetual motion machine. He has gotten nowhere.

Where has *Faust* gotten? Goethe has one more ending in reserve. In the final words of Part II, deliberately matching his vision against the final moment of Dante's *Comedy,* he confronts the paradox of existence and asserts a permanence in the face of change. The Godhead, he suggests, is but another name for the human; the passive, for the active; the many, for the one. Nor do the paradoxes stop there.

> Alles Vergängliche
> Ist nur ein Gleichnis;
> Das Unzulängliche,
> Hier wird's Ereignis;
> Das Unbeschreibliche,
> Hier ist's getan;
> Das Ewig-Weibliche
> Zieht uns hinan.

> (Everything transient
> Is only a likeness;
> The insufficient
> Here comes to pass;
> The indescribable
> Here is done;
> The Eternally Female
> Draws us on.)
>   [12104–11]

The story of Faust goes on forever, and comes to an end.

"The indescribable, / Here it is done." The abiding paradox, the paradox that gives rise to all the others, is the poem itself. With overmastering pride Goethe contradicts Mephistopheles and claims that something has been *done;* the coffin cannot be closed, but the manuscript can be sealed. Whether or not *Faust* rewards its sixty years of expectations, it has been achieved. If its achievement consists only of mutable images, so does the rest of life— "Everything transient / Is only a likeness." If it seems inadequate to its promise, if *Das Unzulängliche* (the inaccessible or unattainable) keeps its secrets, here at the close it takes on the reality of something performed— "The insufficient / Here comes to pass." If beyond interpretation, it sur- passes description to become the thing-in-itself—"The indescribable / Here is done." If it falls short of the ideal, it creates an ideal for others to follow in turn—"The Eternally Female / Draws us on." Goethe does not claim perfection. The seal of the poem will be broken, he knows; everything changes, and the future will read him in its own way. Yet still he has made a whole—the work of his life.

With increasing clarity, in fact, he came to think of *Faust* as the single Great Confession that would draw all his work together. The special priv- ilege of the poet, Goethe thought, was the ability to purge himself of unendurable experiences by reliving them and mastering them in art.

> Und wenn der Mensch in seiner Qual verstummt,
> Gab mir ein Gott, zu sagen, wie ich leide.

> (Though man keeps silence in his pain,
> A god has let me speak of how I suffer.)

These lines, from the last speech of *Torquato Tasso* (3432–33), were used again by Goethe (with "how" revised to "what") as the epigraph for the most personal of his late poems, the great "Marienbad Elegy." Tasso and Goethe, unlike Werther, are inspired to confess their pain and thus continue living. It is in this sense (and probably no other) that Goethe regarded his works as "fragments of a great confession"; each testified to an experience controlled or sublimated through being expressed in art. The creative pro- cess builds scars over wounds. But *Faust* was different. By the end of his life, Goethe wrote to Wilhelm von Humboldt in the last of his letters, he had lived so long with his art that conscious effort could duplicate the results of unconscious creation. "The organs of man, through practice, study, reflection [*Nachdenken*], success, failure, assistance and opposition and again and again reflection, unconsciously connect in free activity the acquired with the inborn, bringing forth a unity that astounds the world." The practical test of this unity would be the seamlessness of *Faust;* readers, Goethe was sure, would be unable to distinguish the early work from the later or the spontaneous from the deliberate. Yet more profoundly, *Faust* would embody every aspect of its poet, both his inner nature and his earned experience. All that Goethe had felt and learned would enter it; there would be nothing more to confess. The completed *Faust* was the poet's destiny, and his absolution.

*　　*　　*

Yet Goethe's harmonium, like Virgil's, proved difficult to follow. Thus Emil Staiger, who spent much of his own life on Goethe, refused even to comment on the last lines of *Faust*. They were a miracle—literally indescribable—and a miracle does not abide our questions. In solving the problem of how to end a work of perpetual activity, Goethe had pronounced the last word. Moreover, he had measured out his work by the span of his own life, his own personal rhythm. *Faust* subordinates all other formal arrangements to the peculiar way that human beings experience time, its sudden gaps and speedings, its annihilation by memory, its weird proclivity for repeating itself. Nor could Goethe have succeeded without the precious length of time made possible by his incredible health and well-being. His aesthetic required it. His constant practice of revisiting the past, of going back to Werther or Wilhelm or Faust, could flourish only where the past was rich enough to reward the return, to disclose previously hidden potentialities. Goethe needed every moment of his long life not only for the time to complete *Faust* but for the time to look at it again through the perspective of ages. "Who is a poet?" Thomas Mann asked, and answered his own question under the spell of Goethe: "He whose life is symbolic." The endless activity of Goethe's life found its appropriate symbol in *Faust*.

Few later poets have been so fortunate. "It is a notable fact that since Goethe our world has brought forth no more classics," E. R. Curtius wrote in 1949, at the end of a study of "Fundamental Features of Goethe's World." "Poets like Hugo and Whitman do not fill out the dimensions. The great problematical writers like Dostoevski and Nietzsche do not do so for other reasons. Whether a classic is still possible in a declining civilization is questionable. All our experience speaks against it. In that case Goethe would be the last classic of Europe as Virgil was the last classic of Rome." By successfully incorporating the literature of Europe into his own life and work, Goethe had achieved the sense of an ending—a "totalization of tradition in an original creation." *Faust* is a summing-up. It achieves its unity, according to Curtius, by pronouncing the last words not only of Goethe but of Western civilization. "Goethe created a universal, positive oeuvre in an era of incipient disintegration." And those who come after cannot expect to make a whole. They must be satisfied with broken pieces—or learn to begin again.

Yet why should the past exert so much control? The constant returns of Goethe, not only to earlier literature but to his own past life, impede another sort of effort: a poem that would project its destiny forward into the future.

Renewal constitutes the theme of *Faust,* but its own renewals are companioned by the unquiet figures of the dead. The new day that dawns in the last scene repeats the opening dawn in heaven. But another kind of creation might be imagined: a morning of time itself, utterly free from the past. Can the work of a great poet consist entirely of beginnings? One poet, at least, seems to have thought so. "A great poem is no finish to a man or woman but rather a beginning. Has anyone fancied he could sit at last under some due authority and rest satisfied with explanations and realize and be content and full? To no such terminus does the greatest poet bring." The words introduce a poem of beginnings: *Leaves of Grass* 1855. Whitman, like Goethe, set out to make a book of his life—one book only. But this book would have no end. Whitman's inspiration, unquenchable as grass, would show that a starting-out and a summing-up could be one and the same: a harmonium made from initiations. The past could not chain him. And a poet of democracy would shake the Fathers from his shoulders and roust the Mothers from their hiding places. Whitman would generate himself. "Thus we presume to write, as it were, upon things that exist not, and travel by maps yet unmade, and a blank. But the throes of birth are upon us. . . ."

Leaves of Grass

> The experience of each new age requires a new confession, and the world seems always waiting for its poet.
> —Emerson, "The Poet"
> There are just two great modern books—Faust and Leaves of Grass.
> —Richard Bucke

At the end of "A Backward Glance O'er Travel'd Roads" (1888), an essay intended to close all future editions of *Leaves of Grass,* Whitman left "two items for the imaginative genius of the West, when it worthily rises—First, what Herder taught to the young Goethe, that really great poetry is always (like the Homeric or Biblical canticles) the result of a national spirit, and not the privilege of a polish'd and select few; Second, that the strongest and sweetest songs yet remain to be sung." The reference to Goethe here has a secret competitive edge; for Goethe, Whitman thought, had not learned Herder's lesson. Subversive ideas are harbored by *Faust*—the ideas of world literature and of an art transcending its time—and a robust American poet could have no truck with them. In one of his final essays, "American

National Literature" (1891), Whitman returned to the attack. "The Goethean theory and lesson (if I may briefly state it so) of the exclusive sufficiency of artistic, scientific, literary equipment to the character, irrespective of any strong claims of the political ties of nation, state, or city, could have answer'd under the conventionality and pettiness of Weimar, or the Germany, or even Europe, of those times; but it will not do for America today at all." America cannot bother with self-sufficient art. She requires instead a National Literature, a *people's* poetry. Far from holding themselves aloof, her poets must participate in the life of the nation; indeed (as Whitman said over and over again in *Democratic Vistas*) a nation *is* her poets. Goethe, from this point of view, enacts the role of Mephistopheles—the sower of doubt. With all his seeming loftiness and independence of spirit, he reminds the reader of the doom that awaits even the best ideals and the greatest nation. He is not impressed by size and power and strength; he has seen them all before. And he knows very well that the classics already in existence are very great and not to be surpassed. The achievement of Goethe falls like a shadow on Whitman and the American future. It is time for another hero: the American Faust. "The strongest and sweetest songs yet remain to be sung."

Yet Whitman's quarrel with Goethe also represents a quarrel with himself. Even as he denounced Goethe for worldliness and conventionality, he could describe him to Horace Traubel in terms of an Ur- or proto-Whitman. "Goethe impresses me as above all to stand for essential literature, art, life—to argue the importance of centering life in self—in perfect persons—perfect you, me: to force the real into the abstract ideal: to make himself, Goethe, the supremest example of personal identity: everything making for it: in us, in Goethe: every man repeating the same experience." If concentration on the self can lead to egotism and abstraction, as Whitman points out, it can also lead to the purest democracy: a federation of all men in one, *e pluribus unum*. Goethe had been a "kosmos"; the work of his life had made him representative, in his intense individuality, of every human being. And what else had Whitman himself aimed after? " 'Leaves of Grass' indeed (I cannot too often reiterate) has mainly been the outcropping of my own emotional and other personal nature—an attempt, from first to last, to put *a Person*, a human being (myself, in the latter half of the Nineteenth Century, in America,) freely, fully and truly on record." *Dichtung und Wahrheit* stands behind *Leaves of Grass*.

Nor could Whitman be confident that he, any more than Goethe, was a poet of the people. If self-absorption, egotism, and a craving for success conspire to block a poet from joining himself to the common man and the national spirit, then the American poet might well accuse himself no less than the German. Whitman was a remarkable man—anything but common. He loved the word "Master," with all its connotations of a poetical hierarchy

115

or craft guild ruled over by a supreme authority, and his fondest hope was that comrades would rise up and cheer his mastery. Indeed, insofar as a single thought may be said to have precipitated *Leaves of Grass,* that thought was probably Whitman's realization that he could be the Great Poet whose coming had been prophesied by many contemporaries—not only by Emerson, famously, in "The Poet," but by Alexander Smith, whose poems drew this manuscript note from Whitman in 1854: "There is one electric passage in this poetry, where the announcement is made of a great forthcoming Poet." The excitement of the 1855 Preface to *Leaves of Grass* clearly derives from a sense that the prophecy has been fulfilled. Whitman characterizes a single figure, "the greatest poet" (sometimes referred to also as "the great master"), described not conditionally but as an accomplished fact. "The greatest poet does not only dazzle his rays over character and scenes and passions . . . he finally ascends and finishes all . . . he exhibits the pinnacles that no man can tell what they are for or what is beyond. . . . he glows a moment on the extremest verge" (716). *Leaves of Grass* announces itself as the book of the greatest poet. The moment of initiation, I have said, often occurs at the point when the poet discovers that his own personal history exactly corresponds with the universal history of mankind. There is no better example than Whitman. Accepting his destiny as the American poet, he at once assumes the role of greatness.

To what extent, however, did the greatness belong to America, and to what extent to Whitman? The rhetoric of the early *Leaves of Grass* depends on an absolute equation between the two sorts of greatness. "The great master has nothing to do with miracles. He sees health for himself in being one of the mass. . . . The master knows that he is unspeakably great and that all are unspeakably great" (720). But the later Whitman had reason to doubt the equation. Americans would not rise to their poet's notions of their greatness. Nor would they buy his books. For Whitman, as Santayana saw so clearly and said so haughtily, could never be a poet of the people. Ordinary people do not dream about democracy but about pure ideals of power and beauty and love. "Their chosen poets, if they have any, will be always those who have known how to paint these ideals in lively even if in gaudy colours. Nothing is farther from the common people than the corrupt desire to be primitive." And Whitman knew this himself. The America that would affectionately absorb its greatest poet would have to be an America imagined in spite of itself. The constant fluctuation in Whitman's poems between a titanic assertion of self and a self-effacing submission to the People or the All reveals a strenuous effort to reimagine the people in the poet's own image. Only then could the greatest poet and the greatest nation be one and the same.

Moreover, the tension in Whitman's work between the self and America increasingly reflected a similar tension in the country around him. The large

116

majority of Americans, however democratic in theory, were in practice as selfish as Faust. By the time of *Democratic Vistas* (1871), Whitman's moving attempt to keep his faith on the brink of the Gilded Age, his vision of a unified people has twisted into an enormous question mark.

> Must not the virtue of modern Individualism, continually enlarging, usurping all, seriously affect, perhaps keep down entirely, in America, the like of the ancient virtue of Patriotism, the fervid and absorbing love of general country? I have no doubt myself that the two will merge, and mutually profit and brace each other, and that from them a greater product, a third, will arise. But I feel that at present they and their oppositions form a serious problem and paradox in the United States.

Whitman's hope that individualism and patriotism would someday merge accords with his hope that the people one day would share his own identity, and that his own great spirit, writ large, would turn out to be the same as the great American poem.

Its name would be *Leaves of Grass.* But the title, like the work itself, hints at how difficult Whitman found the struggle to be one of the people. No matter how much he pictured himself as a representative, anonymous democrat, common as grass, he also dreamed himself a master, inscribing himself and his soul on every leaf. And he dreamed of success, a popular coming-out. The conflict is emblemized by the difference between the first and second editions of *Leaves of Grass*—the first (1855), proudly incognito, with no author's name on the title page or titles on the poems, only the famous portrait of "an American, one of the roughs" (if Whitman had continued that format, modeled on the best-selling *Fern Leaves from Fanny's Port-Folio,* he might eventually have been known as "Walt Grass"); the second, a year later, bearing on its green binding, stamped in gold, not only the name "Walt Whitman" but also the most magnificent blurb of all times: "I Greet You at the Beginning of a Great Career R. W. Emerson," and, inside, copies both of Emerson's letter and Whitman's long reply. That letter *made* Whitman—not Walt the singer but the Good Gray Poet, an American institution. No wonder that Emerson later had second thoughts about his role as Frankenstein. Greetings at "the Beginning of a Great Career" place an almost intolerable burden on the recipient; they "set him up." And Whitman felt the pressure. "Master, we have not come through centuries, caste, heroisms, fables, to halt in this land today." No longer anonymous, he would have to shape a career. On the title page of the final *Leaves of Grass,* the "deathbed edition" (1891–92), the name WALT WHITMAN appears as a bold, authoritative signature.

Yet Whitman did not find his "Great Career" so easy to realize. The stakes had been set so high that no mere modest success would do; he would have to gamble everything on a single throw. In an early, unsigned review

of his own unsigned *Leaves,* Whitman had predicted that the haughty unknown author "is to prove either the most lamentable of failures or the
most glorious of triumphs, in the known history of literature. And after
all we have written we confess our brain-felt and heart-felt inability to
decide which we think it is likely to be." If the vein of self-advertisement
is genuine here, so is the note of self-doubt. What sort of book could follow
such a prediction? American writers traditionally falter at the second try;
the euphoria of a first success fades before an anxious awareness of how
much more is expected. Second books tend to be melancholy. Thus Whitman himself, after his heady start, turned to the darker tones of "Calamus."
In the first flush of recognition by Emerson he had thought that the world
was his for the taking. "The way is clear to me. A few years, and the
average annual call for my Poems is ten or twenty thousand copies—more,
quite likely. Why should I hurry or compromise?" But not many years had
passed before he learned that the public for which he wrote—those hearty
and generous companions—had yet to exist. In 1856 he bragged to Emerson
that the first printing of *Leaves,* a thousand copies, had "readily sold"; years
later, in a different mood, he denied that a single one had been bought. Nor
would he compromise his vision by giving his readers something they
wanted to buy. If forced to choose between being a success and being
himself, it would be, to his credit, himself he chose.

What could he do for an encore? In effect Whitman found a unique
solution to the problem of the second book. He never wrote one; or rather,
he assimilated every new poem into one of the revised editions of *Leaves
of Grass.* The American bard, the American book, would have to stay in
motion. America itself, after all, was a collection of promises, a land of
beginnings. In a little poem which raises the flag, "World Take Good
Notice," the manuscript refers to "thirty four stars," dating it before June
19, 1863; first printed in 1865, the verses admitted West Virginia and Nevada
into "coals thirty-six"; by 1881 the coals had swelled to thirty-eight (the
rhythm will not work out again, in our own variorum, until we add another
state—Whitman himself favored Canada). Where could it end? A growing
nation demanded a growing poem.

Moreover, the author was also changing. When Whitman insisted that
" 'Leaves of Grass' is, or seeks to be, simply a faithful and doubtless self-
will'd record," he was insuring that each new edition would have its own
new subject. Whatever the poet saw became a part of him—and he saw a
great deal. A single pair of covers could hardly enclose all the accumulations,
the carefully wrapped and much-loved baggage that a man gathers in the
course of his life. *Leaves of Grass* would have to make room.

> The past and present wilt . . . . I have filled them and
> emptied them,

And proceed to fill my next fold of the future. . . .
Do I contradict myself?
Very well then . . . . I contradict myself;
I am large . . . . I contain multitudes.

And the poem, as it expanded into the future, would also have to contradict itself and contain multitudes. After the Civil War, most of all, neither America nor Whitman could be the same. They had lost their innocence; they had seen that unity, whether of a nation or a person, cannot be assumed before a debt has been paid in tribulation and blood. The unity of *Leaves of Grass* would have to be earned.

Unity, indeed, eventually proved to be the problem. Young Walt and old Walt did not always have much in common, and the book on which they collaborated—the initiation of the young poet and the harmonium of the old—often was wrenched apart. Nor did Whitman himself know what to make of it. Sometimes he regarded it as a personal ledger, a diary open to any notation, however fugitive: "autobiography pure and simple—in its elemental form." At other times he perceived it as the manifestation of a cosmic order, like the Rocky Mountains or one of those treatises, popular in mid-century America, that decipher the laws governing the whole creation. One work that may have influenced *Leaves of Grass*, for instance, is Andrew Jackson Davis' *The Great Harmonia; Being a Philosophical Revelation of the Natural, Spiritual, and Celestial Universe* (5 vols.; 1850–52). Typically, such authors attempt to demonstrate the unity of all being, the identity of macrocosm and microcosm. Whitman was no exception. Yet he often changed his mind about the principle of that unity. Was *Leaves of Grass* an intimate journal or confession? an *Upanishad* or meditation on the Divine? a language experiment? a collection of recitatives and arias like an Italian opera? a history of mankind through a biography of a representative man? an organic flowering around a seed of death? a conspectus of America? a landscape? an ocean? a summary and furthering of all previous thought? an Emersonian oration? an imitation of the life of Christ? a human body? All these and more. Nothing is more characteristic of the later Whitman than an excited discovery that "I have found the law of my own poems." He hungered for assurance that his life-work had been completed. But the laws he found kept changing; no one metaphor would do.

In one vital respect, of course, *Leaves of Grass* is *not* a single book. Each of the nine editions, stretching over a period of thirty-six years, builds a structure of its own—often a structure radically different from its companions. No one is likely to confuse the version of 1855, that wonderfully fresh beginning, with the inflated and monumental volume of 1891–92, a death-bed edition in more than name. Nor do Whitman's final thoughts necessarily represent his best. Malcolm Cowley has argued eloquently for the superiority of *LG* 1855, Roy Harvey Pearce for the quintessential greatness of 1860. And surely a case can be made for 1856, with the first version of "Crossing Brooklyn Ferry"; for 1867, with the new note of democratic sorrow; for 1872, with *Passage to India;* or for the last words and revisions of 1881 and 1892. The problem is more than merely textual (though the absence of a variorum *Leaves* long constituted one of the major gaps in American literary scholarship). From the standpoint of the reader who wants to know Whitman, *Leaves of Grass,* so far from being a unified whole, hardly exists except in drafts and fragments. Critics who wish to demonstrate the unity of the book ordinarily begin by positing a single edition—usually, though not always, the last—as the essence of *Leaves.* But no one edition can capture the variety of Whitman's achievement, its shifting adaptations to the state of mind and the state of the union. Whatever its virtues, the final version exhibits a waning ebb of creative vitality. The conscientious reader must rather begin at the beginning, with *Leaves of Grass* 1855, and read through each successive edition until Whitman's death in 1892 interrupts his progress. Only then will he know the essential Walt—in a constantly revised edition.

The justification for this procedure is spelled out by the poem itself. Right from the start, in 1855, the poet freely gave advice on how his book was to be read.

> Have you practiced so long to learn to read?
> Have you felt so proud to get at the meaning of poems?
>
> Stop this day and night with me and you shall possess
>   the origin of all poems,
> You shall possess the good of the earth and sun. . . .
>   there are millions of suns left,
> You shall no longer take things at second or third hand
>   . . . . nor look through the eyes of the dead. . . .
>   nor feed on the spectres in books,
> You shall not look through my eyes either, nor take things
>   from me,
> You shall listen to all sides and filter them from yourself.

Virgil and Goethe had carefully sowed their poems with hidden meanings. Each of those poets, already famous, had composed his last work with the full knowledge that connoisseurs and commentators were waiting to unravel the fine points; Goethe in particular enjoyed the prospect of how much hard work he was leaving the philologists. The master poet, like the priest of mysteries, held the keys to correct interpretation. But Whitman had thrown away the keys; *Leaves of Grass* would belong to everyone. Thus a famous

Emersonian passage of *Democratic Vistas* insists that the reader, and the reader alone, has the right to construct a text.

> In fact, a new theory of literary composition for imaginative works of the very first class, and especially for highest poems, is the sole course open to these States. Books are to be call'd for, and supplied, on the assumption that the process of reading is not a half-sleep, but, in highest sense, an exercise, a gymnast's struggle; that the reader is to do something for himself, must be on the alert, must himself or herself construct indeed the poem, argument, history, metaphysical essay—the text furnishing the hints, the clue, the start or frame-work. Not the book needs so much to be the complete thing, but the reader of the book does.

The author who strives to perfect his own book is a kind of tyrant. Far better to abandon it or to die in the attempt.

How then could Whitman finish *Leaves of Grass?* Despite his reluctance to face the question, it absorbed him for most of his life. A democratic poem could not afford to close any of its options; but a poem with all its options open could hardly achieve the sense of unity that America—and the poet—desperately wanted. The attempt to prepare a final edition of *Leaves of Grass* was literally a life-and-death struggle. And its result has generally, I think, been misunderstood. Whitman's own rhetoric of organic unity has tempted critics to search out, and inevitably to find, a single, perfected organizing principle. But the immediate experience of reading *Leaves of Grass* in the Deathbed Edition tends to destroy such impressions of unity. What one poem offers, the next takes back; what the poet builds he can also dissolve. Nor does this shifting of ground exemplify a fruitful, life-affirming spirit of contradiction. Often it suggests instead a death wish, a resignation to the forces of chaos that mock every discovery by proving it cannot last. Whitman's Faustian vision also harbors a Mephistopheles— a spirit of negation. Death is a part of life; every ecstatic moment contains the seeds of dissolution. The boy in "Out of the Cradle" became a poet, his older self reveals, at the instant of grasping the fact of death. A similar logic informs the book as a whole. The source of its order is chaos, a leaf of grass is the symbol at once of life and death.

The formal principle that lies behind the successive editions of *Leaves of Grass,* therefore, is largely that no theme, emotion, or poem can be allowed to stand unchallenged. Constantly changing the contexts, fitting together poems from different periods of his life and different states of feeling, Whitman insured that all his work would stay in flux. Inconsistency is not an accident in his method but the method itself. When the resolutely untitled anonymous poem of beginnings was rechristened "Walt Whitman," when the physical immediacy of "Calamus" (1860) was turned, through an insertion of 1871, to "The Base of All Metaphysics," when *Drum-taps* and

Passage to India, conceived as separate, rival books, were assimilated into *Leaves of Grass,* they helped to show that the spirit of the poetry could not be identified with any one point of view or any one procedure. Even the later chronological arrangement, where the author clearly intends his *Leaves* to imitate the stages of a human life, is shot through with anachronisms, since some of the prefatory verse dates from the weary end of the poet's career and some of the concluding verse from his beginning. More than one poem, in fact, reverses its meaning as it travels from edition to edition. If "Song of Myself" was originally (as Malcolm Cowley argues) a song of not-myself, then it exemplifies its moral even more strongly: the self does not stay the same.

Nor would the poet have been dismayed to hear how often he changed his tune. As *Leaves of Grass* grew, nothing required more labor than preserving its freshness, its crackle of danger and caprice. In 1860 the vagrant growth of *Leaves* could be attributed to the diversity of "American mouthsongs!", each flowing from a different particular person:

> The delicious singing of the mother—or of the young
> wife at work—or of the girl sewing or washing—Each
> singing what belongs to her, and to none else
>
> [19]

Even the dashes, democratically affirming that all punctuation was created equal and that no clause should be subordinate to any other, imply the separate, independent life of each particular. But commas replaced the dashes when "I Hear America Singing" was transferred to "Inscriptions" in 1881, and the "I" became obtrusive. The praise of spontaneity and contradiction often sounds programmatic in the later *Leaves of Grass.* The twenty-four "Inscriptions," for instance, each offering a different justification for the book to come, seem rather too calculatingly random. Detail piles on detail until the whole enterprise threatens to sink of its own weight; the sheer size intimidates the reader. *Leaves of Grass* could easily have become a monument or—worse yet!—respectable.

Thus the final task of Whitman was to deconstruct his book. It could not be allowed to congeal. Unlike earlier poets, he refused to consider his initiation—*Leaves of Grass* 1855—something to be put behind or surpassed. Rather, he regarded it as a work in progress, potentially infinite and therefore never to be abandoned. Like the world, it had not been "plann'd and built one thing after another as an architect plans and builds a house" (394); nor could its time, any more than a man's, be limited to seventy—or seventy million—years. The poem that carries this message began its life untitled in *Leaves of Grass* 1855. The next year it was called "Lesson Poem." In 1860 it became "Leaves of Grass" No. 11; in 1867, No. 3. Then it was absorbed into *Passage to India* (1871), where it received a title it would carry, as one

122

of the "Autumn Rivulets," into the Deathbed Edition. The title, which is also the first line, announces the question that lies behind the whole odyssey: "Who Learns My Lesson Complete?" No one does; no lesson poem is ever complete. And the poet who has learned that much of a lesson will never make the mistake of finishing what he started. Instead, a Penelope waiting for America to come home, he spends his evening unraveling the book of his morning.

Nevertheless, Whitman never gave up his hope that he had fulfilled the prophecy and written the great American poem. Though the poem of Birth and Life had eventually been superseded by the poem of Death, the last would include and justify the first. The final twenty years of *Leaves of Grass* revolve around a single image, an image first explored in "Passage to India" (1871). "There's more of me, the essential ultimate me, in that than in any of the poems," Whitman told Horace Traubel. A note in the Centennial Edition of *Leaves* (1876) indicates why he thought the poem so important.

> As in some ancient legend-play, to close the plot and the hero's career, there is a farewell gathering on ship's deck and on shore, a loosing of hawsers and ties, a spreading of sails to the wind—a starting out on unknown seas, to fetch up no one knows whither—to return no more— And the curtain falls, and there is the end of it—So I have reserv'd that Poem, with its cluster, to finish and explain much that, without them, would not be explain'd, and to take leave, and escape for good, from all that has preceded them. (Then probably *Passage to India,* and its cluster, are but freer vent and fuller expression to what, from the first, and so on throughout, more or less lurks in my writings, underneath every page, every line, every where.)

Without surrendering his ambition or his sense of exploration, Whitman commits himself to death and a voyage of no return. He no longer trusts his power to find a destination; he no longer believes in action. The completion of the Suez Canal, which Goethe had viewed prospectively as a wonder so exciting that an old man must regret he would not live to see it, has an opposite effect on "Passage to India." The poet remembers for how long a time human beings have felt unappeasable yearnings, how inadequate material progress has been to satisfy the soul. "Ah who shall soothe these feverish children? / Who justify these restless explorations?" (415) Only "the poet worthy that name," who has the courage to "steer for the deep waters only" (421). The great American poem, like the poet himself, must loose its sails to the wind.

One figure above all dominates Whitman's later poems: the figure of Columbus. The first edition of *Leaves of Grass,* relentlessly set to the future, had not required that old sailor. Whitman himself, "Voyaging to every port to dicker and adventure," had been explorer enough. But later, in the time of retrospection, Columbus became a precious example of what the poet could hope to accomplish—perhaps had *already* accomplished.

> And who art thou sad shade?
> Gigantic, visionary, thyself a visionary,
> With majestic limbs and pious beaming eyes,
> Spreading around with every look of thine a golden world,
> Enhuing it with gorgeous hues.
>
> [417]

The visionary shade, like the shade in "Little Gidding," represents one aspect of the poet: the discoverer of a new world. Washington Irving's popular *Life and Voyages of Columbus,* which supplied Whitman not only with his general view of the explorer but with many particular phrases, had emphasized the "visionary fervour" of Columbus' imagination, his character as a "poetical projector." Thus Whitman embraces him as a fellow poet, fertile in creation, able to contain multitudes. And like Eliot's shade, the figure of Whitman's imagination reminds him of the gifts reserved for age.

> (Curious in time I stand, noting the efforts of heroes,
> Is the deferment long? bitter the slander, poverty, death?
> Lies the seed unreck'd for centuries in the ground? lo,
>   to God's due occasion,
> Uprising in the night, it sprouts, blooms,
> And fills the earth with use and beauty.)
>
> [417–18]

More than a little self-pity lies behind these lines. Whitman's own days of golden discovery have passed, and he now identifies with the explorer not only as "History's type of courage, action, faith" (417) but as history's victim of persecution and neglect. The parenthetical comment holds out hope for *Leaves of Grass;* one day, perhaps centuries hence, everyone will realize that the poet too had discovered America. Yet the odd insistence on the present tense seems to remove that crowning moment of recognition from history. Only God's due occasion—perhaps an apocalyptic moment in the dark night of the soul—will reveal the fertility of Whitman's poem. Nor can the poet predict when that revelation will occur; he stands "Curious in time." The phrase is ambiguous. Perhaps it refers to a simple chronological sequence, in which the poet *now* comes along, long after the death of Columbus, to inquire into the costs of heroism. But a more complex meaning is possible. Perhaps the poet's curiosity extends to time itself, in which he stands as in a prison or a strange terrain. From this perspective Whitman envisions a moment of heroic reward when time will have a stop and mankind, after the long deferment, will acknowledge him as the pioneer of its free new soul. He chants the praise of a country that has yet to be born.

Three years later, years that had included Whitman's paralytic stroke and the death of his mother, he returned to the image of Columbus. In "Prayer of Columbus" (1874) the poet's identification with the "batter'd, wreck'd" explorer has become explicit, and the question about what all his life-work has accomplished is touched by despair. Though the speaker of the poem clings to God, as though to the spar of a broken ship, he feels his "terminus near"; nor can he be certain that his faith amounts to anything but an illusion.

> Is it the prophet's thought I speak, or am I raving?
> What do I know of life? what of myself?
> I know not even my own work past or present,
> Dim ever-shifting guesses of it spread before me,
> Of newer better worlds, their mighty parturition,
> Mocking, perplexing me.
>
> [423]

At the instant before his death, Columbus does not know what he has discovered. Even God, in the absence of a sign, offers no final consolation. And Whitman participates in the torment of the explorer. He cannot know the fate of *Leaves of Grass,* he cannot be sure whether he has found a new poetic continent or only a series of uninhabitable islands.

Yet Columbus had eventually been justified. "Centuries after thou art laid in thy grave," "Passage to India" had proclaimed, "The shore thou foundest verifies thy dream" (414). The final sentence of Irving's *Life of Columbus* celebrates the afterlife of the hero by offering him a vision of his future.

> And how would his magnanimous spirit have been consoled, amidst the afflictions of age and the cares of penury, the neglect of a fickle public, and the injustice of an ungrateful king, could he have anticipated the splendid empires which were to spread over the beautiful world he had discovered, and the nations, and tongues, and languages which were to fill its lands with his renown, and to revere and bless his name to the latest posterity!

Whitman took notes; he required the same success, the same verification. And at the end of "Prayer of Columbus" the prayer is answered, the vision granted, in one of the poet's most felicitous moments.

> And these things I see suddenly, what mean they?
> As if some miracle, some hand divine unseal'd my eyes,
> Shadowy vast shapes smile through the air and sky,

And on the distant waves sail countless ships,
And anthems in new tongues I hear saluting me.

[423]

Few poets—not even Keats discovering Chapman's Homer—have ever promised themselves a grander future. Imagining Columbus vouchsafed a glimpse of the America that honors and verifies him by its very existence, Whitman simultaneously imagines a glorious posterity of his own, when not only America but the peoples of the world will sing his praises. If the poignant emotion of the stanza depends on self-glorification, it earns forgiveness because the vision is so precarious and, after all, so true. The poet hopes for a miracle. He knows that his satisfaction will not occur in this life.

Indeed, the end of Columbus' prayer may well coincide with his moment of death. The last line blends together two possibilities: the anthems of heavenly choirs or of contemporary Americans (singing, perhaps, "Columbia the Gem of the Ocean"), whose new language differs not only from Italian and Spanish but from English. Columbus goes west. Heaven and America, from his point of view, are the same place. But Whitman knows better. His own apotheosis will materialize only when America has been transformed by spirit, when vast unknown visionary forces emerge to "smile" upon his hopes. He will never reach an end of exploring, he must look to future times to realize his dream. To imagine contentment he must also imagine death.

Another composite figure haunts this stanza: the shade of Tennyson-Ulysses. The diction, meter, and near rhyme ("they," "eyes," "sky," "me,"), unusually conventional for Whitman, associate "Prayer of Columbus" with "Ulysses," a poem (he once noted) that "redeems a hundred 'Princesses' and 'Mauds,' and shows the Great Master." The phrase is significant, for mastery—its burdens as well as its honor—lends both poems a theme. Ulysses, like Columbus, has devoted his life to exploration and now, with old age upon him, might choose to rest. Yet Tennyson, who admitted that the poem dealt with his own "need of going forward and braving the struggle of life" after the death of Hallam, cannot allow such fatalism; it would mean another death. Instead Ulysses chooses to encounter the unknown: "Come, my friends, / 'Tis not too late to seek a newer world." He will die like an explorer. And Columbus, Whitman's own spiritual ancestor, will do the same. "Old, poor, and paralyzed," he resigns himself to one last trial, one more venture into the unknown. That is what it means to be a master: not rest, not a safe harbor and secure rewards, but always another voyage—indomitable to the end.

"Ulysses" resembles "Prayer of Columbus" in yet another respect. The Greek hero, like the American, seeks a "Passage to more than India," an unearthly destination.

> I am a part of all that I have met;
> Yet all experience is an arch wherethrough
> Gleams that untravelled world, whose margin fades
> For ever and for ever when I move.

No amount of searching will ever arrive at a terminus, no experience can touch the boundaries of the imagination. Whitman too had hungered after experience, though, more acquisitive than Tennyson, he had not become "part of all that I have met" so much as a receptacle who assimilated all objects into "part of that child who went forth every day." Yet both poets suggest the merger of their souls with an "untravelled world." Is it experience they seek, at last, or an active collaboration with death? Certainly Tennyson's poem is death-inspired. In a curious way he remains faithful to Hallam by adopting his ethic of social activism at the same time as, recognizing the futility of human effort, he longs to share his grave. Experience and death lie in the same direction, an immersion in the sea.

Moreover, both poets achieve some consolation by converting their private agonies into myth. Ulysses' sorrows are filtered through an immense distance of time. His labors ended long ago, and his pursuit of a better world, admirable in itself, long since has proved an empty dream. Tennyson expects no better reward from his own resolution to live his life to the end. And Whitman takes a similar tack. For the first time in his career he dwells not on the present or future but on "The Past—the dark unfathom'd retrospect!" (411). Columbus represents the freshness and hope of America at the moment when everything still remained to be explored, but the poet meditates instead on the sense of loss, the human wreckage. His work is almost done; he has become, even to himself, largely a myth. "Now Voyager depart" (503). The future invites him not so much for its infinite range of possibilities as because, passing the border, he will rid himself of inessentials and become wholly myth.

He did not die, in fact, for eighteen years. Yet neither did he advance very far beyond this image of himself as the old Columbus, explorer of America and death. Indeed, the last of Whitman's poems, handed to Traubel ten days before the end, also transmits "A Thought of Columbus." The poem exudes an atmosphere of mystery and wonder; specifically, the amazing way that a mere idea, "A mortal impulse thrilling its brain cell," can affect the whole world.

A phantom of the moment, mystic, stalking, sudden,
Only a silent thought, yet toppling down of more than
    walls of brass or stone.
(A flutter at the darkness' edge as if old Time's and
    Space's secret near revealing.)
A thought! a definite thought works out in shape.

[582]

The thinker, of course, was originally Columbus, whose intuition that the earth could be circled has led to "the widest, farthest evolutions of the world and man." Four hundred years of history (in 1892) have been nothing but an unfolding of that thought. But it would not be far-fetched to regard the wonder of the poem as emanating also from another source: Whitman's own "Thought of Columbus." At the end of *Leaves of Grass* (properly, its appendix of "Old Age Echoes") the poet looks back in time and sees with awe how much has issued from his own first conception. Columbus' thought had made America, and Whitman's thought of Columbus—his poetic renewal of the sense of exploration—has made the first American book. Whitman mythologizes himself. He views his work, as he views the ultimate triumph of Columbus, retrospectively, as an immense macrocosm astonishingly predicted by a microcosmic thought.

Soul plaudits! acclamation! reverent echoes!
One manifold, huge memory to thee! oceans and lands!
The modern world to thee and thought of thee!

[582]

Thus Whitman reduces *Leaves of Grass,* at the last, to a thought. The problems of the book, in retrospect, can be ascribed to the incommensurability of thought in relation to the growth of a country and a mind. Explorers cannot know what time will make of their discoveries. The essence of *Leaves of Grass* had been contained in the poet's first sight of it: his initiation. What followed, inevitably, was both more wonderful than that first impulse—since the accumulation of verses and experiences, like the settling of a continent, went far beyond imagination—and disappointing— since the dream lost some of its purity and coherence in the process of being realized. Whitman solaces himself by restoring his book to a condition of pure potentiality. Once he has died his work will merge with his nation, like Ossian, or like grass in a field. Only the thought will survive.

The last editions of *Leaves of Grass* invent, in fact, a new creation myth, a myth not so much of accomplishment as of stripping-away. Whitman interprets his career as a fashioning of "Eidólons" (1876), which a seer (perhaps Emerson) had taught him to make his study.

> Put in thy chants said he,
> No more the puzzling hour nor day, nor segments, parts, put in,
> Put first before the rest as light for all and entrance-song of all,
>   That of eidólons.
>
> Ever the dim beginning,
> Ever the growth, the rounding of the circle,
> Ever the summit and the merge at last, (to surely start again,)
> Eidólons! eidólons!
>
> Ever the mutable,
> Ever materials, changing, crumbling, re-cohering,
> Ever the ateliers, the factories divine,
>   Issuing eidólons.
>
>   [5–6]

We have noted already that Goethe's Helen referred to herself as an "Idol," and an entry in Whitman's "Notebook on Words" relies on the same example: "Ei-do-lon (Gr) phantom—the image of a Helen at Troy instead of real flesh and blood woman." Yet Whitman does not stress, like Goethe, the *inauthenticity* of the image so much as its triumphant representation of the soul. When the body of *Leaves of Grass* has decomposed, its image will come into its own.

> Thy very songs not in thy songs,
> No special strains to sing, none for itself,
> But from the whole resulting, rising at last and floating,
>   A round full-orb'd eidólon.
>
>   [8]

The soul or ghost of the book outlasts its crumbling, mutable materials; and how better can the poet display the eidólon of *Leaves of Grass* than by proving it will survive any number of different versions, any number of changes in material particulars?

Yet Helen's problem remains. If nothing endures but images, if "everything transient is only a likeness," then how can a book hold on to a stable identity? Would *Leaves of Grass* have kept the same eidólon even if every one of its verses had been changed? Whitman suggests a positive answer. Every imperfection of the verse, every rent in its fabric, will only serve to liberate the soul. Moreover, his fascination with the eidólon requires him to transmute his poems from time to time, to see whether the afterimage will abide ("scientifically," the eidólon may be considered a sort of halo or nimbus that floats around objects, "a delicate facsimile register" on the ether). How could the Trojans have determined whether the Helen who moved among them was true or false, the living woman or her facsimile, except by trying to kill her? Whitman performs a similar experiment. He tries to extract the essence of *Leaves of Grass,* not by purging it of impurities but by steeping it in the destructive elements, matter and time. Like the alchemist who burns a rose in the hope of perceiving its afterimage floating on the air, he subjects his book to the fire.

Where then is the Whitman canon? It does not exist, except in whatever we make it. He embraces a manifest destiny—"Omnes! omnes!" The book of Whitman's life does not obey canons, and its refusal to finish or lie down in its Deathbed seems to mock the very notion of a classical career. Whatever his intentions, his practice violates each of the four Virgilian criteria of poetic husbandry. Instead of managing a canon, he habitually pushes new pieces into the chinks of the old (as if the *Appendix Vergiliana* were stuffed between the books of the *Aeneid*). Instead of paying tribute to the past, he often forgets it or repeats it (as if Virgil had abandoned the story of Aeneas to tend the wounded of Augustus' wars). Instead of surpassing himself, sacrificing every irrelevant line for the sake of progressive improvement, he seems to think that any line he writes is as much worth saving as any other, and any self or minute as precious as the most sublime (as though Aeneas had sailed westward past Italy for the sake of the journey itself). And instead of planning ahead he tries to understand retrospectively what he has already done (as though Virgil, ignorant of how his story and Rome would come out, had left the parts of the *Aeneid* in the order in which he first wrote them).

Thus *Leaves of Grass* lays down the pattern of a new vocation for poets. Whitman abandons the false dream of perfection and resolves on an anti-career. The future will complete his work, he expects, just as the unknown free America to come will break and repair the repressive civilization that has stifled all poets ever since Rome. "I was to show that we, here and today, are eligible to the grandest and the best—more eligible now than any times of old were. I will also want my utterances (I said to myself before beginning) to be in spirit the poems of the morning." The greatest master would be content always to begin again. Not for him the finish of Virgil, the stonework, the evening light and shade. All those were *literature,* and literature was precisely the enemy. He had worked all his life, it seems, to accomplish the death of Virgil.

The Death of Virgil

Many later authors have joined in the self-same project. But the death of Virgil has been no easy matter. If Western civilization depends on its poets, then the civilization of poets (as Haecker and Eliot suggested) seems to depend on Virgil: the legacy of a total career more precious than any of its parts. And poets who reject that harmonium have been forced again and again to define themselves against its standard. As Whitman lay on his deathbed, a flock of disciples came round to listen for his last words; they wanted to know the end of the story. A dying poet is supposed to rise to the occasion. And the problem especially troubles those who are not content, like Whitman, to write poems of the morning. A poet who wants to continue into the afternoon and evening must face, in the shadow of middle age, a terrible challenge: to find a new meaning in his work as a whole. So much depends on the last poem. Even in its decay, the life of Virgil imposes an iron logic on the future. Thus the life of Emily Dickinson—she who made the great refusal—was given dramatic shape by her consciousness of that public poetic destiny she would not engage. The idea of a career enables the idea of an anti-career. For two hundred years each generation of poets has sought its own way to put an end to Virgil.

No work addresses the situation more explicitly than the long prose poem whose very title is *The Death of Virgil*. Behind the original form of Hermann Broch's masterpiece an ancient question echoes and echoes to the point of numbness: What value has a literary career? Nor does Broch consider the question at all rhetorical. Writing under the same circumstances that had caused Curtius to despair of seeing any more classics and Eliot to fear that all his work would end in fire—not only the war sweeping across Europe but the disintegration and powerlessness of culture—Broch judges his own poetic futility with deadly seriousness. He first conceived the book, in fact, as a lecture on "Literature at the End of a Culture." When Radio Vienna asked him to read instead "something poetical"—another sign, in the mid-30s, of literary futility—he decided to recast his vision of apocalypse as a short story on Virgil, taking advantage of "the parallels between the first pre-Christian century and our own—civil war, dictatorship, and a dying-away of the old religious forms." The story obsessed him; it swelled from eighteen pages to eighty, then more; soon he could work on nothing else. And then circumstances deepened its meaning. Imprisoned by the Gestapo in 1938, prepared for death at any moment, Broch used the work to clarify his own experience. "The book developed a scope completely detached from the historical figure and work of Virgil. It was no longer the dying of Virgil; it became the imagination of my own dying." Even after Broch's release, he lived in a world made transparent by the prospect of total extinction. *The Death of Virgil*, according to its author, could not be more removed from "literature." A "completely private act," it rises from an abyss where categories of art no longer apply and all careers come to nothing. Death is its subject: the death of a culture; the death of the artist; the death of art.

Indeed, the book itself is an offering to death. Broch takes as his point of departure the legend that Virgil sought to destroy the *Aeneid*. The "plot" revolves around the attempts of the poet's friends to dissuade him. But destruction has the better of the arguments. Broch interprets the legend not as a sign of the poet's will to perfection, his reluctance to allow his masterpiece to exist in any but a final finished state, so much as evidence of Virgil's sense of inadequacy, his decision to repudiate his whole career. The *Aeneid* is not merely unfinished; it is *wrong*. Or so Broch's Virgil argues. The epic enshrines the imperial values: confident mastery of life; a hierarchy that stretches from gods to slaves; beauty in the service of things as they are; a sense of destiny; the Law. Yet Virgil knows that all these things belong to the past. Prophetically sensing the coming Christian era, he sees that his own time is suspended between a vanishing antiquity and a religious mystery yet to be realized. "No longer and not yet." What can a poet do amid such uncertainties? His best course, according to the Virgil of Broch, is to prepare his own extinction. Only by sacrificing his life-work, by giving himself over wholly to the understanding of death, can the poet overcome the irresponsible aestheticism that, tantalizing men with the illusion of beauty and order, prevents them from grasping the truth.

> For the perception of life, earthily bound to the earth, never possessed the power to lift itself above the thing known and to endow it with unity, the unity of an enduring meaning. . . . For only he who through his knowledge of death became conscious of the infinite was able to retain the creation, to retain the single part within the whole creation and the whole creation in every single part.

The poem of life had been exhausted. It was time (as Whitman had said) for the poem of death.

All the art of *The Death of Virgil*, therefore, goes into preaching a paradoxical moral: the insufficiency of art. *Das Unzulängliche, / Hier wird's Ereignis.* Accepting the theme of Haecker's *Virgil, Father of the West,* which had canonized Virgil both as the harbinger of Christianity and as the foremost representative of Western culture, Broch brilliantly inverts the argument by involving the Roman poet in the failure of culture. He lived, like us, in a time of crisis; like us, he did not know what dispensation would replace him. "No longer and not yet." Nor does Broch remain aloof from the criticism. His own use of the *Aeneid* demonstrates the extent to which he has been saturated by its poetry, rehearsed so long that it has become a part of his inner ear and internal culture. Yet he also disapproves of Virgil. The poet's disgust at his own artistic irresponsibility, which furnishes so large a part of his interior monologues within the book, clearly stems from the modern poet who has reimagined him only in order to kill him. There are greater truths than those of the *Aeneid;* so Dante knew, and so Broch also knows. Yet extinguishing Virgil means for Broch, as it meant for Dante, also doing away with a part of himself.

Thus *The Death of Virgil* sets out on a great project of annihilation—a project that includes the author and his protagonist as well as the reader. Even the form of the book, with its musical structure, its continual repetition and development of a limited number of themes and words, its endless fine-spun sentences, its lack of action, shows a contempt for ordinary artistic conventions. The difficulties are enormous. Broch spurns the linear sequence of a story, where a chain of incidents leads to a destined end (as Aeneas presses toward his fate), and substitutes the circling of thoughts and images around an insoluble dilemma—"the dialogue of the mind with itself." Like Arnold's *Empedocles on Etna,* its near relation, *The Death of Virgil* can find no vent in action. Even the single point of suspense—will Virgil succeed in burning the *Aeneid?*—is casually cast aside, not only because the answer is preordained but because the poet's decision results less from conviction than from an impulsive submission in the face of Augustus' anger. In the long and magnificent debate between the poet and his emperor, a struggle for the fate of the poem, the logic of destruction triumphs. Indeed, only the reduction of the issue to its simplest human terms allows the *Aeneid* to be saved. The emperor, losing his head, becomes merely human, so that Virgil makes him the gift of the poem as a personal gesture, not an imperial tribute. Significantly, at the moment of decision the poet yields to "Octavian" rather than "Augustus"—the godlike honorific replaced by a vulnerable mortal name. Words count for more than actions. And the survival of the *Aeneid,* if not a matter of indifference, is largely a matter of chance.

The project of annihilation also determines the style. At the heart of *The Death of Virgil* (and structurally at the center) five elegies on Fate contemplate, and try to surpass, the Virgilian sense of destiny.

> . . . . Steht hinter dir, grösser als du,
> Unentrinnbarer, unerschaubarer noch
> Ein anderes Schicksal und weiter und weiter
> Schicksal an Schicksal, Leerform an Leerform gereiht,
> Das nimmererreichbare Nichts, der gebärende Tod,
> Dem nur noch der Zufall entspricht?

> (. . . . Standing behind you, greater than you,
> More inescapable, more imperceptible, is there
> Another destiny still, and further and further
> Destiny on destiny strung, blank form on blank form,
> The never-attainable nothing, the birth-giving death,
> Whose only companion is chance?)

The answer is yes. Beyond Fate another Fate, composed of nothingness and death, awaits the poet. (In Broch's terms, welded together from classical and Christian elements, Fate must be assimilated to Logos, myth to truth.) Virgil must surrender the clarity and chiseled elegance of his style, and acknowledge mortality by incorporating the fluidity and incomprehensibility of chance within his language. And Broch shows him the way. Dissolving the fixed lines of the *Aeneid* into hypnotically extended, labyrinthine figures, he also dissolves the character of Virgil. The poet's consciousness, within the book, regularly assumes the present tense (an effect not reproduced in Jean Starr Untermeyer's English translation); barred from the safe historical past, he must test his ideas at every moment against the chaos and flux of modern life. Broch allows no nostalgia; *The Death of Virgil* belongs to the present. It is as if a poet had attempted to construct his whole harmonium from the materials of the final speech in *Faust,* with Faust himself annihilated into a realm of pure possibility and the language refined to its absolute, paradoxical, nonreferential essence.

Indeed, Broch seems to have intended precisely this effect. In a penetrating essay on "The Style of the Mythical Age" (1947), he defines the "style of old-age" as a new level of expression, ripened by the foreshadow of death and characterized by a kind of mathematical "*abstractism* in which the expression relies less and less on the vocabulary, which finally becomes reduced to a few prime symbols, and instead relies more and more on the syntax." Examples include Bach's *Art of the Fugue,* Beethoven's last quartets, the final paintings of Titian, Rembrandt, and Goya. But the primary literary reference is to "Goethe's last writings, the final scenes of *Faust* for instance, where the language discloses its own mysteries and, therefore, those of all existence." In Goethe's *Faust* the subject matter or "vocabulary" dissolves, leaving behind a pure "syntax" consisting wholly of archetypes and myths— a Logos whose internal relations capture the structure of the universe. Goethe found himself (according to Broch's analysis) in an epoch whose values had shattered. He was forced to create, in the style of his old age, a new model of truth. And Broch assumes the same task. He tolls out the old dead myths of culture; he rings in the new.

Yet Broch, unlike Goethe, lacks confidence in the power of the individual to affect his fate. Romanticism had insisted on the union of subjectivity with nature, the single private case of Faust with the largest aspirations of mankind; but modern times have shown the futility of such a vision. The gods no longer care for Faust. "The personal problem of the individual has become a subject of laughter for the gods, and they are right in their lack of pity." Nor do the gods concern themselves any longer with such a small matter as the destiny of a poet. The name of Virgil is merely a proper noun in the vocabulary that a syntax of old age must replace. Whether or not Homer ever existed, he survives forever "as the mythical old man, the eternal paradigm of an epoch which demands the rebirth of myth." Virgil, and Broch himself, must learn a similar self-effacement and transform themselves into a paradigm. No poet can achieve a harmonium; no cunning of art can ever rebuild the harmony of the world on which art relies. This lesson was known, among modern artists, to Kafka alone.

> Kafka, in his presentiment of the new cosmology, the new theogony that he had to achieve, struggling with his love for literature, his disgust for literature, feeling the ultimate insufficiency of any artistic approach, decided (as did Tolstoy, faced with a similar decision) to quit the realm of literature, and asked that his work be destroyed; he asked this for the sake of the universe whose new mythical concept had been bestowed upon him.

Broch takes up the work of destruction. Like Virgil, like Tolstoy, like Kafka before him, he renounces his art and drowns his book.

Why then should a poet preserve his harmonium? Broch gives no certain answer. When asked why he had not destroyed *The Death of Virgil*, he cited the many people whose help—saving his life as well as his work—had obliged him to reward their faith (as Virgil, within the book, spares his epic not for his own sake but as a personal gift to Octavian). Moreover, he had followed the Virgil of his imagination right to the end. "I have renounced the thought of completing the book in a genuinely artistic way, because in this time of horrors I could not dare to put still more years into a work that, with each additional page, would have become increasingly esoteric; and with this I believe that I have definitely finished my poetic career." As Virgil, according to tradition, had resolved to abandon poetry for philosophy, so Broch turned to other pursuits: tireless activities on behalf of refugees, a treatise on mass psychology, a political "Bill of Duties." No time remained for literature. Culture itself was dying; the poet's time was no longer—or not yet.

Nevertheless, *The Death of Virgil* achieves its own sort of resolution. It survives as a model of the modern harmonium, the eternal "style of old-age." First of all, despite its emphasis on decomposition, the book is everywhere suffused with a passion for summing-up. Virgil interrogates the universe until it reveals its secrets. Like a German metaphysician, he will not die before he has reached ultimate conclusions about the significance of everything he has done. Nor can we ignore the fact that the solitary dying man is, after all, Virgil. Broch's condemnation of aestheticism requires a great antagonist, one whose supreme devotion to art sets the terms by which art is disowned. To burn the *Aeneid* would be to destroy the thousands of poems, the millions of lives, that have been built on it—a holocaust devouring the very basis of civilization. *The Death of Virgil* could not have been written about a minor author. Its every line depends on an idea of literary greatness, a greatness so unquestionable that the act of questioning it represents a tortured heroic ideal. And Broch associates himself with such heroism. The depth and size of *The Death of Virgil* assert their own claims to greatness and authenticate the author's right to judge Virgil as unforgivingly as he judges himself. If Broch rejects the *Aeneid,* even the rejection demands a total commitment to unity of being, a total perception of life and death. "The true piece of art, even though it be the shortest lyric, must always embrace the totality of the world, must be the counterweight and the mirror of that universe. This is felt by every true artist, but is creatively realized only by the artist of old age." Broch, like Virgil, accepts the challenge. He attributes his own knowledge to the classical poet and condemns him by the highest standards of the future. Hence Virgil's own wish to be a prophet is redeemed, within the modern book, through an ultimate circular vision: he foresees the death of the culture he founded.

Yet his end is also a beginning. That is another respect in which *The Death of Virgil* may be seen, despite itself, as a characteristic harmonium. All its labor of deconstruction, all its sacrifices and renunciations, serve only to prepare the way for another ideal of art: the book that is left when all its words are finished. Erasing everything trivial and adventitious, Broch creates a pregnant empty space. Nor does that emptiness—the poet's *Ewig-Leere*—contradict the nature of the harmonium. Perhaps every great harmonium includes, at the end, the possibility of its undoing, a moment of exhaustion or a rival creation. Virgil consigns his work to the shades; Dante's words fail him; Chaucer retracts; Milton descends from Eden; Pope speaks an uncreating word; Goethe reluctantly allows the moment to stay; Whitman becomes "as one disembodied"; Mallarmé salutes the rule of chance; Eliot embraces the fire. When the total pattern of words has been accomplished, the poet longs for something more than words. Hence the idea of recantation—*unsinging*—preoccupies many great poets in their final moments. The poet dispossesses his work of himself, as if to leave room for a later, different incarnation. Syntax, in Broch's terms, replaces vocabulary; the personal meaning of the work must be unwritten. If the *Aeneid* is to survive its burning and Virgil his death, whatever dies must be allowed to pass away. In the effort to define that saving recantation, Broch not only sums up his own career but invents a myth of creation and uncreation.

The final section of *The Death of Virgil,* its "Homecoming," carries the poem of death to its consummation. Reversing the direction with which the book had started (the poet sailing into harbor), Virgil voyages out like Whitman into the unknown. And then the world dissolves. The poet's need to destroy the *Aeneid* merges imperceptibly with the undoing of the whole creation. Moment by moment, as if the clock of time were running backward, species and objects are annulled, life is erased into darkness. The past tense deposes the present. Yet just at the moment of final blindness—is it

the instant of Logos, or death?—Virgil is permitted to turn around. Rid of
his work, detached from his name and career, perfectly nothing, he hears
another word:

> the word of discrimination, the word of the pledge, the pure word; so
> it roared thither, roaring over and past him, swelling on and becoming
> stronger and stronger, becoming so overpowering that nothing could
> withstand it, the universe disappearing before the word, dissolved and
> acquitted in the word while still being contained and preserved in it,
> destroyed and recreated forever, because nothing had been lost, nothing
> could be lost, because end was joined to beginning, being born and
> giving birth again and again. . . .

He has come beyond the Logos, beyond art. The ghost that has always
haunted Virgil, the shape of his work as a whole, withdraws from his spirit.
He cannot change the *Aeneid* any longer, it is over and done. And in that
moment of recantation the soul of the poet relaxes. His quest for a perfect
word has been transmuted to a myth; Logos and Fate, Broch suggests, have
become the same. Now Virgil's destiny belongs to others, to do with as
they will. The final harmonium exists as a pure ideal, retreating from us
perpetually, like the Eternal Feminine, to draw us higher. Nothing more
is required of the poet but to die; the final word cannot be spoken. And the
last word belongs to Broch:

> . . . . and he, caught under and amidst the roaring, he floated on with
> the word, although the more he was enveloped by it, the more he
> penetrated into the flooding sound and was penetrated by it, the more
> unattainable, the greater, the graver and more elusive became the word,
> a floating sea, a floating fire, sea-heavy, sea-light, notwithstanding it
> was still the word: he could not hold fast to it and he might not hold
> fast to it; incomprehensible and unutterable for him: it was the word
> beyond speech.

But the destiny of the poet did not end with the death of Virgil.

III

TOMBEAU

"Quisque suos patimur Manes . . . ."

Jonson on Shakespeare

When a great poet dies, the immediate critical question is often where to bury him. In the choice between the public tomb and private resting place, a prominent quarter in Westminster Abbey or the weed-choked corner of a foreign graveyard, posterity makes its first decision about how the poet will be remembered. And often enough the result has been a scandal. Each of Mallarmé's three most famous *tombeaux* recounts a particular disgrace: the twenty-six years that Poe's countrymen left his grave unhonored; the twenty-five years that had already passed, in 1892, without a monument to Baudelaire; the insignificant burial spot where only a friend would know that "he is hidden in the grass, Verlaine." Not even a proper burial can guard against infamy. Milton's bones, for instance, were dug up at the end of the eighteenth century for souvenirs, just as fragments of his early poems had been exhumed and confiscated by minor poets. Neglected at first, eventually competed for, like Homer, by contending cities, the poet goes to meet his shades. But not unsung. With his dying breath, frequently, an industry springs up around him—memorialists, literary undertakers, chiselers, epitaph-makers. The custodians of his fame take charge of manuscripts and the will. He enters his tomb.

First, however, he must be placed. Few significant poets die without an elegy from a spokesman for the next poetic generation: an estimate of what they leave. Such elegies are the heart of literary history, at once a memorial of the past and an attempt to improve upon it or put it to use. Nor is criticism ever more intense than when one poet tries to see what he can take from another. In the hands of a great poet-critic, the form that Mallarmé called the *tombeau* can define a poet's legacy more elegantly and practically than any other. Indeed, until comparatively recent times (the seventeenth century, let us say) such poems account for the greater part of that criticism we call "practical"or "descriptive" or "close reading." There is no sharper analysis of the styles of Aeschylus or Euripides than Aristophanes' elegiac burlesques in *The Frogs,* no better contemporary literary criticism of John Donne than the elegy by Thomas Carew. Poetic criticism like this, which weighs the reputation of an author line by line, has little in common with the mere obituary. Instead it asks the question What survives? The tomb of the poet is built by other poets; their verses take him in.

They may also make him unrecognizable. Every *tombeau* represents a collaboration between two poets, the dead and the living, and the interests of the two do not necessarily coincide. The dead poet demands tribute, the living must look to his own art. To some extent these alternatives are posed by the very word *tomb,* which can stand either for the burial place or for the monument erected over it. Poets may try to design their own memorials, but all they can be sure of is the body of their work; the monument, the way the work will be remembered, must be left to other hands. Very quickly the poet ceases to control his fate.

Consider, for instance, Shakespeare's progress. In sonnet after sonnet the poet himself boasts of the claims he is creating upon eternity—

> Not marble, nor the gilded monuments
> Of princes, shall outlive this powerful rhyme. . . .

In his eyes, clearly, his verses are the monument he leaves, preserving his love forever. Posterity will have little authority over the matter; the lines will live "So long as men can breathe, or eyes can see." But Ben Jonson's tribute, prefixed to the First Folio, introduces a slight change of emphasis.

> Thou art a Moniment, without a tombe,
> And art alive still, while thy Booke doth live,
> And we have wits to read, and praise to give.

Shakespeare himself, according to Jonson, is his own best monument. Or rather, the monument is Shakespeare's reputation, the poet (preserved in his book) as he appears to others. Jonson erects a cenotaph—a monument without a tomb, in honor of someone buried elsewhere—and suggests that verses cannot make themselves immortal, by breath and sight, unless critics cooperate by bestowing their own wit and praise. Already posterity arrogates the poet to its own needs.

By the time of the Second Folio, to which John Milton contributed his first published English poem, the process of idolatry had gone still further.

> Thou in our wonder and astonishment
> Hast built thyself a livelong Monument.
> . . . .
> Then thou our fancy of itself bereaving,
> Dost make us Marble with too much conceiving.

Shakespeare's monument, Milton argues, consists of his readers, frozen into marble through astonishment (a word once derived from "stony," i.e., "petrified") at his "hallowed reliques." In such lines Shakespeare is transformed into material for a metaphysical conceit. Indeed, the young Milton deliberately contrasts his own rather heavy-handed style with his idol's— "to th'shame of slow-endeavoring art, / Thy easy numbers flow"—presumably to coax himself into an easier vein. Here Shakespeare's verses and Shakespeare himself have become less significant than the use to which the younger poet can put them. Jonson had addressed Shakespeare intimately in his elegy, as a friend and colleague; but Milton speaks of *my* Shakespeare, immortally internalized: every man's property, a tomb within the mind.

The living poet always wins the day, of course. The dead cannot choose their own monuments, Virgil has no authority to destroy the *Aeneid.* Yet the struggle in the *tombeau* can be fierce, and the living poet does not always dominate his poem. Characteristically, the *tombeau* incorporates many reminiscences of the poet it memorializes—style, verse forms, images, specific lines—and it may even try, eerily, to impersonate his voice. *Anima hominis,* in Yeats' terms, converses with *anima mundi.* Sometimes that conversation can lead to strange reverberations, a bitter debate. The problem does not arise when a great poet commemorates one markedly inferior; *Lycidas,* for example, obviously deals with Milton's own poetic aspirations, not with the poetry of Edward King. Nor does a minor poet necessarily suffer by comparison when he pays tribute to a master. Carew's elegy on Donne draws on a vein of Donne-like "masculine expression" that seems to rebuke the elegist's own charming lyrics; but Carew, inspired by his master to hew out weighty and provocative lines, never wrote a better poem. A different situation may come about, however, when one great poet writes about another. Here an implicit comparison between the dead and living masters can never be wholly disowned. The author's compassion for the spirit who has gone may well vie with his sense of spiritual competition—marvelously so at the end of *Adonais,* where Shelley, "borne darkly, fearfully, afar," implies that Keats, already immortalized, is much luckier than he. Critically, the living poet is driven to search out weaknesses as well as strengths, something he can improve. Thus praise itself must leave room for a fault. Beneath the monumental surface of the *tombeau,* sometimes old scars crack open; respect and animus contend.

Is it praise or animus, for instance, that motivates Jonson's offering "To the memory of my beloved, The Author Mr. William Shakespeare: and what he hath left us"? Certainly many readers, from the first, have suspected that the poem secretly intends to attack Shakespeare for wanting art. Even John Dryden, usually sympathetic enough to Jonson, thought the verses "an insolent, sparing, and invidious panegyric." To some extent these suspicions may derive from unfounded gossip, as well as from conflating the poem with Jonson's far harsher comments in *Timber:* "hee flow'd with that facility, that sometime it was necessary he should be stop'd. . . . His wit was in his owne power; would the rule of it had been so too." Yet even by itself the poem might foster doubt. Jonson summons forth his Shakespeare like an old competitor and rival, the *other* great British playwright. Nor does he put aside the argument of nature versus art, of invention versus learning, that he had been debating with many rivals for a generation. The old wounds have not healed. Ben Jonson interleaves his tribute with a sermon, and everywhere assumes the right to sit in judgment.

Nor should we underestimate Jonson's finesse, his ability to insinuate misgivings even while he seems to commend. The ruler and patriarch of a legion of sons and disciples, this poet knows how, and how not, to praise. He can make a poem curl back to question itself. Consider his "vision" of Drayton.

> It hath beene question'd, *Michael,* if I bee
> A Friend at all; or, if at all, to thee.

Even the most careful reading of these verses does not answer the question. Drayton's own editor, in fact, concludes that Jonson intended a covert satire. The bombastic puffing of mediocre work rebounds against its perpetrator, and the ending slyly notes that Drayton has never thought to write a poem to *Jonson,* nor counted him an ally:

> And, till I worthy am to wish I were,
> I call the world, that envies mee, to see
> If I can be a Friend, and Friend to thee.

Can Jonson be a friend? Has he come to praise Drayton or bury him? The poem is too self-involved, too deft, to allow an easy answer. At any rate, the poet himself draws a strong distinction between true and false friends, true and false praise. The distinction becomes still more obtrusive in the first part of the poem to Shakespeare.

> To draw no envy *(Shakespeare)* on thy name,
> Am I thus ample to thy Booke, and Fame.
> . . . .
> Or crafty Malice, might pretend this praise,
> And thinke to ruine, where it seem'd to raise.

Such lines foment distrust; suspicions that naturally turn back upon "honest Ben."

Indeed, Jonson's eulogy seems calculated to remind us who gives, as much as who receives, the honor. Many readers, coming to the poem in hope of finding the way that a great contemporary perceived Shakespeare's greatness, have been taken aback to find that the first sixteen lines look past

Shakespeare to debate the proper mode of praising him. The eulogy itself, oddly enough, commences only at line 17.

> I, therefore will begin. Soule of the Age!
> The applause! delight! the wonder of our Stage!

Jonson emphasizes the "I," partly to contrast his poem with William Basse's inferior elegy on Shakespeare and partly to present himself as a model. And subsequently we learn very little about Shakespeare either as a man—the one piece of personal information is the famous comment that "thou hadst small *Latine,* and lesse *Greeke*"—or as a poet. No specific work, or even line of poetry, is mentioned. Instead Jonson reviews the history of tragedy and comedy, describes (rather abstractly) the qualities of a good poet, and transforms the "Sweet Swan of *Avon,*" with judicious compliments, not only into a monument but into a constellation. The living Shakespeare tends to recede into a "Starre of *Poets*"; the tributes, though affectionate, are so formal that they might apply to any great author. Above all we remain conscious of Ben Jonson: doling out justice, rising to the occasion.

He also wields a scourge. The teachings of the poem do, in fact, depend on animus, directed not against Shakespeare but against those who would praise him for the wrong reasons. Jonson, unlike Basse, will not mix the ashes of his dead friend with "disproportion'd *Muses*" like Chaucer and Spenser. That would involve a promiscuous confusion of genres. Instead the name of Shakespeare, stretched by a pun, is brandished at the eyes of Ignorance. The ignorant actors who, according to *Timber,* honored their friend for never blotting a line must here learn better: natural ability counts for little unless matched by art. Jonson assumes the censorious role of Quintilius in his own version of Horace's *Art of Poetrie.*

> If to *Quintilius,* you recited ought:
> Hee'd say, Mend this, good friend, and this; 'tis naught.
> If you denied, you had no better straine,
> And twice, or thrice had 'ssayd it, still in vaine:
> Hee'd bid, blot all: and to the anvile bring
> Those ill-torn'd Verses, to new hammering.

Poor work, bad praise, must all be blotted. And Shakespeare himself, in the verses in his honor, becomes the engine of this moral. The necessary union of art and nature, Jonson's favorite critical theme, was never more elegantly stated.

> Yet must I not give Nature all: Thy Art,
> My gentle *Shakespeare,* must enjoy a part.
> For though the *Poets* matter, Nature be,
> His Art doth give the fashion. And, that he,

> Who casts to write a living line, must sweat,
>   (Such as thine are) and strike the second heat
> Upon the *Muses* anvile: turne the same,
>   (And himselfe with it) that he thinkes to frame;
> Or for the lawrell, he may gaine a scorne,
>   For a good *Poet's* made, as well as borne.
> And such wert thou. Looke how the fathers face
>   Lives in his issue, even so, the race
> Of *Shakespeares* minde, and manners brightly shines
>   In his well torned, and true-filed lines.

Negatively, Jonson scorns those who would scorn the laurel by attributing everything to nature; positively, he exhorts any talented young man "who casts to write a living line" to work at his art. The example of Shakespeare reproaches the ignorant, instructs the industrious. Moreover, Shakespeare exemplifies the paradox (touched on in his own plays) that the good poet's nature *is* art. A poet must turn himself on the Muse's anvil, making his inherent mortal gifts immortal; he reworks insensible lines until they come alive and refines his own life until he becomes a star. The word "race" deepens this paradox. It means not only "the flavor of the soil" (as in wine) but "rush" or "swiftness"; the speed of Shakespeare's mind, so highly valued by the players, paradoxically shines most in lines slowly turned and filed by labor. The race or flavor of poetry, Jonson says, is not to the swift. A great poet must be hare and tortoise, nature and art, together.

The primary meaning of "race," however, is "ancestry"; and Shakespeare's race, in this sense, constitutes the main subject of the poem. Jonson cares far less about those traits that distinguish Shakespeare from other poets and playwrights than about those excellences that all great authors hold in common. In the universal family of poets, the features of the newest prodigy call all the ancestors to mind. Thus Jonson envelops Shakespeare in a ring of comparisons, from the ancient Greek tragedians to the leading British playwrights of the age just past:

> . . . how farre thou didst our *Lily* out-shine,
>   Or sporting *Kid,* or *Marlowes* mighty line.

The puns on Lyly and Kyd should alert us to a parallel pun on "line" (the third object of the verb "out-shine"). Shakespeare has surpassed not only Marlowe's magnificent blank-verse line but all its inheritors, the tribe or line of Elizabethan dramatists descended from Marlowe. He brooks no comparison. A genius for comedy, above all, proves this English bard one of "Natures family," incomparably better than the antiquated comedians of Greece or Rome.

> He was not of an age, but for all time!

In this line Shakespeare ascends to take his rank above the classics; no longer the soul of the current age, he becomes ageless as an ancient. Jonson can bestow no higher praise.

> Triúmph, my *Britaine,* thou hast one to showe
> To whom all Scenes of *Europe* homage owe.

Yet such praise, even as it elevates Shakespeare, keeps him at a distance. To whom does the "triumph" belong? Our first impression, that the triumph is Shakespeare's, cannot sustain a careful reading. Rather, "my *Britaine*" triumphs, and Shakespeare is only the object of that pride. The point may be more significant than first appears. As a connoisseur of "triumphal forms," as in the symmetrical structures of his masques, Jonson was well aware that the person to be honored (the emperor or king, in standard triumphal ceremonies) deserves the central pride of place. The center is crucial; and the word "Triumph" occurs, in fact, exactly at the midpoint of Jonson's poem. But a slight numerological finesse is needed to adjust the balance. Since the poem consists of eighty lines, the precise center would fall between the fortieth and forty-first ("Triumph" begins line 41). Yet line 80 does not conclude the poem. Beneath it, a few additional words lend just the proper weight:

BEN: IONSON

The signature is not an accident. Not only does it draw the equation tight, it also claims a share of the triumph. Shakespeare is too important to be left to his own devices. Instead his achievement reflects luster on his nation and his critic. My *Britaine—Jonson's* Britain—stands at the center.

The interest of the *tombeau* to Shakespeare, then, hangs upon self-interest. Jonson reconstructs Shakespeare in his own image, metamorphosing him into, if not a Son, then a Brother of Ben. Indeed, the poem seems most intense when it deals with Jonson's own problems. The first of those problems, artistically, must have been simply his commission: to write a prefatory encomium, a more or less official endorsement of the First Folio, with national and professional honor at stake. But Jonson went beyond the call of duty by focusing on another problem, one that had always absorbed him: could a modern author compete with an ancient? He never tired of that question. His whole career, his criticism and his self-esteem, depended on a positive answer. Hence Shakespeare offers his colleague a perfect test case of what a modern can do; and he passes the test. In comedy, Jonson would

> Leave thee alone, for the comparison
> Of all, that insolent *Greece,* or haughtie *Rome*
> Sent forth, or since did from their ashes come.

144

Significantly Jonson used the same words another time, in *Timber,* when he wrote that Sir Francis Bacon had "perform'd that in our tongue, which may be compar'd, or preferr'd, either to insolent *Greece,* or haughty *Rome."* The comparison itself counts for more than the particular writers used to enforce it. Insolent Greece and haughty Rome must bow to the modern Muse. Englishmen—if only they will allow themselves to be instructed—need fear no comparison. And the poem before them, displaying the right kind of praise, the right critical principles, will help to instruct them.

What then remains of Shakespeare? No more than an example. Ironically, he could not have estimated his own virtues, since he lacked the Latin and Greek (we are told) to have known those authors he rivaled. Jonson's monument tends to make Shakespeare into a legend, less English than universal, a bit unreal. The true companions of this shade, for instance, include Pacuvius and Accius, Roman tragedians known only through Horace's mention of them. Distilled, perhaps denatured, Shakespeare changes into a humanist's ideal. If the eulogy asks (as in its subtitle) what he has left us, its answer is, an emblem: the new constellation Cygnus, starry neighbor of Orpheus' Lyra, which shows that an Englishman as well as a Greek may be fit for translation.

> Shine forth, thou Starre of Poets, and with rage,
> Or influence, chide, or cheere the drooping Stage.

Such influence, of course, could hardly be understood without an interpreter, someone to read the stars. Fortunately the English stage need not look far for that diviner. Ben Jonson, poet-critic, will know how to chide and cheer it.

Yet not all the honors go to Jonson. Almost despite himself, the poet who pays tribute must pay it in the coin of his subject. Hence Jonson's criticism bends to Shakespeare's nature. The emphasis on *race* implies that natural wit and genius can carry everything before them and even issue forth in art. The swan is born knowing how to sing. If Jonson adjusts the usual homage to Shakespeare's genius in the direction of art, he also tempers his own usual stress on art with admiration for those gifts that Shakespeare did not have to learn. A dearth of Latin and Greek cannot disqualify that greatness. In this respect the eulogy is nicely balanced: neither the honor due the dead nor the kind of praise needed to instruct the living is granted an undisputed sway. And if the last word belongs, quite literally, to Ben: Ionson, he earns it by showing that he knows how to praise.

Jonson's poem to Shakespeare has the mark, in short, of a classic *tombeau:* its honors are divided. The eulogist's respect, the critic's animus, each is given voice. Partisans of Shakespeare may feel, to be sure, that Jonson might have effaced himself a little more. Though the poem asserts that Shakespeare has no competition, the voice of *one* competitor does surface from time to time. Yet Jonson has no choice but to remain true to himself, most of all at the moment when his values confront the one modern poet capable of challenging them. Jonson must write his own poem; tombs are designed by the living. Out of the meeting between the poet who has died and the poet who carries on his work, a new project springs, the dead hand redirected to some living purpose. Nor can the tense dialogue between the poets ever be quite suppressed.

Collins on Thomson

> Come then, expressive Silence, muse his praise.

No one can accuse William Collins, certainly, of lacking humility toward his predecessors. Almost without exception, each of his best poems abases itself before some great poet of the past—Spenser, Tasso, Shakespeare, above all Milton—whose success, we are told, preempts and intimidates the votary until he scarcely dares break silence. At the heart of each poetic mode, Collins finds an elegy: an elegy for a master who has gone, for a world no longer sustaining poetry, for gods and passions that once were stronger. It is not surprising, then, that his last published work should have been a pastoral elegy on a poet: "ODE Occasion'd by the DEATH of Mr. *Thomson*" (1749). Few *tombeaux* have ever been so reverent, so genuinely considerate of the spirit to be honored.

> In yonder Grave a DRUID lies
> > Where slowly winds the stealing Wave!
> The Year's best Sweets shall duteous rise
> > To deck *it's* POET's sylvan Grave!

> In yon deep Bed of whisp'ring Reeds
> > His airy Harp shall now be laid,
> That He, whose Heart in Sorrow bleeds
> > May love thro' Life the soothing Shade.

The scene is the Thames at Richmond, where Thomson had been buried not long before, and where he and his friend Collins had both settled. Thomson is called a Druid for many reasons—he was a rural poet-priest, a spokesman for English liberty, an inspired teacher of natural religion—but not least because his own *Castle of Indolence,* published in the year of his death (1748), includes an eloquent Druid bard. The year offers flowers to "its" poet, of course, because as author of *The Seasons* he owns the year.

In the following stanza the Aeolian Harp is an appropriate reminder of
Thomson, since he not only helped to popularize it but wrote, in *The Castle
of Indolence* and "An Ode on Aeolus's Harp" (1748), famous descriptions
of its music. And since those passages (as so many Romantic poets were
to remember) suggest mysterious affinities between nature and the soul, it
is only fitting that the harp should console Collins by soothing him with
a "shade" that represents at once the eternal spirit of Thomson and a shady
natural grove.

Such tribute could be paid only by an author thoroughly imbued with
his subject. Collins' love for Thomson and for Thomson's verse saturates
the poem; it cannot be mistaken by anyone who cares enough for eighteenth-
century verse to read it with attention (unfortunately, not a very large
number of readers). Nor does the rhetoric of pastoral diminish the note of
sorrow. Samuel Johnson's famous charge against the elegiac mode of "Lycidas"—"Passion plucks no berries from the myrtle and ivy, nor calls upon
Arethuse and Mincius. . . . He who thus grieves will excite no sympathy;
he who thus praises will confer no honor"—falls away from Collins' "Ode."
The details, even the feelings, of the poem are firmly situated in a specific
time and place: not the never-never land of pastoral but a spot of countryside
along the Thames. Thus the "hinds and shepherd-girls" of stanza 10 live
not in Arcadia but in Richmond, and they will tend an actual grave. Even
the structure of the ode derives (as Thomson's structures often do) from
the scene and the occasion: a boat with its mourner moves slowly past the
shore where Thomson lies, and the day turns into evening. (According to
an eighteenth-century editor, Collins wrote his elegy during "an excursion
to Richmond by water.")

Significantly, the progress of the author's grief follows the same natural
rhythm. Collins carefully, if somewhat archaically, works his poem into a
Druid circle. The last line echoes the first, and the stanzas are arranged
symmetrically around a figure buried at the center. As in many "triumphal
forms," the sovereign character appears only at midpoint; here, in the sixth
stanza of eleven, the boat passes Thomson's grave before returning. But
the proximity of the dead poet only heightens Collins' grief. Even the
closest friend, he is reminded, remains infinitely far from the reality of
death.

> But Thou, who own'st that Earthy Bed,
>   Ah! what will ev'ry Dirge avail?
> Or Tears, which LOVE and PITY shed
>   That mourn beneath the gliding Sail!

And the stream carries Collins back to the only consolation that nature
affords: increasing distance. The ode centers, emotionally as well as nu-
merologically, on Thomson. It ends as it began, with the Druid in his grave,

and it spurns the thought that life will be continued tomorrow in "pastures new."

Like most pastoral elegies, however, the ode on Thomson has another theme: the vocation of the poet. When a shepherd dies and his piping is heard no more, his songs may soon fade away. Collins is haunted by the question asked in "Lycidas."

> Alas! what boots it with uncessant care
> To tend the homely slighted shepherd's trade,
> And strictly meditate the thankless Muse?

The answer, of course, is that the poet can hope to be immortal. "Maids and youths shall linger" near Thomson's Aeolian Harp and seem "to hear the woodland pilgrim's knell"; "Remembrance oft shall haunt the shore"; and a friend shall weep. If these dirges do not "avail" Thomson, nevertheless anyone without a heart of stone will feel compelled to join in them.

> Yet lives there one, whose heedless Eye
> Shall scorn thy pale Shrine glimm'ring near?
> With Him, Sweet Bard, may FANCY die,
> And JOY desert the blooming Year.

Collins delicately rephrases some lines from Thomson's own "Hymn on the Seasons"—

> For me, when I forget the darling theme,
> Be my tongue mute, may fancy paint no more,
> And, dead to joy, forget my heart to beat!

—deflecting them from the poet himself to the enemies of poetry. Sidney's *Apology* had voiced a similar curse: "if you have so earth-creeping a mind that it cannot lift itself up to look to the sky of Poetry, . . . when you die, [may] your memory die from the earth for want of an epitaph"—a sentiment repeated by Thomson's own apology for poetry, the Preface to "Winter." Yet Collins' anathema is far more melancholy. If one man scorns Thomson's shrine, he suggests, fancy and joy may die with their poet. Indeed, the situation seems very bleak, since Thomson, whose poetic spirit had kept fancy alive and celebrated the joys of the year, has now gone, and even his shrine grows "pale." Sidney and Thomson had radiated confidence about the future of poetry, its power to survive even in unpoetic times, but Collins seems to anticipate a time when poetry itself shall prove mortal.

The following stanzas of the ode subtly develop this melancholy suggestion.

> But thou, lorn STREAM, whose sullen Tide
> No sedge-crown'd SISTERS now attend, .

> Now waft me from the green Hill's Side
>   Whose cold Turf hides the buried FRIEND!
>
> And see, the Fairy Valleys fade,
>   Dun *Night* has veil'd the solemn View!
> —Yet once again, Dear parted SHADE,
>   Meek Nature's CHILD again adieu!

The nymphs have departed from the sluggish Thames (Wordsworth and Keats would remember these lines); the fairy valleys, once hospitable to fancy, are curtained by a night that allows no poetic view. Thomson has already vanished into fairyland. As he recedes, he changes from an earthy, buried friend into a shade from that past time when divinities and poetic spirits still roamed the earth. Critics have differed about whether the naiads have ceased to attend the Thames "nowadays" (as opposed to the days when people still believed in them) or "now" (since the death of Thomson); but the ode itself clearly draws no such distinction. Just as Collins commemorates Thomson both as his own dear friend and as an ancient "Druid," so he regards him as a modern poet who miraculously recaptured the animating spirit and faery powers of earlier generations. Fancy, as the poets of Collins' generation so often lament, is veiled from modern eyes; now, with the passing of her "sweet bard," she fades into the past. Wafted away on a forlorn stream of time, Collins bids farewell to poetry. A sacred mystery shrouds the dead; they keep their own secrets.

If poetry is veiled by night, moreover, soon men will cease to appreciate it. Once the nymphs depart, their evocation in verse becomes rather morbid and pathetic, the ritual of a religion whose meaning has been lost. In this light the first of Collins' two epigraphs to the ode, from Virgil's Fifth Eclogue, acquires a sad irony.

> Haec tibi semper erunt, et cum solemnia vota
> reddemus Nymphis, et cum lustrabimus agros.
>
> (These rites shall be yours forever, when we offer
> yearly vows to the nymphs, and when we purify the fields.)

"Forever," under such conditions, may not last very long; Thomson's votaries will soon drift away like the nymphs'. The immortality of the poet survives only so long as posterity keeps faith, and posterity is notoriously fickle. Yet the epigraph may be read in other ways: as Collins' own vow to keep faith with the memory of his friend ("Me, too, Daphnis loved," the second epigraph recalls) and, more comprehensively, as an implication that whenever men observe the seasons of nature they will be honoring Thomson too. A true poet is immortal, Collins supposes, whether or not men read his poems; he lives in the seasonal processes or passions he has described. "Nature's child," Thomson becomes a part of nature.

The final stanzas of the ode press this pathetic fallacy to its consummation.

> The genial Meads assign'd to bless
> Thy Life, shall mourn thy early Doom,
> Their Hinds, and Shepherd-Girls shall dress
> With simple Hands thy rural Tomb.
>
> Long, long, thy Stone and pointed Clay
> Shall melt the musing BRITON's Eyes,
> O! VALES, and WILD WOODS, shall HE say
> In yonder Grave YOUR DRUID lies!

After Collins has said his last adieu, he is succeeded by other mourners: the meads that once gave birth to Thomson and now provide a place of rest. Landscape absorbs the poet and his poems; he vanishes into the earth. The maids and youths of stanza 3, who linger near the Aeolian harp in pity of "the woodland pilgrim," are presumably poetry-loving tourists, day-trippers from London who know enough about the poet Thomson to associate him with his harp. But the hinds and shepherd girls who dress the tomb belong to the meads; they pay their vows not to a poet but to a spirit of the place. Though Thomson was actually buried in the parish church, Collins situates him indefinitely amid meadows and vales. Older and more primitive than Christianity, the rites in which the dead man partakes remove him to the ageless rounds of the earth.

The last stanza carries this implicit pantheism to daring lengths. The musing Briton addresses the vales and wild woods directly, and Thomson becomes *your* Druid, fully assimilated to his natural surroundings. Even the tomb joins in this ritual: as "stone and pointed clay," it seems more allied to a Druid circle than a Christian vault. Collins deliberately superimposes an ancient scene of mourning upon a modern one. Translated into modern terms, the stanza affirms that for a long time to come Britons will visit Thomson's tomb to pay respects to the greatest national poet of nature. Yet the ancient scene, without reference to Thomson's poetry, worships him rather as a pagan god. Collins estranges his friend from the contemporary world, burying him so deep in landscape and past time that he seems less a historical figure than a pervading presence.

To preserve Thomson this way, however, it is also necessary to lose him. Collins pushes the dead poet so far back into nature and night that he strangely fades away. Mrs. Barbauld, more sensitive than later readers to Collins' habitual mixtures of Christian with pagan, complained that "To the sanguinary and superstitious Druid, whose rites were wrapped up in mystery, it was peculiarly improper to compare a Poet whose religion was simple as truth"; and her charge (like Johnson's against "Lycidas") makes more sense than most later critics have admitted. Thomson's Druid bard, in *The Castle of Indolence,* speaks like a Christian and a philosopher (at the time, the Druids were commonly believed to be early Christians). Moreover, the conscious archaizing of that poem, with its cheerful Spenserian diction, insures that no reader will mistake its romance for truth. By contrast, Collins weaves truth and fiction so closely together that Thomson is enfolded in prehistoric pantheism. The poet of *The Seasons,* the poet whose own most famous elegy celebrates Sir Isaac Newton, had tried to make poetry congruent with reason: scientifically accurate, religiously instructive. He did not fear that Enlightenment would mean the death of fancy. On the contrary, he thought, the poet bold enough to open his imagination to truth would find sublimity everywhere he looked—whether in the night of philosophic melancholy or directly in the sun. Thomson associates poetry with gazing through a veil; Collins, with drawing one closed. The later poet pauses, hesitant and fearful, on the brink of the sublime; he does not trust himself to see the light. And his tribute to his friend, for all its sincerity and pathos, exquisitely dispels his truth.

Collins, that is to say, remains a poet of his own generation and his own kind. No amount of reverence for Thomson and his verse can close the distance between them. Nor is any hypocrisy involved in the process of mystification, of subtle distortion, by which a poet of natural religion is transformed into a fairy bard. Indeed, Collins keeps a remarkable good faith, according to his lights, with the memory of his friend. No word of criticism or self-aggrandizement intrudes upon the ode. Yet the form of the *tombeau* inexorably draws Collins to reveal the deepest criticism of Thomson that he knows: something has gone out of nature, and the poet who would continue to write in modern times must come to terms with his sense of loss. That perception, all the stronger because the ode embodies rather than states it, defines the essential tension between the two created spirits of the ode: Thomson as he appears to Collins, safely passed over into a world of fancy; and Collins as he appears to himself, helplessly drifting down the sullen tide of modern life. The two cannot speak. Pursuing his lost companion into the vale of death, Collins finds only himself. Yet the journey leads him to an image of poetry he can use: half an enchanted Druid circle, half the grave of a friend—a tomb where nature and poetic fancy join. Collins is true to Thomson in his fashion. At a time when poetry comes hard, he draws from him, at any rate, a poem.

Auden on Yeats

If even the closest friendship between poets harbors this sort of tension, however, what can we expect from a *tombeau* predicated on opposition?

Surely the battle, though one-sided, must be fierce. But in practice such a *tombeau* may not be so one-sided as a reader might expect. Even as the living author attacks the dead, he must pay him some attention; the devil must be given his due. And often that deference allows surprising counterattacks, a sudden half-heartedness.

> They but thrust their buried men
> Back in the human mind again.

A poet who criticizes the verse of another must expect his own verse to show the strain. Even a hatred of vulgarity (as in the verse of Pope or e. e. cummings) may vulgarize the satire it touches, and an obsession with the faults of the great almost inevitably results in imitating them. In the *tombeau* the dead can strike back. When two poets confront each other across the abyss, it may well happen that neither will return quite whole.

Few confrontations in literary history have been defined more sharply than Auden's with Yeats, in the *tombeau* "In Memory of W. B. Yeats." For this sharpness of opposition the older poet must be given much of the credit; for Yeats wrote his own *tombeau*. "Under Ben Bulben" may originally have been intended to begin *Last Poems,* but for compelling reasons it insists on concluding every selection from the poet's work. Yeats tells us exactly how he chooses to be remembered. With almost brutal simplicity he states his creed, instructs succeeding poets to carry on his work, marks out his place of burial, and writes his epitaph. Nothing is conditional, there is no concession to futurity. Even his death is recorded as an accomplished fact.

> Under bare Ben Bulben's head
> In Drumcliff churchyard Yeats is laid.

(Since Yeats died and was first buried at Roquebrune, on the Riviera, more than nine years passed before these lines came true.) Like his great precursor Swift, who also wrote his own epitaph (much admired and brilliantly translated by Yeats) as well as his own best memorial, "Verses on the Death of Dr. Swift," Yeats enjoys picturing himself dead. He will not allow pity or revision. He will remain, in death, a hero.

Indeed, "Under Ben Bulben" fairly gleams with arrogance. Much of it is written in the imperative, as if the poet could command posterity to do his bidding:

> Swear by what the sages spoke. . .
> "Send war in our time, O Lord!". . .
> Poet and sculptor, do the work. . .
> Irish poets, learn your trade. . .

and, of course, the epitaph itself,

Cast a cold eye
On life, on death.
Horseman, pass by!

Yeats once thought of calling the poem "His Convictions"; "His Directives" might do as well. Yet the pride is justified, surely, by conviction. "Under Ben Bulben" presents a confident, many-stranded argument for personal immortality. Yeats faces death without fear because he believes that his time will come round again, in the twin eternities of race and soul, and because he believes that artists, working toward the "Profane perfection of mankind," are the true masters of the earth. Since death is only a sort of violence through which a man "completes his partial mind," since the poet above all men can "Bring the soul of man to God, / Make him fill the cradles right," the artist claims reincarnation as his due. Yeats expects to lose none of his authority in the grave. Rather, dying will perfect him, making him one with the ancient Irish race and his accomplished soul.

The claim for immortality is fixed, at the last, by the poet's directions for his burial. The place inherits special value from its ancestral associations. Yeats' great-grandfather had been rector of Drumcliff, the poet spent most of his childhood in nearby Sligo and remembered it as the scene of his first visions, and the mountain Ben Bulben, which towers over it, is intricately involved with Irish history and legend—the Fianna, Dhoya, and other faery horsemen, we are told, may still sometimes be viewed emerging from a magic gateway in its side. In a curious way Yeats even identified himself with the mountain. It is not clear whether "Old Rocky Face," who looks forth in "The Gyres," is intended to stand for Ben Bulben or Yeats—each of them holds the same things dear—and the man who converses with the echo "Rocky Voice" in "The Man and the Echo" may well be talking to himself. Mountain and man alike hold allegiance, deep within them, to ancient memories, and each of them, battered but unbowed, looks out on the world with a certain reserve. Aristocrats, they cast a stony eye on life, on death, refusing to distinguish between them. Yeats first began his epitaph "Draw rein; draw breath"; but those words were too inviting to suit his deathly mood. Moreover, they also suggest too explicitly that the horseman is alive. Yeats expects his grave to be visited, but some of those visitors will be superhuman,

That pale, long-visaged company
That air in immortality
Completeness of their passions won.

Once his own immortality has been completed, fixed "On limestone quarried near the spot," he will be as indifferent to death as to time. Proud and unconventional to the last, he commands the spirit of the place. He will be a mountain, nothing will move him.

Yeats died on January 28, 1939. On February 3 "Under Ben Bulben" (completed the previous September) was first published. "In Memory of W. B. Yeats" appeared in the March 8 issue of the *New Republic*. When Auden wrote his *tombeau*, Yeats' own must still have been ringing in his ears, and, intentionally or not, his argument responds to Yeats' at every point. First of all, and perhaps most decisively, he robs Yeats of property rights in his own death. In place of the rural landscape near Sligo, with its peasants and "Hard-riding country gentlemen," he substitutes an urban scene, complete with airports and stock exchange, whose silence ironically seems to derive more from a latent political insurrection than from the pastoral mourning that the elegiac meter might lead us to expect. In place of Yeats' indomitable Irishness, the first section of Auden's poem deliberately internationalizes its subject; we might be in any dark cold modern city, any of those indistinguishable places without character or feature. In place of that particular spot under Ben Bulben, most of all, Auden substitutes a different kind of burial:

> Now he is scattered among a hundred cities
> And wholly given over to unfamiliar affections.

Less a tomb than a cremation, the elegy demonstrates the essential unimportance of tombs. We shall visit Yeats whenever we like, in spite of his commands, by casting our minds upon his work.

Indeed, rather than completing himself in death, Auden argues, the poet utterly disperses. At the moment of his passing "He became his admirers"; his personal death was kept from his poems "By mourning tongues" that recite Yeats' verses in barbaric accents like English and American; he will be judged by "a foreign code."

> The words of a dead man
> Are modified in the guts of the living.

Yeats had insisted that he could not be kept buried, but Auden makes his resurrection impossible by scattering his remains to the winds. Similarly, he denies that the poet has brought his work to perfection. In *The Dyer's Hand,* commenting on Yeats' statement that the intellect must choose between "Perfection of the life or of the work," Auden says flatly that "This is untrue; perfection is possible in neither."

The elegy proves its point, in this first section, by the very character of its verse, the utterly un-Yeatsian way in which it commemorates Yeats. Auden modifies Yeats' words in the guts of his poem. The music of the verse, with its deliberate flatness and slack rhymes (agree/day, tongues/poems), represents everything that Yeats had deliberately rejected—as in the *Oxford Book of Modern Verse* he had rejected Auden himself. Even in its themes the elegy runs through Auden's whole modern repertoire: the powerlessness of individuals, however heroic, to affect the state; the aura of the ordinary that surrounds even something "slightly unusual," like the death of the greatest living poet; the chasm between public and private worlds; the pathology of isolated lonely men; the poetry of cities. Considering how much Yeats detested the bourgeoisie, it would probably be difficult to think of a metaphor more likely to offend him than that by which his physical collapse becomes "Silence invaded the suburbs." Similarly, nature's mourning for Yeats, like the convulsions of Ireland, is reduced to "weather."

Auden means no disrespect, of course. That the world carries on its business as usual during the fall of Icarus or the fall of Rome may serve to sharpen the poignance of personal human concerns; *we* care, all the more because the world does not. Thus the instruments that record a dark cold day, while they do not suffer for Yeats, remind us of the limitations of instruments (as Auden's revised version of the line suggests, they are only "what instruments we have"). Yet Yeats' effects are different. The coldness of his eye is the sort that can stare down any instrument. In an extraordinary paragraph of "A General Introduction for My Work" (1937), Yeats associates his own style with everything cold and icy. In great art "all must be cold; no actress has ever sobbed when she played Cleopatra, even the shallow brain of a producer has never thought of such a thing. The supernatural is present, cold winds blow across our hands, upon our faces, the thermometer falls, and because of that cold we are hated by journalists and groundlings." If the day of his death was cold, Yeats might have said, that was because his spirit had made it so. Poetry is not the still small voice that reproaches history, according to this poet, but history itself.

The issue is joined directly in the meditation later added to "In Memory of W. B. Yeats," its second section: "poetry," Auden says, "makes nothing happen." In an essay contemporary with the elegy, "The Public v. the Late Mr. William Butler Yeats," he made his position still more explicit: "art is a product of history, not a cause. . . . the honest truth, gentlemen, is that, if not a poem had been written, not a picture painted, not a bar of music composed, the history of man would be materially unchanged." Interestingly enough, it is "The Council for the Defence," not "The Public Prosecutor," who offers this argument. If poetry *did* make something happen, the prosecuting side of Auden would be quick to point out, Yeats would have much to answer for. "In the last poem he wrote, the deceased rejected social justice and reason, and prayed for war," like a Fascist. This accusation could not easily be dismissed—not in 1939. As defender of Yeats, Auden can dismiss it by separating the "silly" opinions of the man from the artistic excellence of the poet. Prosecutor and council agree that "we are here to judge, not a man, but his work," and the opinions expressed by the work do not matter, since poetry makes nothing happen.

> He was silly like us: His gift survived it all.

The problem with this line of defense, of course, is that it succeeds only at the cost of making Yeats seem silly. The poet himself, with his theory of masks that fulfill by opposition the deepest yearnings of a man, his belief that all images begin "In the foul rag-and-bone shop of the heart," would hardly have accepted the facile distinction between a man and his work that is invoked to save him. His last poems insist instead on the legacy a poet leaves when his life-work is completed, Anima Hominis entering Anima Mundi. Poets give men and nations their souls, and a dying poet must face the responsibility for what his dreams have begun: "Did that play of mine send out / Certain men the English shot?" Civilization itself, Yeats believes, depends on the artist's sense of "measurement." Poetry makes everything happen.

Auden's indifference to this argument may derive partly from his reaction to the propagandistic verse of the thirties, partly from the common impression, especially keen in England, that nothing ever happens in Ireland— nothing, at least, but "weather," endless rounds of the same old pugnacity and romanticism:

> . . . mad Ireland hurt you into poetry.
> Now Ireland has her madness and her weather still.

(Prosecutor: "It is true that he played a certain part in the movement for Irish Independence," but "Of all the modes of self-evasion open to the well-to-do, Nationalism is the easiest and most dishonest.") More central to Auden's critique, however, may be his powerful sense that poetry must live in the present, its function to remind us that we are creatures of the moment, fugitives. In the title poem of *Another Time* (1940), the volume that includes "In Memory of W. B. Yeats," he mounts a direct attack on the possessiveness, the living lies, of those who try to live in past or future,

> Bowing, for instance, with such old-world grace
> To a proper flag in a proper place,
> Muttering like ancients as they stump upstairs
> Of Mine and His or Ours and Theirs. . . .
> No wonder then so many die of grief,
> So many are so lonely as they die.

Yeats, of all poets, most deserves this criticism. He does choose to live in a place wholly possessed, another time.

> Cast your mind on other days
> That we in coming days may be
> Still the indomitable Irishry.

Against this heroic and romantic "madness," Auden puts another ideal of poetry: immediate, private, changeable, consoling. It is the ideal, above all, of an expatriate, an "inconstant one." Such poetry inhabits a landscape that has nothing to do with the towering ancestral altitudes of Ben Bulben. Rather, it flows

> From ranches of isolation and the busy griefs,
> Raw towns that we believe and die in; it survives,
> A way of happening, a mouth.

When Auden wrote these lines, he was in transit to America, and his interior landscape seems to draw on outback and cow town, anonymous places always in process of formation. For all his ancestry, the poem says, the time has come for Yeats too to set out on his journey westward. An isolated human being, he now belongs less to his countrymen than to any lonely reader to whom his work gives "a mouth." He has left the past and future behind; he lives today.

Yet the case for and against Yeats cannot be resolved so simply. In spite of Auden's trenchant criticism of Yeats' provincialism, a part of him responds to it. Yeats' scorn for modern formlessness—"When I stand upon O'Connell Bridge in the half-light and notice that discordant architecture, all those electric signs, where modern heterogeneity has taken physical form, a vague hatred comes up out of my own dark"—finds a faint echo, perhaps, in the motive that led Auden to exclude "Petition" from his *Collected Shorter Poems:* "I once expressed a desire for 'New styles of architecture'; but I have never liked modern architecture. I prefer *old* styles, and one must be honest even about one's prejudices." For all his tolerance and liberalism, Auden is not at home in raw towns, the failed civilization of capitalist democracy "in which the only emotion common to all classes is a feeling of individual isolation from everyone else." Without accepting the cure offered by Yeats' poems, he accepts their diagnosis: "From first to last they express a sustained protest against the social atomisation caused by industrialism, and both in their ideas and their language a constant struggle to overcome it." Auden writes from between two worlds—Old and New, the thirties and forties, Eden and Babel.

As behooves a poet, however, Auden's strongest response is reserved for Yeats' language. Here at least, Council for the Defence argues, "the poet is a man of action." Yeats can make language happen.

> However false or undemocratic his ideas, his diction shows a continuous
> evolution towards what one might call the true democratic style. The

157

social virtues of a real democracy are brotherhood and intelligence, and
the parallel linguistic virtues are strength and clarity. . . . The diction
of *The Winding Stair,* is the diction of a just man, and it is for this reason
that just men will always recognize the author as a master.

Against his own modern logic, which tells him that the complexity of
civilization makes it necessary for a poet to be difficult (in Eliot's famous
phrase, "to force, to dislocate if necessary, language into his meaning"),
Auden betrays a yearning for a simpler language, a poetry based on democratic brotherhood. Yeats' faith in the mission of the poet rings true in the
realm of language; when one man speaks strongly and clearly, all men who
speak his language meet him on common ground. Can heart speak to heart,
brotherhood be forged in words, without political repercussions? Few poets
would like to think so.

In the remarkable last section of "In Memory of W. B. Yeats," Auden
tries to put Yeats' linguistic virtues to use. As first published in the *New
Republic,* in two parallel sections printed in a double column, the elegy
visibly reforms upon the page. The language simplifies; the broken, hesitant
rhythms and urban images of the beginning are healed into daring, old-
fashioned quatrains. Suddenly we hear Yeats' voice.

> Earth, receive an honored guest;
> William Yeats is laid to rest:
> Let the Irish vessel lie
> Emptied of its poetry.

Yeats returns to the earth. No longer scattered among cities, the anonymous
poet dispersed in foreign climates, he is allowed a name and place of rest.
Auden's manner becomes both simple and ceremonial. Shearing Yeats of
his middle name, he makes him sound like a common man—compare
"William Butler Yeats shall rest"—or a poet whose common touch insures
that he will live forever. Auden strives for public eloquence; he mourns the
dead man, no longer with a private shudder but with authoritative justice.
He even speaks for Time, which, as three stanzas (later canceled) insist, will
pardon Yeats, since it "Worships language and forgives / Everyone by
whom it lives." Eventually Auden may have thought himself rather high-
handed in these stanzas—to "pardon" Kipling, Claudel, and Yeats for their
views is also to patronize them—yet he does catch Yeats' own familiar high
tone: the elevated yet direct speech that everyone can understand; "what
poets name / The book of the people."

There are many precedents for the public manner of these plain-spoken
tetrameter couplets—Marvell and Blake come immediately to mind—but
their direct source, of course, can only be "Ben Bulben." Like his prede-

cessor, Auden lectures the poet, and calls him to his public function. Yeats' commands—

> Poet and sculptor, do the work,
> Nor let the modish painter shirk
> What his great forefathers did,
> Bring the soul of man to God,
> Make him fill the cradles right.

—are adapted to a new exhortation:

> Follow, poet, follow right
> To the bottom of the night,
> With your unconstraining voice
> Still persuade us to rejoice.

Auden's imperatives may be less hectoring, less "constraining," than Yeats', but he does seem to regard poets at this moment as physicians for society's ills. On the brink of war, with mankind infected by hatred and "Intellectual disgrace," the artist still retains power to heal.

> With the farming of a verse
> Make a vineyard of the curse,
> Sing of human unsuccess
> In a rapture of distress.
>
> In the deserts of the heart
> Let the healing fountains start,
> In the prison of his days
> Teach the free man how to praise.

Many of Auden's recurring axioms join in these lines: mankind is sick, free will is illusory, only a change of heart can save us. It is even possible, in the traces of biblical imagery and the hint of prayer, to see a foreshadowing of his turn from psychiatry to Christianity as the medium of cure. The burden of the passage, however, falls elsewhere. What Auden prays for is a poetic language so pure and truthful—so strong and clear—that all men will heed it. Out of equivocal feelings, the layer of irony on irony that recognizes the root even of rapture in distress, he hopes to make a clear poetic line.

The end of the elegy pays tribute to Yeats in more ways than one. Auden captures some of the resources of Yeats' verse: the rhythm whose momentum drives ahead of meaning, the simplicity of language that weaves opposing thoughts into a single thread. Indeed, the mode of the poem, as well as its versification, derives from the poet it commemorates: Auden thought that a kind of personal, occasional elegy given public meaning (as in the "gallery poems") was Yeats' most significant formal innovation. But what Yeats teaches Auden above all, perhaps, is how to praise. The constant theme of the *Last Poems,* that the poet can call us to rejoice even amid the "numb nightmare" of history, that the inexorable tragic play in which every man is locked can be transfigured by joy, here turns back upon its author. Yeats, Auden has suggested, was more a victim of history than he knew; nevertheless his poems show us how to be free. The way to freedom is praising: to perceive the tragedy of an era or the frailties of a man with a clarity that conceals nothing yet indomitably sings. For Auden himself, so conscious of the psychic and political prisons that enclose the mass of men, so knowing about the lies that poison our ideals, an unequivocal gesture of praise does not come naturally. But he makes that gesture at the last— in memory of W. B. Yeats.

To claim that in the course of writing the elegy Auden became converted to Yeats' position would be, to be sure, more ingenious than true. Auden's public manner lacks the obsessive power, and perhaps the conviction, of Yeats'. It seems almost always in danger of veering into sentimentality. The essentially private voice that speaks through it cannot risk grand effects without putting us on notice, through strains of rhetoric, that part of the truth has been suppressed. Notoriously, Auden dropped his other venture in the Yeatsian mode, "September 1, 1939," from his canon because of its "incurable dishonesty." Nevertheless, "In Memory of W. B. Yeats" does establish a momentary equilibrium between the two poets it joins. For all their differences, they unite as lovers of strong and clear poetic language.

> Lovers, like the dead,
> In their loves are equal;
> Sophomores and peasants,
> Poets and their critics
> Are the same in bed.

And when the critic is himself a poet, he can signify his love by welcoming its object into the texture of his verse. Under the equalizing force of death Yeats must relax and become his admirer, with one condition: his admirer must also become Yeats. That equation marks the logic of the *tombeau;* of literary history itself.

The Tombs of Mallarmé

For poets are the carriers of literary history. They hold the past within them like a seed or an infection; they pass it on. The dead poet is communicated

by the living. In no other human activity, it seems, are ancestors so continually present; if Aeneas had been a poet he might have been forced to
shoulder Anchises forever, as Virgil carried Homer. The burden lies heaviest
in language. When Auden speaks of Yeats he yields to Yeats' own way of
speaking. In this respect the *tombeau* epitomizes a paradox that many modern
linguists consider the essence of language: every statement is at once determined by innumerable constraints—the rules of grammar, the history of
usage, the context in which speech occurs—and yet a wholly new creation.
The poet, especially, must speak with a double voice. A destroyer and
preserver, he cannot be less than the caretaker of language but cannot be
less than original and free. He serves the remains of speech by making them
new. Language, like poetry, consists of fossils; the *Oxford English Dictionary*
resembles a vast *tombeau*. But a living language emerges not from the dictionary but from a continuous response to new situations. The poet must
close the book and speak for himself. Coming to terms with his inheritance,
he makes a language of his own.

The history of poetry is composed of such choices. A long chain of
tombeaux stretches generation through generation from the ancients to the
present, preserving a vital record of what poets inherit. When one great
poet dies, another assumes his mantle—not always without opposition.
Thus, on the death of Sir Philip Sidney (1586) a flock of would-be successors
competed to sing his praises and capture his spirit. None tried harder, surely,
than his friend Fulke Greville (Lord Brooke), whose later *Life of Sidney*
makes plain his effort to imitate the life of the poet as a saint might imitate
the life of Christ. But devotion is not enough. Posterity has favored another
claimant, Edmund Spenser, who hitched his wagon to Sidney's star with
repeated tributes to "Astrophel."

> So there thou livest, singing evermore,
> And here thou livest, being ever song
> Of us, which living loved thee afore,
> And now thee worship, mongst that blessed throng
> Of heavenlie Poets and Heroes strong.
> So thou both here and there immortall art,
> And everie where through excellent desart.
> ["The Ruines of Time," 337–43]

There, amid the angelic choir, Sidney may sing just as he pleases; but *here*
on earth only the songs of his worshipers will keep his name alive. Spenser
enters a lien on Sidney's immortal part. The king is dead! such poems
declare. Am I the king?

Sometimes a war of succession may be required to determine the answer.
When Ben Jonson died, for instance, so many good poets wrote *tombeaux*
of so many different kinds that the dust did not settle for a generation. But

more often, as in the case of Sidney and Spenser, the title is clear. The phoenix may serve as an appropriate emblem. Indeed, the famous volume called *The Phoenix Nest* (1593), which elegizes Sidney three times over, defines his leavings with its very title. England's most brilliant poet has burned to ashes, but there in his tomb a nestling starts to quiver. The phoenix will rise again. Somewhere in England an immortal poet—Sidney reborn—awaits his chance to blaze. And the spirit of Sidney's poetry will pass on and be renewed inextinguishably into the future. *Tombeaux* rekindle the poet; the phoenix never dies.

A history of poetry could be strung together, in fact, from *tombeaux* alone. What Lydgate learned from Chaucer and Surrey from Wyatt and Carew from Donne and Herrick from Jonson and Cowley from Crashaw and Denham from Cowley and so on and so on . . . what each of them learned was his trade. The sequence stretches on. Nor is this sequence less reliable, for all its loops and patches, than the histories of poetry that scholars write. *Tombeaux* can help to remind us of some obvious truths that literary critics and historians (especially in the past few centuries) have tended to forget: the art of poetry consists essentially of knowing how poems work, not of ideas about poems, and literary history begins with the effort of one poet to learn from another, not with the retrospective constructions of the scholar. A good line of poetry is immortal, as poets have always said, so long as it can come to life again in someone else's poem. Poets engage in tomb-work. Moreover, that labor is replicated to some extent by every good critic, even by every ordinary good reader. As readers we intuitively submit to the poem; we try on its style. It is notorious that most of us, when we study an author deeply, begin (quite helplessly) to imitate his writing. Good poets cast a spell. And the accumulation of such spells, the continuing life reflected in *tombeaux,* defines the only past that poets can use.

The tomb of the poet, that is to say, registers not only his death but his renewed existence. He surfaces again in certain words, in certain rhythms. Even when the successor attempts to erase or expunge him, as Broch with Virgil, the buried poet rises up into the mind. *Tombeaux* insure the life-after-death of the poet. Hence Dante and Broch translate Virgil into a man of their own times, and Goethe teaches Tasso German. Only thus can the life of the poet be carried on, when his legacy has become so independent of particular works or manifestations that it can enter into works by other hands. Moreover, both poets profit from the exchange. The modern fear or anxiety of influence, suffered no less by critics than by poets, often seems to imply that an author in his ideal state would be circumscribed only by his own individuality, self-originating, self-aggrandizing. But the history of poetry suggests an opposite truth. Dante became most himself when he learned to speak like Virgil. And the same thing happened to Broch. The life of the undead poet requires a living soul to harbor it, and, when it finds one, it is capable of blessing. Such is the lesson, at any rate, suggested by a poet who made *tombeaux* a way of life: Stéphane Mallarmé.

No poet is more original than Mallarmé; no poet is more obsessed by other poets. As a schoolboy, after meeting Béranger, he was seized (he confessed in his "Autobiography") by "a secret desire someday to replace" him; the poems of his teens include one "Sur la tombe de Béranger." In his mature years he devoted a high proportion of his slender *oeuvre* to elegies on artists: the "Toast Funèbre" to Gautier, "Hommages" to Wagner and Puvis de Chavannes, and above all the crucial works he called *tombeaux,* honoring Poe, Baudelaire, and Verlaine. Mallarmé defines his vocation as a poet, and to some extent modern poetry itself, by constantly bringing news of the dead. He describes with great exactness the grave, the tomb; with futile patience he searches every cranny for the lost poet. Compulsively the poems reiterate a question: Where now is Gautier? Poe? Baudelaire? Verlaine? These are the works, most clearly, in which Mallarmé tries to find himself.

The morbid originality of the *tombeaux,* their haunting of the dead, is at once their paradox and subject. Not wholly divorced from compassion, Mallarmé nevertheless turns his attention elsewhere, toward the aesthetic challenge that a vanished poet offers his successors: What is there left? The first and longest of the major elegies, the "Funeral Toast" (1873) to Gautier, poses such questions most insistently. Mallarmé presented his toast, by invitation, as part of a vast public tribute to Gautier, to be recited at the funeral and eventually published in *Tombeau de Théophile Gautier,* a volume stuffed with testimonials from eighty-three poets. The public occasion of the poem provokes not only its rather ceremonial rhetoric but also its underlying irony. For what has all this to do with Gautier? Surely the ceremony can only remind us of an emptiness, of who and what is missing in the spirit.

> Et l'on ignore mal, élu pour notre fête
> Très simple de chanter l'absence du poète,
> Que ce beau monument l'enferme tout entier.

> (Nor are we unaware that, chosen for our very simple
> Gathering to sing the absence of the poet,
> This splendid monument shuts up the whole of him.)

Gautier has gone; all possibilities are at an end for him, "nothing of his destiny remains." Indeed, the pomp of the funeral fête only emphasizes the grim disparity between man's pride and the dust to which it returns. Far from raising up the poet, who in death becomes "Magnifique, total et solitaire," the mourners shrivel by contrast into skeletons temporarily masked by flesh.

Cette foule hagarde! elle annonce: Nous sommes
La triste opacité de nos spectres futurs.

(This haggard throng! it announces: We are
The sad opacity of our future specters.)

Within the tomb, where everything mortal rests in silence and night, Death
claims his subjects: Gautier and us.

Singing the absence of the poet, however, has a vital creative function
for Mallarmé. For only when freed from everything mortal—his destiny,
his meanings, his dreams, himself—can the poet become "pure." The mortal
Gautier has escaped into his words; now they alone, in "a solemn agitation
through the air," survive. That is how a poem ought to be. Mallarmé
restlessly strips the dead of all false consolations—the immortality of the
soul, the honor paid by the living, the power of influencing others—just
as he would strip a poem of a narrative line or paraphrasable content.
Distilled into pure symbol and music, the poet attains some of the quality
of the best verse. Poetry came into Eden, Mallarmé suggests, in that infinitely strange moment when things were first given their names; with a
shudder the disquieting miracle of mere existence was tamed. Adam, the
first poet, learned to rule all things with words, though only at the cost of
knowing that his rule, essentially arbitrary, confirmed an eternal divorce
between things and what we call them. Every poet recreates that moment.
Gautier, "The Master" of a verbal Eden, "awakens / For the Rose and the
Lily the mystery of a name." And the mortal thing that Gautier was has
also become a name. Mallarmé toasts an empty tomb. In the absence of the
poet, he finds a necessary precondition for the pang of divorce from the
natural world that every poem endures.

Poe

If the absurd distance between the poet as a person or celebrity and the poet
purified into his words absorbs Mallarmé at Gautier's tomb, it is still more
appropriate and oppressive at the tomb of Poe. The first line of "Le Tombeau
d'Edgar Poe," perhaps the most frequently quoted line in modern French
literature, carries the logic of purification to its apotheosis.

Tel qu'en Lui-même enfin l'éternité le change,
Le Pöete suscite avec un glaive nu
Son siècle épouvanté de n'avoir pas connu
Que la mort triomphait dans cette voix étrange!

Eux, comme un vil sursaut d'hydre oyant jadis l'ange
Donner un sens plus pur aux mots de la tribu

Proclamèrent très haut le sortilège bu
Dans le flot sans honneur de quelque noir mélange.

Du sol et de la nue hostiles, ô grief!
Si notre idée avec ne sculpte un bas-relief
Dont la tombe de Poe éblouissante s'orne,

Calme bloc ici-bas chu d'un désastre obscur,
Que ce granit du moins montre à jamais sa borne
Aux noirs vols du Blasphème épars dans le futur.

(Such as into Himself at last eternity changes him,
The Poet rouses with a naked sword
His century frightened not to have known
That death triumphed in that strange voice!

They, like a vile start of the hydra hearing of yore
The angel give a purer sense to the words of the tribe,
Proclaimed in full cry the enchantment drunk
In the honorless flood of some black brew.

Out of opposing earth and sky, what shame!
If our idea should not carve a bas-relief
With which to adorn the dazzling tomb of Poe,

Calm block dropped here from a mysterious disaster,
May this granite at least point out forever a bound
To black flights of Blasphemy scattered in the future.)

Once again a public occasion prompted the tribute. It was composed, according to Mallarmé's later recollection, for the dedication of a monument erected at Poe's grave in 1875, and an early version was published in *Edgar Allan Poe: A Memorial Volume* (1877). Considering that Poe had been reviled and neglected in his native land since his death in 1849, however, it might well strike his French admirers that America's wreath for her poet was too little and too late. An eternity, indeed, had passed; and only now was Poe beginning to come into his own. Much of the sonnet turns on Mallarmé's resentment of "them," the hydra-headed crowd that had pursued its angelic poet past the grave with blasphemous accusations of alcoholism and un-healthiness. Time reveals "them" now in all their loathsome hypocrisy. "Très haut" (not only loud but proud) in pretensions, they are really serpents capable of no more than the basest leap ("un vil sursaut") of imagination. By contrast, Poe is a shining knight, an angel, Himself, pure, dazzling, calm. Mallarmé reverses the reputation of Poe as a dark spellbinder and hurls the charge of blackness back at the accusers: the blackest flights of

Blasphemy are *theirs*. The Poet has mounted above such human pettiness. Eternity has changed him into a poetic essence; he triumphs in death.

This apotheosis, however, conceals a certain doubleness of meaning. Poe may be interpreted, through the words of the sonnet, not only as Mallarmé's pure angel but as Baudelaire's genius of the perverse. Thus the Poet frightens his readers because his strange voice celebrates (or "hymns," as in an earlier version) the triumph of death (3–4); he deals in charms and spells, if not black magic (7–8). Is the "obscure disaster" of line 12 Poe's death, which leaves this monument behind, or his life, the disastrous and mysterious personal history that somehow produced the "calm block" of his work? The climax of these ambiguities occurs in the closing lines. Their primary sense, I have suggested, seems to be that the monument now erected will put a curb to the blasphemous attacks on Poe by "bourgeois mediocrity." But another interpretation is possible: Poe's own "black flights of Blasphemy" set a new standard for what such art can achieve, and the monument (and poem) commemorate that bourn of blackness which none shall ever surpass. Both senses are as necessary to the sonnet as to Poe's reputation. He must remain a subversive Olympian, Orpheus in the underworld, even though his monument falls as though from a star ("désastre," from *astre, "star"*). In our idea of him the earth wars with the sky as physical mortality with the immortality of the poet. Poe's evil destiny, the palpable mystery and darkness that surround him, supplies Mallarmé with exactly the contrast he requires for the shining purity of art. The more adulterated the elements of life and subject matter, the greater the poetic triumph that refines them away. At last, in the *tombeau,* Poe's blasphemy evaporates into a kind of holiness. In spite of everything he merely was, he now becomes Himself, the dazzling star made by eternity—and Mallarmé.

The contrast between Poe's terrestrial and eternal aspects is reflected, in fact, by every detail of the sonnet. The influence of the dead poet—his peculiar logic and style—hangs heavy upon his survivor. Thus the *tombeau* takes the form of an attack upon the stifling prejudices of society partly because of Poe himself, that adversary of society to whom the very existence of his country (Baudelaire had said) was like the foul air of a prison. With the monumental block of basalt, Mallarmé commented many years later, "America weighted down the poet's light shadow, in order to make sure that it would never reappear." But the poem cleverly transforms the block into a true memorial: a mysterious apparition, fallen from the sky, that reminds us of the cryptic messages Poe so much enjoyed concocting and decoding. Nevertheless, Mallarmé accepts the image only on condition of displacing its meaning from the earth to the sky. This cipher admits of no solution.

The main influence and displacement, however, occur in the realm of language. Almost every word of the poem might be traced to a source in

Poe. To confirm this point without pedantic listing, let us imagine Mallarmé's lines guided back into the original by the dead hand of his master.

> Translated now and come into his own,
> The Poet quickens with a naked blade
> His all-unknowing century afraid
> That death with that strange voice has reared its throne!
>
> They, as a startled hydra might halloo
> Hearing our words made pure by Israfel
> Proclaimed that he had sung so wildly well
> By weltering in some Plutonian brew.
>
> Disgrace! if from the earth and sky at war
> Our thought should not carve out a metaphor
> To deck the scintillating tomb of Poe,
>
> Calm block dropped here from some dark meteor,
> The ultimate dim Thule may you show
> To Blasphemies like ravens of the future.

Here ghosts of Poe's own writings rise to the surface, as in his own favorite image of the prematurely buried soul who will not stay below. The lady Ligeia, the House of Usher, Ulalume, Dream-land, the City in the Sea, the angel Israfel, the Raven—all these had haunted Mallarmé's imagination from his early years. He taught himself English in order to read them in the original, he labored at translating the poems into French, and they conditioned his ear forever.

The language suffered a sea change, to be sure, on its passage overseas. The thrilling-rotten quality of Mallarmé's own English version of "The Tomb of Edgar Poe" suggests that part of his fascination with Poe's mysteries may result from the mystery that *any* English held for him. The French author "Edgar-Poë," as is well known, only faintly resembles his American cousin. Yet Mallarmé's subversions of Poe (like the version of Mallarmé above) are also based on a principle: the necessity of a *total* translation. The eternal aspect of the poem requires the sacrifice of its personality. Hence the French poet breaks down the language of his master, deliberately unsettling every word by changing its context or by rendering the subtext at the expense of the surface meaning. To become Himself, Poe must vanish. In this respect Mallarmé performs the service demanded by a famous passage in his "Crisis in Verse":

> Work that is pure involves the disappearance of the poet's voice, which cedes the initiative to words, propelled by the shock of their bumping together. They kindle reciprocal reflections like a trail of fire on precious

stones, replacing the hard breathing of bygone lyric inspiration or the individualistic enthusiastic shaping of the phrase.

Mallarmé sets out, in short, to "purify" Poe, to carry on the task of giving "a purer sense to the words of the tribe." Poe's mode of expression, like his career, passes through a refining process that strives to reduce it to its peculiar diction, its obsessive meters, its suggestion of cosmic immensities, without its encumbrance of story, psychology, and thought. The letters recover the initiative. Thus Poe's very name, through the magic of letters, conjures up "Le Poëte." Similarly, "Tel" reverses itself at the onset of "l'éternité," only to emerge again when the final "té" runs into the following "l." And throughout the poem (as critics have painstakingly noticed) Mallarmé rings the changes—or tintinnabulates the bells—not only of internal sound effects but of his own previous texts. One word produces or evokes another, as if without the intervention of human speech.

The danger of this procedure is that it risks falling into nonsense. Do the words of the tribe make sense in any of the known languages? Mallarmé's own best poems often sound as if translated from some unknown dialect— a tongue more obscure and rarer than any man has spoken. Yet the "Tomb of Edgar Poe" is saved from evaporation by the influence of Poe himself. It was Poe, after all, who taught the later poet his tricks with letters. *Tel* and *l'ét* reflect the *dim mid* region of Weir, and "Raven" spelled backward is "never"—at least when pronounced with a French accent. More important, Mallarmé draws his indignation and passion directly from scenes in Poe's biography. The effect is far from pure. Whatever the "translation," the pressure of Poe *as he was* upon the poem, its constant suggestions of blasphemies, of wilder words, of something not so "calm," lends it an air of menace. Beneath the static triumph of the tomb there are hints of a restless, impure poet.

Indeed, all *tombeaux,* as Mallarmé conceives them, aspire to a stasis that their tensions belie. Partly this must result from the nature of language itself, which abhors "purity" as nature abhors a vacuum. Words and their associations take on new life with every reader. Nor can a poem be utterly stripped of meaning; the meaning of "Le Tombeau d'Edgar Poe," for instance, can certainly be paraphrased and explicated (though not of course exhausted) by banal prose. But another source of tension comes from Mallarmé's attempt to fix his progenitors in a frozen immortality. The rhetoric of his *tombeaux,* if not their sometimes indefinite syntax, suggests that poets cease to be problematical in death. Our ideas, precise enough to carve a bas-relief, capture the artist in his eternal form; the sum of all his words together composes a calm, immovable block. Poe equals Poet. But to achieve this perfection Mallarmé must rigorously exclude every accident or idiosyncrasy, every possibility of living confrontation with the "blasphemous" physical world, from his idea. Each *tombeau* performs a sacrifice of the dead poet. His individual experiences and proclivities are purged away; he changes into an artifice of eternity. (In Frank Kermode's terms, he becomes an autonomous "Image.")

Yet the work of the poet, stubbornly irreducible, resists the sacrifice. Phrases and images from his body of writing, not yet laid to rest, reappear in the lines of living poets; scandal, metamorphosis, the threat of resurrection keep the tomb in flux. Poems that dwell on the static purity of death almost inevitably break down their own immobility; one might cite the underwater earthquake of Poe's "City in the Sea" or the wind that springs up at the end of Valéry's "Le Cimetière marin." Similarly, a breath of the spirit of the dead poet invades each of Mallarmé's *tombeaux*. Poe's strange voice, though absent, imposes its accents on the words of the tribe; Baudelaire's vitality, in death, undermines every attempt to bury him.

Baudelaire

It is this theme, above all, that dominates "Le Tombeau de Charles Baudelaire" (1895). Mallarmé's early prose poem, "Symphonie Littéraire" (1864), had frankly exalted the author of *Fleurs du Mal*, construing him as a luxurious ancient church where one could breathe no other word than *Alleluia*. But "Le Tombeau de Charles Baudelaire" performs a far more ambiguous service—not only worship but exorcism. Indeed, many critics suspect the poem, like Jonson's on Shakespeare, of harboring a secret animus, informed, at best, by a "cold and intellectual" praise and, at worst, by reflective malice. Perhaps Baudelaire has been dead too long. Something is rank.

The point may be clarified by comparing Mallarmé's sonnet with "Ave Atque Vale" (1867), A. C. Swinburne's quite classic *tombeau* in memory of Baudelaire. Galvanized into immediate homage by a premature report of the poet's death, Swinburne imagines a visit to the grave, loads every line with allusions to Baudelaire's poems, proclaims his immortality, comforts him with having escaped from the troubles of life, and submits himself to his spirit. The tenth stanza is representative.

> Not thee, O never thee, in all time's changes,
>> Not thee, but this the sound of thy sad soul,
>> The shadow of thy swift spirit, this shut scroll
> I lay my hand on, and not death estranges
>> My spirit from communion of thy song—
>> These memories and these melodies that throng
> Veiled porches of a Muse funereal—
>> These I salute, these touch, these clasp and fold

169

As though a hand were in my hand to hold,
Or through mine ears a mourning musical
Of many mourners rolled.

Despite his regrets at never having met Baudelaire, the English poet claims him as a brother. He offers to translate him in every way—most of all by assimilating "the sound of thy sad soul" into his own music. ("Veiled porches," in this context, may represent not only the portal to immortality and the proper monument for Baudelaire's funereal genius but Swinburne's own receptive ears.) It is all too sweet for comfort. Swinburne almost forgets to mention the sense of menace that he so much admired in Baudelaire. Yet the poem is undeniably reverent and beautiful; and Mallarmé praised its music.

Twenty-eight years later, however, the situation had changed. Now Baudelaire was truly a classic, and no French poet could avoid the question of where to place him. Nor was the question merely figurative. A committee of poets, including Mallarmé, had recently been delegated to remedy a scandalous neglect of Baudelaire's grave by designing a monument in his honor. In this light the octave of "Le Tombeau de Charles Baudelaire" probably qualifies as the most audacious committee report ever submitted. Mallarmé proposes two designs.

> Le temple enseveli divulgue par la bouche
> Sépulcrale d'égout bavant boue et rubis
> Abominablement quelque idole Anubis
> Tout le museau flambé comme un aboi farouche
>
> Ou que le gaz récent torde la mèche louche
> Essuyeuse on le sait des opprobres subis
> Il allume hagard un immortel pubis
> Dont le vol selon le réverbère découche

> (The buried temple bares its mouth, displaying
> Through drains sepulchral drooling mud and rubies
> Abominably some idol of Anubis
> Muzzle ablaze as in ferocious baying
>
> Or if the new gas twist the shifty wick
> Wiping up insults yielded to and known
> It lights a wild immortal pubic bone
> Whose flight is bedded by the streetlamp's arc)

Once again the dead poet is pillaged for images and phrases that can be used to shore him up or tear him down. The book of Baudelaire reveals, when opened, Anubis, the jackal-headed Egyptian god of death, an idol who mixes the human with the animal, mud and rubies, spleen and ideal. Then a hint of smoldering sewer gas leads to a second "monument," the pubic bone of a prostitute (or Baudelaire's mistress, Jeanne Duval) shamefully illuminated by the recently installed gaslights of the city as she flits from lamppost to lamppost.

Baudelaire, that is to say, has designed his own monument. He has taught us to see beauty in extremes, in the urban underworld, tucked into sewers from which we used to avert our eyes. His very grave, dug up again, would yawn into beastly splendor. Yet the tribute also contains a drop of poison. Is there perhaps a touch of parody in the extravagant opening divulgence of Anubis, with its abominable extremes and litter of self-referring *b*'s (". . . bavant boue et rubis / Abominablement")? The sonnet, as scholars have often noticed, sounds the first letter of Baudelaire's name no fewer than eighteen times. Mallarmé himself commented elsewhere on the secret significance of *b*, the letter of "production or childbirth, of fecundity, amplitude, bloating and bending." It is all quite indulgent. Mallarmé emphasizes Baudelaire's prodigious self-consciousness, his intoxicating hothouse images, and hints that such flowers, now overripe, are fading. Having purified the language and renewed its stock of symbols, the dead poet himself becomes an idol. The city changes. Gaslights pervade it with new clarities and shadows; new gods arrive. Nor does the *tombeau* allow the poet much human sympathy. "Absent" (like Gautier), he dries into a ghost.

What does remain, then, of Baudelaire? The sestet broods upon his legacy.

> Quel feuillage séché dans les cités sans soir
> Votif pourra bénir comme elle se rasseoir
> Contre le marbre vainement de Baudelaire
>
> Au voile qui la ceint absente avec frissons
> Celle son Ombre même un poison tutélaire
> Toujours à respirer si nous en périssons.

> (In cities without evening what dried petals
> Could offer blessing like the one that settles
> Against the marble of Baudelaire in vain
>
> Veiling its absence with a wreath of thrills
> That Shade of his a tutelary bane
> Always to be breathed by us although it kills.)

Flowers of Evil, Mallarmé suggests, do not provide a fit wreath for Baudelaire's tomb. The beauty he created, now classic, has begun to wither like foliage; his shady cities, lighted by gas and lorn of Baudelaire, no longer have evenings (not *votive* evenings, at least, if we take "votif" to modify "soir"). Indeed, the mere remains of the poet, such as they are, rest in a cemetery—"cities without evening." We do wrong to look for him in such places. The poet survives not there but in his Shade: the air we breathe.

Two alternative images of what a poet leaves conspire in the final lines of the sonnet. On one side there is Baudelaire's "marble," the finished, perfect tomb of his life-work that celebrates his absence. Yet around that marble, circling it with shudders, a veil hovers like a miasma—the still-dangerous Shadow that refuses (even syntactically) to take form. The poems of Baudelaire resist subsiding into "literature" or a final edition; instead they enter our most secret inner life. Mallarmé marvelously suspends "That Shade of his" in a grammatical limbo from which it casts its influence several lines before being named. Something that blesses and settles and girds, it moves ever closer in its verbs until at last we breathe it in. But the blessing conferred by Baudelaire's influence could hardly be more mixed. It spreads between two oxymorons, "tutelary/poison" and "breathe/perish." The easy sequence of sounds that rearranges the letters r, e, s, p, i into p, e, r, i, s almost induces us to forget that the essence of this beauty is death. One cannot approach the tomb of Baudelaire without danger.

Many of the themes of the *tombeau* gather together in the word "tutelary" (in French, of course, a rhyme for Baudelaire). The glorious dead poet, it conveys, is now a god; not the florid Anubis-idol, safely antique for all its horrifying fusion of sensuality and divinity, but a guardian deity that inhabits those whom it protects. Yet the means of its protection is poison, the cost to those it inspires is smothering. We honor Baudelaire by drawing him into us; he rewards us by touching us with a hellish shudder of immortality. His poetry makes a mockery of life. Nor does Mallarmé know an antidote. Once having been exposed to Baudelaire, the *tombeau* warns, we cannot return to older, safer kinds of poetry; we need his atmosphere, the contagion of a beauty steeped in menace, in order to breathe.

Yet Baudelaire himself has disappeared. Mallarmé patiently reduces him to an ever-diminishing symbol—the letter b, our own internal sense of an "absent presence." Gradually the dead poet fades entirely into Mallarmé's drift of thought. New poems cannot repeat the rhetoric of an earlier generation; they require a certain forgetfulness. And poetry itself can thrive only by erasing Baudelaire—his smudged reality—as he had erased others. Mallarmé acknowledges the influence of the dead master by immersing himself in his language as in a destructive element, at last indistinguishable from himself. Baudelaire lives on as nothing more than an ironic choice of words, a shadow in a pool of light. Only when absent can he enter us. He becomes "acutest at his vanishing."

Verlaine

Nor does Mallarmé shirk his responsibility of helping dead poets to vanish. The last of the *tombeaux,* the sonnet dated January 1897 to commemorate the first anniversary of the death of Verlaine, addresses this problem with special intensity. For what could be more ridiculous than a monumental Verlaine, a Verlaine encased in stone and immune to changing? That was not the poet who had been Mallarmé's friend. Instead Verlaine must have another memorial, a distraction that will allow his quicksilver spirit to escape. Mallarmé had already made the point a year earlier, in a funeral *médaillon* read over Verlaine's fresh grave. "The tomb prefers immediate silence. Acclamation, renown, lofty words cease, and the sobbing of abandoned verses should pursue his hiding place no further, discreetly, lest it offend his glory with a presence. . . . The genius of Paul Verlaine has escaped to the future, the hero remains." The grave holds a "hero," surrounded by idolators; but the light and solitary genius of the dead poet will not abide our praise. Verlaine must keep in motion. Evidently the incongruities of the scene at the Batignolles Cemetery—the contrast between a winter landscape and a fertile poet whose very name contains a touch of green *(vert),* between the reverent crowd and the absent lone wolf, between ritual and iconoclasm, gravity and flightiness, the public and private voice—made a strong impression on Mallarmé. A year later he recreated the scene forever.

> Le noir roc courroucé que la bise le roule
> Ne s'arrêtera ni sous de pieuses mains
> Tâtant sa ressemblance avec les maux humains
> Comme pour en bénir quelque funeste moule.
>
> Ici presque toujours si le ramier roucoule
> Cet immatériel deuil opprime de maints
> Nubiles plis l'astre mûri des lendemains
> Dont un scintillement argentera la foule.
>
> Qui cherche, parcourant le solitaire bond
> Tantôt extérieur de notre vagabond—
> Verlaine? Il est caché parmi l'herbe, Verlaine
>
> À ne surprendre que naïvement d'accord
> La lèvre sans y boire ou tarir son haleine
> Un peu profond ruisseau calomnié la mort.
>
> (The black rock wrathful to be rolled by cold
> Wind will not stop though pious hands should stroke
> Its likeness to the frailties of our folk
> As if to bless some stultifying mold.

173

Here almost always if the ringdove coo
This immaterial sorrow will crush down
In nubile folds the ripe star yet unknown
Whose shimmering will silver all the crew.

Who seeks, by tracing out the lonely bound
Just now outside of this our vagabond—
Verlaine? He is hidden in the grass, Verlaine

Only to find in naïve unison
With lip not drinking nor with unslaked breath
A superficial river slandered death.)

The black rock, at once gravestone and storm cloud, refuses to be fixed in place by those pious hands that would freeze its significance, either by sermonizing blindly on the poet's sorry life-story (literally *feeling out* its resemblance to ordinary human woes) or by carving conventional sentiments on his tomb. Here lies the poet Paul Verlaine—no! he does not lie here! Insofar as his life does contain a message for the "crowd," it is as subtle and natural as the cooing of the ringdove, whose mourning song prefigures a time when all humanity will realize that Verlaine's poems have altered the world. (The "nubile folds," in this context, may represent either a wedding veil that signals "tomorrow's" marriage of the poet and the public—the mourners converted to wedding guests—or a veil of clouds, derived from the Latin *nubilus* or "cloudy," through which the translated Verlaine will eventually burst like a star.) Certainly the poet is very restless in his grave. And Mallarmé rescues him from premature burial by relocating him in every element of the scene.

Verlaine continues his bouncing in the sestet. The tomb cannot hold such a vagabond; he hides out in the grass and surprises his own unquiet reflection like Narcissus in the face of a brook. But Mallarmé saves his boldest stroke for the end. Here the French idiom *calomnie ramassée dans le ruisseau,* "slander picked up in the gutter," reminds us not only of the notorious gossip associated with the name of Verlaine but of the actual gutters where the drunken poet had sometimes been found lying. Evidently death has not changed his habits. Yet death itself, according to the poem, might be considered a kind of gutter, essentially shallow and benign. Or rather, we slander the underworld, the Heraclitean river of perpetual flux and motion, by labeling it with a term as static as "death." What remains of Verlaine, down there in the grass, has not drunk the waters of forgetfulness nor dried into breathlessness. Instead it continues on its way, recognizing the fluidity of the afterlife as a type of its own. We have not heard the last of Verlaine. Newly baptized and circulated, he will reappear in our verses or vital sources whenever we least expect him.

Indeed, the *tombeau* denies death in many ways. Mallarmé flatly refuses any religious pieties or obituaries that would wrap Verlaine up. He insists that the tomb has not pressed the poet to its mold, that the new day of poetry, far from completed, has yet to ripen, that somewhere interior the vagabond still is leaping, and that even the word "death" does not apply. Moreover, the whole conception of the poem is mobile. Rather than preach a sermon, Mallarmé evokes each crotchet and quaver of the burial day: the moving clouds that mock the deadly stillness of the rites, the hands in prayer, the cold wind and trickling of waters, the cooing of the ringdove that somehow sets the tone for the occasion, and even the physical presence of the body as the mourners think the unthinkable and imagine what it feels like to be buried. Could we escape? The poem suggests that we could, partly by joining the earth in its endless changes and partly by transforming every appearance of nature into matter for poetry. Hidden in the grass and scattered into pieces, Verlaine performs the work that Mallarmé had once told him was the poet's sole duty: "the Orphic explanation of the Earth."

Perhaps Mallarmé is also denying, in the year before his death, that he himself will die. He converts the ephemeral into the eternal in two ways: by stretching the tomb to accommodate all the atmosphere of one particular moment, even its weather, and by incorporating Verlaine's own spontaneous, shimmering effects within a different kind of poetry, monumental and obscure—a black rock rolled by the wind. Thus he insures Verlaine a place in that canon within which his truest inheritor, of course, is Mallarmé himself. To us in the future, the *tombeau* points out a line of succession that would otherwise have been by no means clear. Verlaine and Mallarmé, despite their surface differences, will constitute a party in the hereafter. At the same time, moreover, Mallarmé writes his own work into history. Praise for the much-misunderstood dead poet implies a superior understanding, which the living poet has put to use and transcribed for the next generation. So long as Mallarmé stays alive, the significance of Verlaine's achievement will not fade. And by the same logic Mallarmé designs himself a tomb in posterity with many chinks for breathing. There is room for more than one poet down there below.

Mallarmé's skepticism about death, however, goes far beyond a personal hope for survival. Instead it expresses the poet's deepest analysis of all *tombeaux* and, consequently, his understanding of death, life, language, and poetry (in ascending order of importance). Like any great exploration of a poetic form, Mallarmé's *tombeaux* collectively define the essence and the possibilities of the genre. To begin with, each of them insists on the fundamental, childish questions: What happens to people when they die? Do they go down into the ground or up into heaven? Mallarmé coolly considers the matter. The hostility between earth and sky, explicit in "The Tomb of Poe," also furnishes an underlying imagery for each of the other tombs (as in the "bedded flight" of Baudelaire or the flying rock and crumpled star of Verlaine). In this respect the *tombeaux* fit firmly in tradition. Consider the magnificent climax of "Lycidas," for instance, where two warring versions of King's poor body—hurled about in the ocean or wafted by dolphins to shore, sunk low beneath the waters or mounted high into heaven—are superimposed on each other. Most elegies describe a similar ascent. Yet Mallarmé changes the direction. The "block" of Poe falls to earth, Baudelaire's shade finally "settles," and Verlaine, for all his lightness, hides in the grass. Mallarmé will not allow us to forget that the tomb still holds a body. The facile religious consolations of "heaven" are not granted even to poets.

Yet neither does the grave hold poets captive. Orpheus turns the tables, after his dismemberment, by sowing himself into every bit of the earth and explaining it; henceforth he will be "the genius of the shore." The prospect of nonexistence does not terrify Mallarmé, that is to say, because he pays so little respect to mere existence. The earth would be nothing indeed without its poets. None of his pronouncements was intended to be more scandalous, or more literal, than the famous maxim that "everything in the world exists in order to end up in a book" ("tout, au monde, existe pour aboutir à un livre"). More scandalous still, he meant it. As a poem exists not through direct presentation or description of things but through suggestion, contemplation, and evocation, so the world is constituted for Mallarmé by those who author it or evoke it most finely. Hence a great poet— a Poe, a Baudelaire, a Verlaine—can author even his own death, compelling us to read it in the light of his poems. The life-in-death of the *tombeau* makes it the most typical of all poetic forms. Thus the problem that I have defined as central to the *tombeau*—the struggle between the dead and the living, between the body of the poet and the monument erected over it—becomes, for Mallarmé, merely an instance of a common fallacy: a belief in existence without a book or in a tomb where the body is independent of its monument. The Orphic poet knows better. Poe's works *are* his tomb, at least in their new translation, and so are the works of every poet who resists a superficial entombment by his society. "In my view the state of the poet, in this society that does not permit him to live, is the state of a man who isolates himself in order to carve out his own proper tomb." The outcast poets whom Mallarmé commemorates had spent their lives in carving out their tombs. The earth had not captured them; they had captured the earth.

By folding existence into a book, moreover, they had also made themselves available for translation. In one respect dead poets *do* go to heaven: they become constellations. Throughout the long tradition of the *tombeau,* no pattern is more characteristic than the final turn from the body of the poet, in his resting place, to a new celestial sphere. "The earth his bones, the heavens possesse his gost," Surrey concluded of Wyatt, and almost every elegist of a poet is drawn to the same conclusion. Stellification is a very safe method of disposal. Nor does Mallarmé refuse to avail himself of the tradition. As Jonson translates Shakespeare into the Swan, Shelley elevates Keats into Vesper, and Goethe telescopes Byron into the shooting star Euphorion, so the *tombeaux* exalt an astral Poe, a tutelary Baudelaire, and a starry Verlaine. Great poets leap over the earth. At the last trumpet, Dryden assured the shade of Anne Killigrew,

> The Sacred Poets first shall hear the Sound,
> And formost from the Tomb shall bound:
> For they are cover'd with the lightest Ground.

Mallarmé would have approved the sentiment.

Yet he also revises the idea of a *constellation*. The word itself was favored by Mallarmé with many uses. He liked it so much, in fact, that he capitalized it in the center of the last page of *Un Coup de Dés*, as if to crown with it his own career. But the special virtue of a constellation, he thought, was its superiority to any hint of substance. Only when the individual stars have lost their interest, only when the astronomical facts have been submerged in a pure pattern of relations *between* stars, does the constellation assume its ideal form. The dance begins when the dancers forget themselves. And so with poets. Their life begins when every material circumstance of being has been purged away, when eternity has changed them at last into themselves, when existence itself has been pressed and folded into a book, when the constellation at last receives its name. Ideally, therefore, the *tombeau is* a constellation, translating the poet into his next stage of life. One evening, after a long acquaintance with Mallarmé, his young friend Paul Valéry suddenly understood the goal of all his efforts: "He has tried, I thought, *to raise a page at last to the power of the starry sky!"*

That power, though strong, is distant. The page that has been raised so high, like the poet who has been dispersed into the air we breathe, may quickly grow hard to read. Mallarmé's notion of the *tombeau* concedes a great deal to flux. Yet it is precisely that acceptance of change, he thinks, that keeps our stars immortal. The atoms of the body shift in the earth, the letters of old texts recombine in startling new formations, and even a pair of dice, as they whirl through space, may seem to assume a classic pattern. A similar destiny awaits poets, according to Mallarmé. Though forever in motion, like stars, they trace the illusion of a human significance upon the sky. We read them as we read the heavens, to glimpse a shape that might foretell our future. Perhaps that shape results from an internal harmony, the laws that govern all celestial bodies in enduring relations; perhaps it results from nothing more than our need to impose meaning on whatever we read. Yet the constellations have survived the death of the myths that once sustained them, the persons or gods who inhabited them. We still know their names.

On the other side of the tomb, according to the last of Rilke's *Duino Elegies*, new stars fill the sky, the stars of Griefland. Each of the constellations named there—*Rider, Staff, Fruitgarland, Cradle, Way, The Burning Book, Doll, Window*—has a personal meaning for the poet. They are *his* emblems, the things translated to eternity by his poems. But one constellation stands slightly apart from the rest.

> Aber im südlichen Himmel, rein wie im Innern
> einer gesegneten Hand, das klar erglänzende *M,*
> das die Mütter bedeutet. . . .

> (But in the southern sky, pure as in the palm
> of a consecrated Hand, the clear shining *M,*
> which signifies Mothers. . . .)

The ultimate emblem of destiny, Rilke suggests, is curiously intimate. It has accompanied and protected us from childhood and remains as close to us as the palm of the left hand (where palmistry had taught the poet to perceive the lines of an M). Certainly no constellation could be closer to *him*. Yet at the same time the shining, magnified "Mothers" refers to one of the most famous passages in German poetry: the "Dark Gallery" scene in which Faust searches for the deepest truths of existence by descending to primal, mysterious goddesses—*Die Mütter.* Rilke redirects the quest by pointing it upward and inward. Perhaps he is even "correcting" Goethe and Faust by suggesting that the Mothers live within us. Our destinies are not to be attained by striving; we hold them in our hands. Nor is the world beyond the tomb a foreign country. The land of death belongs to the poet, because he alone has spent his life learning how to preserve all things by making them invisible. The poet contains the sources of all myths, Rilke believes, as surely as he houses his mother's genes. Indeed, the two are aspects of each other (at least in German, where *Mütter* and *Mythe* entwine in a plausible pun). The great constellations are internal. Yet this one watches over Goethe as well as Rilke, the dead poet as well as the living. Even at the moment when Rilke names his favorite constellation and designs his emblem for posterity, he is rifling the tomb of a master.

"We make out of the quarrel with others, rhetoric," Yeats wrote, "but out of the quarrel with ourselves, poetry." Yet the two quarrels (as none knew better than the author who joined "Anima Hominis" with "Anima Mundi") are really the same. When the quarrel with others touches on deep concerns, its rhetoric becomes internalized; we carry on the argument within ourselves and sometimes make it poetry. A great poet rereads himself, quarrels with himself, and finds new meanings in himself until he dies. And then another quarrel begins. The poems are disinterred, reread, and shaped into another constellation; every line can be freshly translated. Hence Virgil survives, in spite of Broch, from generation to generation; survives most of all by provoking Broch to a quarrel. Poets are too restless to stay in their tombs. Where then is Mallarmé? He is hidden in the sky, Mallarmé, waiting for his page to be turned. When a great poet dies, the poets he has yet to be begin their journey.

ENDING

This Living Hand

Keats did not finish his career. The garners were never filled. The mighty epic that would advance the grand march of human intellect, the "few fine Plays" that represented his "greatest ambition," had to be set aside. Other words were reserved for his tombstone: "Here lies one whose name was writ in Water." But posterity has not agreed, of course, with Keats' verdict. Each succeeding generation, each new biography, has labored to shape his life and his career as a poet into a satisfying whole. It seems almost a moral obligation. If Keats himself was robbed of the chance to end what he had begun, all the more reason for the rest of us to give him back his destiny and repair his loss of time. The perfect Keats lives in us.

Yet where does his story end? No issue is more significant, in closing the book on Keats' life as a poet, than choosing a poem to conclude. Many plausible contenders have been offered. "The Fall of Hyperion," for instance, leaves us a Keats still groping toward the altar of poetry in an arrested motion and apocalyptic striving like one of his own urn figures—"For ever wilt thou love, and she be fair!" "To Autumn," on the other hand, suggests a final resignation and acceptance of destiny, the life of the poet dropping into timelessness like a ripe fruit. But traditionally the place reserved for Keats' last poem has been occupied by something much stranger and more problematical, a little fragment without a name.

> This living hand, now warm and capable
> Of earnest grasping, would, if it were cold
> And in the icy silence of the tomb,
> So haunt thy days and chill thy dreaming nights
> That thou would wish thine own heart dry of blood
> So in my veins red life might stream again,
> And thou be conscience-calm'd—see here it is—
> I hold it towards you—

No one can say exactly when or why these lines were written. Indeed, we cannot say with any certainty even that Keats meant them to be a poem. Jotted in the manuscript of his faery burlesque, *The Jealousies* (or *Cap and Bells*), and thus presumably dating from the end of 1819, they were not published until 1898; nor is there any indication that the author thought them complete or fit for the press. They resemble none of his other poems. The direct address to an unknown "thou," the broken final line, and above all the monumental self-assertion—so unlike Keats' usual modesty about his claims on immortality—convey a most un-Keatsian agitation or "positive capability." Hence critics have often sought to place the lines in some dramatic context that would explain them. Perhaps they were intended as a morbid reproach to Fanny Brawne; perhaps they represent a speech assigned to a character in some projected historical play or melodrama. We cannot know. Whatever significance the fragment may once have held for Keats himself, it now belongs only to that Keats whom every reader is free to reconstruct in his own mind.

To deny that the context of the lines can be recovered, however, is not to deny its relevance for interpretation. The meaning and effect of "This living hand" depend entirely, in fact, on context. Indeed, the fragment constitutes one of the best examples in literature of a radical ambiguity or "rabbit-duck"—an artifact that can be read in two fully coherent yet mutually exclusive ways. If we take the lines as a speech in a play (perhaps the most likely possibility), then both the auditor and audience can actually *see* the hand. Holding his living hand forth, the speaker forces the listener to imagine a cold dead hand superimposed on it and moving forward. The effect is chilling; only a very strong-willed auditor could keep from flinching. Indeed, that would be the purpose: to jolt and trouble the conscience. If Leicester were addressing Elizabeth, for instance (as has been suggested), he would intend the speech to shock her into mercy—or at least to frighten her. The hearer's blood runs cold.

If we take the lines as a poem addressed to a reader, however, the meaning completely reverses. Now we *cannot* see the hand. Yet knowing that Keats is dead—for any reader, of course, he would always have been *absent*—we nevertheless respond to his gesture; he induces us to imagine a living hand rather than an icy corpse. The effect is touching and pathetic. Far from flinching, most readers will strain toward Keats in sympathetic grasping. When the lines are quoted in a biography of the poet, they can create a rare feeling of intimacy; for once Keats speaks directly to us without formality or mask. Momentarily we should indeed give our blood to bring him back to life.

Both versions of the fragment are effective—the first perhaps a little too melodramatic yet a brilliant theatrical stroke, the second hypnotic and original if less controlled. Yet we cannot compromise between them. Consider a third possibility: the lines addressed (as scholars used to fancy) privately to Fanny Brawne. Now something from both versions will have to enter the interpretation. Fanny, like Elizabeth in the presence of Leicester, seems accused of indifference or heartlessness toward her lover. When he is gone, he suggests half-gloatingly, she will be stricken with guilt and remorse. As a reader, moreover, who like other readers must recreate the hand and the words in her own imagination, she would also sense the tenderness implicit in this oddly insinuating effort to touch her beyond the grave. No one had been offered Keats' hand so often as Fanny. Such a reader, therefore, might well be simultaneously moved and frightened. Yet the fragment largely fails of its effect, it seems to me, when read through Fanny's eyes. Its tone becomes bullying and painful, its mixture of horror and pathos appears too selfish to carry a message of love. The two versions tend to cancel each other out when combined. If Keats *did* address the lines to Fanny—and we cannot prove that he did not—then one can only say that he did them no service. Lovers of the poet will prefer to think "This living hand" a gift to them.

Accepting a gift, we also accept the reality of the donor. Both versions of the fragment do obey, at least in one respect, the same artistic principle: the power of a speaker to control and manipulate our imaginations. In his presence he enforces a sense of absence, in his absence presence. The superimposition of one hand on another and present time on future time serves to remind us that reading can be a dangerous experience. Our imaginations are not wholly ours, the living hand belongs to another. Nor is this effect entirely an optical illusion, the reader's willing connivance in his own deceit. The critic Jonathan Culler, who considers the fragment "perhaps Keats's most fascinating poem," has recently argued that the success of "This living hand" involves an irresistible mystification: "The poem baldly asserts what is false: that a living hand, warm and capable, is being held toward us, that we can see it." But in fact we have no reason to doubt the speaker's assertion that he is holding his hand toward us. Even if we rule out all contexts (Culler does not mention them) in which the speaker might be addressing someone other than "us," we can hardly deny that he might actually have made (be making, at the time of composition) his gesture. Indeed, the very act of writing might be thought to confirm that a warm and capable hand is moving toward a reader. No reader who remembers "this warm scribe my hand" in "The Fall of Hyperion," the culmination of many such references by Keats, will forget that writing used to require an active, grasping hand. Nor does the poet's prompting us to "see" assert a falsehood, "that we can see it." The claim is quite different. From the speaker's point of view, what could be more clearly contrary to fact than supposing himself to be dead? His return to his own present moment— "see here it is"—brings a jolt of truth. The hand exists *here,* in immediate reality, not in some imagined tomb or future. Nothing could be more true than that the poet sees it.   •

Yet the reader, of course, does not. Or rather, the reader will perceive the hand only to the extent that he or she succeeds in looking through Keats' eyes. Perhaps for a moment the illusion may take hold and a living hand begin to swim into our sight. But the gap cannot be closed. The poet's return to his own reality—a return made especially forceful by his abandonment not only of the conceit of death but of conventional poetic language, meter, and even closure—only reminds us that our own reality is elsewhere. "This living hand" goes as far as a poem can go toward encroaching on a reader's space, or abrogating the distance between poet and reader. And a sympathetic reader might want to respond by moving toward the poet in turn or by actually visualizing the hand. But Keats' life is not ours. The hand that, straining, we see held toward us is moving away from him.

Somewhere in that divide between poet and reader—between what he sees and what we see—the life of the poet comes to an end. Keats can go no further. Imagining his future, his life after death, he labors under the same disadvantage as a reader who tries to imagine the living hand of Keats. The past and future are sealed to each other. Only through a willful and perhaps arbitrary decision can we so much as declare "This living hand" to be a poem by Keats. And insofar as it qualifies as such a poem, it offers only the vaguest and dimmest of hopes for poetic survival. By investing his hope in the reader's conscience, not in his own imperishable work ("This monument will outlast metal and I made it / More durable than the king's seat, higher than pyramids" wrote Ezra Pound, outboasting Horace), Keats resigns his fate to strangers. At best he must trust in our "wish."

Yet Keats' imagination of his destiny did not turn out to have been an optical illusion. The potential "Keats" he so often pictured in both poems and letters is still, by and large, a good likeness of the Keats in our minds; the "character in whose soul I now live" now lives in the souls of others. The hand wrote in men. Its eventual fate has yet to be worked out, to be sure, in the complex negotiation between the poet and posterity which alone can determine how a living hand will be remembered. That is why the fragment fits so snugly at the end of Keats' poems: to emphasize that the process of his work can never be completed save by our own responsive acts of attention. But it also serves to emphasize the reciprocal nature of such acts. We imagine Keats' life as a poet so well largely because we know that Keats imagined it first.

He also paid the price. A poet so in love with his destiny must face the consequences of ambition: the constant pressure to grow and build; the sacrifice of modest successes and ordinary pleasures; the extraordinary self-consciousness that drives him to watch his own hand in the process of writing; the unending internal voice that tells him that nothing he has done or can do will ever be good enough. Even his best work may become hateful to him—a record of unpurged images and missed opportunities. His fears will be realized. Before his hand can trace "Huge cloudy symbols of a high romance" that would immortalize his name forever, he knows he will cease to be. Rereading his work, comparing it to what it might have been, he will always half suspect that he has written on water.

Lowell

Most ambitious poets harbor such suspicions, such fears. The life of the poet is achieved at the cost of many other possible lives; it fixes the poet in place like a worm in amber. Nor have poets in modern times always concluded that a sense of destiny is worth its price. The consciousness of a past and future time can easily impoverish the present, the immediate passing moment where a poem "*is* an event, not a record of an event." Hence Robert Lowell agrees with Culler that "This living hand" is "Keats's most fascinating poem" precisely because it "eschews apostrophe for direct address" and produces an event. No longer striving to perfect his work (on this view), just before death the poet voices his raw will to survive. Life is stronger than destiny. "See here it is"—"Keats" surrenders to Keats. Or perhaps to Lowell. Focusing upon the impulsiveness and immediacy of "This living hand," we convert it to proto-Lowell. Certainly few poets have ever had a more ironic sense of destiny. Nor have many been more eloquent than Lowell on the doubts that accompany "Reading Myself."

> Like thousands, I took just pride and more than just,
> struck matches that brought my blood to a boil;
> I memorized the tricks to set the river on fire—
> somehow never wrote something to go back to.
> Can I suppose I am finished with wax flowers
> and have earned my grass on the minor slopes of Parnassus. . . .
> No honeycomb is built without a bee
> adding circle to circle, cell to cell,
> the wax and honey of a mausoleum—
> this round dome proves its maker is alive;
> the corpse of the insect lives embalmed in honey,
> prays that its perishable work live long
> enough for the sweet-tooth bear to desecrate—
> this open book . . . my open coffin.

Lowell repudiates his life as a poet. Performing what this book has re- garded as the essential action in bringing about a new stage of poetic life— rereading his work to find another meaning in it—he discovers not life but death. His technique has consisted of "tricks," his flowers are wax, his whole career congeals into a mausoleum. Nor is it his work alone that revolts him. The deliberate ambiguity of the title, which can apply either to reading poems (whether silently or in public) or to "reading" character, suggests that the petrifaction of the work is related to a psychological weak- ness. The poet has cared too much about building a great career. As a result he has wanted too much to please. Inflamed with pride, he thought to prove himself alive by erecting a dome of words, only to realize that death shows itself most proudly, as in a cathedral, when most denied. And in the mean- time life has escaped him.

"Reading Myself" does not represent Lowell's final verdict on his career. The image of the book as mausoleum later tended to be replaced by more vital images, the fishnet or "eelnet made by man for the eel fighting." Nor did he stop reading himself and others. The eel, for instance, with all its vitality, derives not only from Montale's great poem but from Lowell's own earlier imitation of it. And even "Reading Myself," notwithstanding its nausea in the face of classicism, might well be considered a classical type of modern poem—the failure of its "tricks" related to "The Circus Animals' Desertion," the bee and sarcophagus borrowed from Rilke, the open book, its pages so in need of ruffling and its equation with death so manifest, beautifully adapted from "Le Cimetière marin." Yet readings like these should not be allowed to distract us from the genuine note of recantation in Lowell's own reading. He looks at his early work and does not find it good. He would not go back to it. Attempting to unlearn the brilliant formal structures and powerful rhythms with which he had once thought to storm Parnassus, he opened his book to the day-by-day, to events and history and family and politics and chance and America and the mistakes of a lifetime. His verse became a continuing journal, hesitant, vulnerable, and sometimes slack. The broken-backed unrhymed sonnet form of "Read- ing Myself," octave and sestet reversed to allow a long fall from the climax, is the staple of Lowell's later career. It is not a heroic form—"The line must terminate." Refusing to let his lines deny death any longer, he sought to make his life as a poet identical with his life.

The project, as more than one critic has noted, derives from Whitman's. But Lowell puts far less confidence than Whitman in his readers—even when the reader is himself. The opening lines of "Reading Myself" exhibit an author who is very uneasy about resembling "thousands." Who are those thousands? The context implies them to be the whole herd of ambitious authors, carried away with their own eloquence and sense of future great- ness. Yet clearly Lowell is not the poet to join a crowd. From another point of view the thousands seem associated with a political rally or protest, whose pride in solidarity the poet has helped to inflame. His lack of respect for this accomplishment is sufficiently defined by his view of how one stirs an audience: "I memorized the tricks." A similar uneasiness hovers round the "sweet-tooth bear," whose power to desecrate poetry can refer either to devouring time or a hungry public. To be read at all, Lowell appears to hint, is to risk being inauthentic. Nor does his reading of himself allow any more comfort. For all his democratic mistrust of formalism, heroism, or an embalmed poetic, he does not seem to think of poetry as something to be shared with strangers. "The proof of a poet," Whitman had proudly concluded the preface to *Leaves of Grass,* "is that his country absorbs him as affectionately as he has absorbed it"—a declaration that would plague him later, when it became evident that his affections were not returned. But Lowell resists absorption. Taking just pride not only in his ability to move an audience but in his knowledge of what it costs, he withdraws from the race. Hence America, whose disorders at first seem monstrous counterparts to the poet's own psychological demons, ultimately turns into a foreign country. Even his early poems, reread, seem foreign.

In the image of the bee and the honeycomb Lowell's equivocal attitude toward his career receives its fullest expression. The organization of this particular hive is very peculiar. Surely no bee's labors have ever seemed more isolated or useless. Like a pharaoh aspiring to raise his pyramid by himself, this highly unsocial insect has no coworkers, no progeny, and no object but self-memorial. His own work keeps him prisoner. The dome of the honeycomb might stand for a human skull, whose outward calm conceals feverish, obsessive thoughts. But the figure that presides over the whole, above all, is death-in-life. Though three successive lines insist that the work and its maker "live," a heavy irony surrounds each use of the word; it is only a corpse that "lives." Lowell seems to regard his work and career as burying him alive. Perhaps he also takes some secret pleasure in what he has accomplished; not every poet, after all, succeeds in building a mausoleum. "To die is life," an old man of Lowell's own creation had remembered while "Falling Asleep over the Aeneid." Yet the reading suffers woefully from its lack of issue. The old poems offer no nourishment and will not lead to new ones.

If the life of the poet depends on posterity, that is to say, Lowell considers it far from worth the cost. The sense of destiny withers when the future approaches like a tawdry motorway: "The Aquarium is gone. Everywhere, / giant finned cars nose forward like fish." Why should one sacrifice one's life on an altar where no one worships? Lowell draws the logical conclusion. He writes for himself and tries to be true to himself, not greater than he is. He does not offer us his living hand.

Yet another conclusion might be drawn from Lowell's reading of himself. If the analysis of his career brings him no satisfaction, nevertheless it provides a new self-understanding. Perhaps a modern poet can hope for no more. In these terms the test of a true accomplishment may be less whether the poet has lived up to his dream of what he might be than whether he has perceived that nothing he has done is accidental. To perfect one's life as a poet, Lowell seems to say, would mean accepting full responsibility for it—the weakness as well as the strength. A poetic autobiography has the right to play with the truth, but it cannot afford to pretend that the past has not happened. Lowell's ruthlessness with his previous work (including his depredations of *Near the Ocean*) reflects his decision to judge himself again at every turn. His integrity, the shape of his career itself, consists of sparing nothing.

At the end of *The Dolphin,* the sequence that Lowell chose to conclude his *Selected Poems,* one line is separated from the rest. The fifteenth line of a sonnet, overflowing the space and standing alone, it may have been intended by Lowell as an epitaph for his life as a man and his life as a poet:

> my eyes have seen what my hand did.

I know what I have done, the poet says; and everything these poems record comes out of my own experience. Nor does he excuse himself. The terrible things a hand can do, the guilt of a Cain or the cunning stratagems of his creator, all burden the line. It holds a potential for horror. The disjunction between eyes and hand, between seeing and doing, is reminiscent of a stock Gothic effect: the murderer who observes himself in the act of murder, the criminal disconnected from his crime yet powerless to stop it. Exacerbated self-consciousness may be the ultimate horror. "See here it is." And it is possible that a poet who confesses to this disconnection in his own life, who may even regard the death-in-life of his poetry as both the cause and product of such disconnection, is asking not compassion but acceptance of what he has done.

Perhaps he is also accepting himself. To see what one has done is not to make amends; but responsibilities begin with clarity of vision. At least he has not averted his eyes. In the little world of the author and his page, moreover, where nothing matters more than coordinating the eye and hand, a proper vision of one's writing is all-important. It may even involve a transformation, as in Eliot: "to arrive where we started / And know the place for the first time." Lowell does not claim so much. He sees his handiwork without approving it. Yet the line that he chooses to close his book and his career sounds almost religious—not the religion of Whitman and so many other great poets who believe in reincarnation, nor the religion of Dante and Eliot, who trust in the resurrection, but the religion of a poet who hopes only to be honest with himself. The past cannot be contravened and the future may never exist; there is only the present. If Lowell does not approve his life as a poet, nevertheless he puts his signature to it, his hand turned toward himself. Not "here it is," he says at last, but "here I am."

Rilke

Many other poets, especially in this century, have found a vocation in the same attempt: putting themselves on record. In modern times the realms of gold lie inward. Starting with an image of greatness, such poets gradually learn that destiny has no face except their own writ large, or that the refining fire is life itself. The life of the poet, seen in these terms, consists of a progressive unveiling or gradual stripping-away of illusions. "Now that my ladder's gone, / I must lie down where all the ladders start, / In the foul rag-and-bone shop of the heart." Yeats has no difficulty in reconciling this enterprise with a mighty claim on posterity, because he believes his heart is very great. But lesser poets have often been in danger of reducing their work to ashes. If life is the refining fire, then the residue it leaves may well be not a tempered soul but simply death. Ever since Wordsworth, those poets who have taken their own experience both as the source and the goal of their work have had to contend with exhaustion. What remains when the last veil is lifted?

Another life, more true; something invisible. That is the answer, at any rate, of one modern poet whose career has often been regarded as exemplary: Rainer Maria Rilke. No poet, not even Virgil, has ever possessed a stronger sense of destiny. Indeed, to speak of Rilke's "career" seems almost blasphemous, so fierce was his desire to consume everything belonging to himself in the interest of his greater project of transmuting the world. He had been born not to celebrate himself but to ease the things of this earth in their passing, to translate a coarse and vanishing reality into something angelic. The poet, mankind itself, could have no higher purpose. "It is our task to imprint this provisional, perishable earth so deeply, so patiently and passionately in ourselves that its reality shall arise in us again 'invisibly,' " he wrote in a famous letter to his Polish translator, Witold von Hulewicz. *"We are the bees of the invisible."* Rilke conceives himself an intermediary for angels, the dead, and the Mothers, those who have already accomplished the transformation to a higher order of reality. He thus takes full responsibility not only for his own life but the life of everything he touches. The very survival of the world depends on his cross-pollination and the sweet, invisible substance—essence of poetry—he produces within himself.

The conversion begins, of course, with self-transformation. In the great "Archaic Torso of Apollo," the poem he chose to introduce the second part of his *New Poems* (1908) and new poetic career, Rilke states the explicit terms of his bargain with the invisible: "You must change your life" *(Du musst dein Leben ändern)*. More precisely, it is the torso itself that makes this demand; a necessary distinction, since the poet's new faith requires him to sacrifice his own individuality in favor of assisting his subjects—the panther, the roses, the statue—to speak for themselves. And everything they speak is a reproach. The intense life that harbors even in certain inanimate objects exposes the poet to his own waste of so much life. Now he must change. The things of this world and the other world cry out to him to give them voice. Their words are too passionate to ignore; Rilke submits to the challenge. Hearkening to Apollo, he thrusts his own life as a poet into refining fire.

The process of transformation, however, is also destructive. Angels, according to the first *Duino Elegy,* cannot always tell whether those they move among are living or dead, and neither can Rilke. The shape of destiny that haunts him through all his hours has a face that resembles a death's-head. In his fictionalized work of initiation, *The Notebooks of Malte Laurids Brigge* (1903–10), the poet describes the personified death that dwells within every life that has not been ready-made—in lovers most of all. Life preserves death "as a fruit its kernel." Or as a later fragment has it: *"Leben* und *Tod:* sie sind im Kerne Eins" (*"Life* and *death:* they are one at the core"). To some extent, it seems, a young poet must develop by gradually realizing his death. He burns away everything false, he purifies his work, until at the last, in the words of Malte, "quite at the end, one might perhaps be able to write ten lines that were good." Rilke aspires to a similar life as a poet. But he also believes that those ten lines, with all the authority of death behind them, could permanently change the world. To borrow the image of the bee back from Lowell: the poet is embalmed at the center of the round dome all his work has erected over him, but at the final stage of purification the work becomes invisible, revealing the dome of the sky with a new light shining through it. The bee, converting everything to a transparency, at last converts itself.

Not every poet could endure such burning. Even Rilke's sense of his high destiny can sometimes falter, as the things and people of this world tempt him with earthly sweetness. "Earth's the right place for love," a more practical poet has said, and at times Rilke seems to agree—especially when he is living in Paris or writing in French. Then his roses tend to become quite visible. But the most subtle temptation of all for Rilke is his desire for a personal death, a death peculiar to him alone. "Help me to my own death, I don't want the doctor's death—I want my freedom," he asked a friend during his last weeks. Reasonable as it might sound in the mouth of

Malte, this plea contains a threat to Rilke's fate as a poet. For the later works insist that a great poet becomes anonymous at the end, metamorphosing into the totality of that world and that unseen poetic existence which he has helped to save. Rilke believes, like Shelley, that all significant poets since the beginning of time have collaborated in a single poem. "The poet, there where the great names, Dante, let us say, or Spitteler, no longer matter,—it's the same thing, it's the poet; for, in the ultimate sense, there is only one, that infinite one who, here and there through the ages, asserts himself in some spirit that has been subjected to him." The name of that one poet is Orpheus: he who became the familiar of death and, by being dismembered and dispersed, at last insinuated himself into every particle of nature. The *Sonnets to Orpheus* record that vision. The poet dies to live, and reappears in every future song: "Ein für alle Male / ists Orpheus, wenn es singt." Hence Rilke's fiery individuality, the burning spirit that regards even death as its own possession, threatens to hold him back from the final stage of self-immolation. Orpheus demands the ultimate sacrifice. Having written his own name everywhere, even in the stars, the poet must learn to forget himself and dissolve into air.

The lesson is never easy. A poet who has spent a lifetime gaining control of his world, and who at length contrives a perfect shape for his life as a poet, will seldom acknowledge that his own destiny, the loveliest and fullest of all his creations, must pass from his control. Yet angels and audiences are inexorable. They cluster round the very deathbed of the poet, translating everything he has done into terms of their own. "Tel qu'en Lui-même enfin l'éternité le change. . . ." Whether the life of the poet belongs, as Rilke thought, to the indwelling spirit of the universe or, as so many critics think today, merely to the poet's readers, it will not belong for long to the poet himself. Indeed, it cannot; for no poet can step outside his work and see its totality. The living hand is always in motion, and only when it stops can it be grasped. In Rilke's terms, the condition for preserving the world is to make it invisible. The same condition applies to the life of the poet. The intensity that allows an individual human being to become a great poet, burning away every trace of the prosaic and external, finally turns on itself, flame eating flame until the last trace of individuality has vanished. The life of the poet culminates in no life at all. No one knew this better than Rilke. And no one fought against it harder.

In the autumn of 1926, cutting roses in his garden, Rilke pricked himself on a thorn. Soon the infection spread; it was the onset of leukemia. The "incommensurable anonymous pain," like a fire scattered through the whole body, quickly reduced the poet to a spectator of his own dissolution; nor would he accept any drugs. He developed a new internal sense and felt himself die. The end came on December 29. Less than two weeks before, Rilke had composed the last entry in his last notebook, a poem addressed to that death within him. He who had so often invoked the image of refining fire confronts a final irony: a fire that erases everything he is and absorbs his life into its own. "Bin ich es doch, der da unkenntlich brennt?" ("Is it still I, unknowable, who burns there?") His destiny requires him to vanish in full awareness. And Rilke rises to the challenge. He greets death as something beyond him: the angel of immortality that cuts him off from memories and even his own body. In that moment he becomes anonymous at last. As characterless as a printed page or an unnamed constellation, he submits to the eyes of strangers and that stranger death; he loses his privacy. "Niemand der mich kennt" ("No one who knows me") awaits him on the other side. No longer hungering for greatness, he renounces his life as a poet, gives over his name, and enters a world without future—all fire.

Here is the way it begins.

> Komm du, du letzter, den ich anerkenne,
> heilloser Schmerz im leiblichen Geweb:
> wie ich im Geiste brannte, sieh, ich brenne
> in dir; das Holz hat lange widerstrebt
> der Flamme, die du loderst, zuzustimmen,
> nun aber nähr' ich dich und brenn in dir.

> (Come, you, the last one, you I usher in,
> comfortless ache within the bodily weaving:
> as once I burned in spirit, see, I burn
> in you; the wood has long been striving
> against acceptance of the flame you kindle,
> but now I nourish you and burn in you.)

Notes and Glosses

All translations in the text are my own unless otherwise noted.

PREFACE

vii **divorced from the poems** A pirated Dublin edition first collected the prefaces as *The Lives of the English Poets,* unaccompanied by poems, in 1779–81, inducing Johnson's own publishers to issue the *Lives of the most eminent English Poets* (4 vols.) in 1781.

death **of the poet** "La mort de l'auteur" (1968), tr. Stephen Heath in Barthes' *Image—Music—Text* (New York: Hill & Wang, 1977), pp. 142–48. Barthes' burial of the Author did not prevent him, of course, from writing his own account of *Roland Barthes* (Paris: Seuil, 1975). The effort to erase the "author-function" from discourse—"What difference does it make who is speaking?"—has been extended still further by Michel Foucault, "What Is an Author?" (1969), tr. D. F. Bouchard and Sherry Simon in Foucault's *Language, Counter-Memory, Practice* (Ithaca, N.Y.: Cornell University Press, 1977), pp. 113–38.

viii **hardly been studied** Though theories and commonplaces about poetic careers are not in short supply, so far as I am aware no scholar has ever looked at the topic as a whole. This book should be regarded as a preliminary attempt to define the ways in which a poet may shape a career.

begun to crack See the influential reexamination by Irvin Ehrenpreis, "Personae," in *Restoration and Eighteenth-Century Literature,* ed. Carroll Camden (Chicago: University of Chicago Press, 1963), pp. 25–37.

ix **initiation ceremonies** Standard accounts include Arnold Van Gennep, *Les Rites de passage* (Paris: E. Nourry, 1909), and Mircea Eliade, *Rites and Symbols of Initiation,* tr. W. R. Trask (New York: Harper & Row, 1965).

killing the others "The Perfect Critic," Eliot's opening essay, imitates Frazer's own beginning by performing a ritual slaying or *envoûtement:* "Coleridge was perhaps the greatest of English critics, and in a sense the last. After Coleridge we have Matthew Arnold; but Arnold—I think it will be conceded—was rather a propagandist for criticism than a critic . . . ; modern criticism is degenerate" (*The Sacred Wood* [London: Methuen, 1920], pp. 1–2).

x **Freud** The work of Erik Erikson, for instance *Young Man Luther* (New York: Norton, 1958) and *Identity and the Life Cycle* (New York: Norton, 1959), has lent new strength to Freudian analyses of literary careers. I have discussed Erikson's method in "Analyzing Burke," *Eighteenth Century* 20 (1979): 71–74.

a literary calling For Johnson's attitude toward careers, see my *The Ordering of the Arts in Eighteenth-Century England* (Princeton, N.J.: Princeton University Press, 1970), esp. pp. 454–61, and "Learning to Read Johnson," *ELH* [English Literary History] 43 (1976): 517–37.

xi **considerable uneasiness** The problematic nature of modern careers is a central theme of Edward Said's *Beginnings* (New York: Basic Books, 1975), esp. pp. 226–28.

xii **erasers in order** "Homage to Sextus Propertius" (1917), lines 10–11; *Personae* (New York: Boni & Liveright, 1926), p. 207. The Latin equivalent is Propertius III. i. 7–8:

> a valeat, Phoebum quicumque moratur in armis!
> exactus tenui pumice versus eat

Pound has undoubtedly exaggerated Propertius' reservations about Virgil; see J. P. Sullivan, *Ezra Pound and Sextus Propertius* (Austin: University of Texas Press, 1964), pp. 74–76, 103.

Robert Graves "Careerists are the plague of poetry. . . . Good poets are exceedingly rare; 'great poets' are all too common" ("Legitimate Criticism of Poetry," in Graves' collected essays *On Poetry* [Garden City, N.Y.: Doubleday, 1969], p. 225). See also "The Anti-Poet," on Virgil, in the same volume, pp. 301–22. Winters' fullest statement on the superiority of short poems to long is "Problems for the Modern Critic of Literature" (1956), in his *The Function of Criticism* (London: Routledge & Kegan Paul, 1962), pp. 9–78.

xiii **a career ideal** The contrast between the publicist's and the craftsman's notions of careers, along with the many ironies that attend either choice, is brilliantly expressed by Pound's *Hugh Selwyn Mauberley* (1920).

BEGINNING

3 **"taking possession"** The phrase is Hunt's, *Lord Byron and Some of His Contemporaries* (London: H. Colburn, 1828), vol. 1, p. 410.

4 **a peak in Darien** *The Poems of John Keats,* ed. Jack Stillinger (Cambridge, Mass.: Harvard University Press, 1978), p. 64. Quotations from Keats' verse refer to this edition.

"personally itself" *The Letters of John Keats,* ed. H. E. Rollins (Cambridge, Mass.: Harvard University Press, 1958), vol. 2, p. 102. Hereafter cited as *Letters.*

"honourablest things" *An Apology for Smectymnuus* (1642), in *Complete Prose Works of John Milton,* ed. D. M. Wolfe (New Haven: Yale University Press, 1953), vol. 1, p. 890.

superb biographies A very short list must include Aileen Ward, *John Keats: The Making of a Poet* (New York: Viking, 1963); W. J. Bate, *John Keats* (Cambridge, Mass.: Harvard University Press, 1963); and Robert Gittings, *John Keats* (London: Heinemann, 1968). The work of Bate, in particular, has influenced my views not only of the life of Keats but of the life of the poet in general.

5 **"his first introduction"** Charles and Mary Cowden Clarke, *Recollections of Writers* (London: Low, Marston, Searle, & Rivington, 1878), p. 130.

"an Era in my existence" *Letters,* 1:113. The emergence of the poem from its sources has been traced by J. M. Murry, *Studies in Keats* (London: Oxford University Press, 1930), pp. 15–33; B. I. Evans, "Keats's Approach to the Chapman Sonnet," *Essays and Studies of the English Association* 16 (1931); C. L. Finney, The Evolution of Keats's Poetry (Cambridge, Mass.: Harvard University Press, 1936), pp. 124–27; and Carl Woodring, "On Looking into Keats's Voyagers," *Keats-Shelley Journal* 14 (1965): 15–22.

6 **"create itself"** 8 October 1818, *Letters,* 1:374.

"I now live" 27 October 1818, ibid., p. 378.

"into the Sea" 8 October 1818, ibid., p. 374.

"the heavens" John Bonnycastle, *An Introduction to Astronomy* (London: J. Johnson, 1811), p. 354.

7 **"golden world"** "A Defence of Poetry," *Miscellaneous Prose of Sir Philip Sidney,* ed. Katherine Duncan-Jones and Jan van Dorsten (Oxford: Clarendon Press, 1973), p. 78.

Clarke *Recollections of Writers,* pp. 128–30.

8 **no poison** The noun "serene" derives from Latin *serenum,* a clear sky, and poets like Thomson and Coleridge had already spoken of the "pure serene." The unusual image of *breathing* the serene, however, suggests that Keats may have been familiar with another "serene": a deadly mist supposed to descend after sunset (derived from French *serein* or Latin *seranum,* "evening"). This sense of the word was not uncommon among the Elizabethan poets admired by Keats; it occurs, for instance, in the double sestina of Sidney's *Old Arcadia,* lines 41–42, "I feele the comfort of the morning / Turnde to the mortall serene of an evening." Read this way, "pure serene" might be understood as an oxymoron: an innocuous noxious fume. Fancifully associated with the mist of influence or astral *influenza* (as Harold Bloom would call it), or with the "tutelary poison always to be breathed although we perish from it" *(un poison tutélaire / Toujours à respirer si nous en périssons),* which Mallarmé regards as all that survives of Baudelaire, the phrase would then evoke the double nature of Homeric influence—at once benevolent and deadly.

never look back Compare the exalted sight of the ocean of Poetry in "Chapman's Homer" with the crisis brought on by a similar vision in the contemporaneous "Sleep and Poetry":

An ocean dim, sprinkled with many an isle,
Spreads awfully before me. How much toil!
How many days! what desperate turmoil!
Ere I can have explored its widenesses.
Ah, what a task! upon my bended knees,
I could unsay those—no, impossible!
Impossible!

[306–12]

"Adam's dream" 22 November 1817, *Letters*, 1:185.

Robertson William Robertson, *The History of America* (London: A. Strahan, 1803), vol. 2, p. 314. The passage derives from Bernal Díaz' famous *Conquest of New Spain*.

9 **"in the grave"** "The Fall of Hyperion," Canto I, lines 16–18. "A balm," line 201.

"the time being" 3 May 1818, *Letters*, 1:281, 282.

10 **metamorphosis of the gods** See the fine accounts of the change by M. H. Abrams, *Natural Supernaturalism* (New York: Norton, 1971), and E. S. Shaffer, *"Kubla Khan" and the Fall of Jerusalem* (Cambridge, Eng.: At the University Press, 1975).

sixteen years later According to Frost himself, "The Tuft of Flowers" already existed in 1897, when it was submitted as a class exercise at Harvard. It was published first in *The Derry Enterprise*, 9 March 1906, and then in *A Boy's Will* (1913). The mixed reception of that book, according to the poet, provoked him to write many of the poems in *North of Boston* (1914), among them "Mending Wall." See Lawrance Thompson, *Robert Frost: The Early Years* (New York: Holt, Rinehart & Winston, 1966), pp. 318, 432, 562.

Frost becomes Frost As more than one critic has pointed out, the "Something there is that doesn't like a wall" is veritably frost.

INITIATION

13 **Blake's designs** *Illustrations to the Divine Comedy of Dante by William Blake* (London: National Art-Collections Fund, 1922). Albert Roe, *Blake's Illustrations to the Divine Comedy* (Princeton, N.J.: Princeton University Press, 1953), supplies a useful commentary.

Vanni Fucci *Inferno* xxix. 97–129.

Plate 84 *Purgatorio* xxvii. 1–18.

14 **Olivia Shakespear** 27 October 1927, *The Letters of W. B. Yeats,* ed. Allan Wade (London: Hart-Davis, 1954), p. 731.

"wing on wing" For the revisions see *The Variorum Edition of the Poems of W. B. Yeats*, ed. Peter Allt and R. K. Alspach (New York: Macmillan, 1957), pp. 124–25.

an imaginative art *Essays and Introductions* (London: Macmillan, 1961), p. 130. In 1924 Yeats added a postscript to this essay, originally written in 1897, for a new edition of *Ideas of Good and Evil*.

15 " 'infinite and holy' " *Essays and Introductions,* p. 140.

"In my beginning is my end." The opening of Eliot's *East Coker* reverses the motto of Mary Stuart, "En ma fin est mon commencement."

Bengali See "Who Sits behind My Eyes," *A Tagore Testament,* tr. Indu Dutt (London: Meridian, 1953), pp. 3–23.

16 "Book of Memory" C. S. Singleton, *An Essay on the "Vita Nuova"* (Cambridge, Mass.: Harvard University Press, 1949), pp. 27 ff.

"Book of Revelation" Barbara Nolan, "The *Vita Nuova:* Dante's Book of Revelation," *Dante Studies* 88 (1970): 51–77.

principia S. Foster Damon, *A Blake Dictionary* (Providence, R.I.: Brown University Press, 1965), p. 262.

anatomy Northrop Frye classified the *Marriage* as a satire like those of Rabelais and Apuleius in *Fearful Symmetry* (Princeton, N.J.: Princeton University Press, 1947), pp. 193–201, and defined the Menippean mode in *Anatomy of Criticism* (Princeton N.J.: Princeton University Press, 1957), pp. 308–12; Harold Bloom applied the term to the *Marriage* in *Blake's Apocalypse* (Garden City, N.Y.: Doubleday, 1963), pp. 71–72.

alphabet Letters, pp. 624–27.

"marmoreal reverie" Harold Bloom, *Yeats* (New York: Oxford University Press, 1970), p. 179.

"youth" Italian scholars tend to insist on the restricted meaning of the title, though English-speaking scholars often read it allegorically. J. E. Shaw devotes one of his *Essays on the "Vita Nuova"* (Princeton, N.J.: Princeton University Press, 1929) to the question.

Portrait The beginning of this century was a particularly fertile period for such works. A short list might include, in addition to Yeats and Joyce, Rilke's *Notebooks of Malte Laurids Brigge* (1910), Pound's *Hugh Selwyn Mauberley* (1920), and William Carlos Williams' *Spring and All* (1923).

17 "lead or iron" *Biographia Literaria,* ed. J. Shawcross (London: Oxford University Press, 1907), vol. 2, p. 116. Coleridge refers specifically to Boethius' *Consolation of Philosophy.*

Singleton *Essay on the "Vita Nuova,"* pp. 25–54.

18 whole libraries Yeats' encyclopedic drawing of a twenty-two-petaled Cabbalistic rose has been described by Donald Pearce, quoted by Helen Vendler, *Yeats's "Vision" and the Later Plays* (Cambridge, Mass.: Harvard University Press, 1963), pp. 14–15.

"to write criticism" *The Stubborn Structure* (Ithaca, N.Y.: Cornell University Press, 1970), p. 176.

19 "dead and gone" "September 1913," Yeats' *Poems,* pp. 289–90.

"a morning star" The last line of *Walden.* It may be worth noting how many of Milton's major poems end with a similar glance at the future.

20 "metaphors for poetry" *A Vision* (New York: Macmillan, 1956), p. 8.

"those histories" *A Vision*, p. 9.

21 **"do the same"** *La Vita Nuova* xxv. 8 (my translation). The standard text of the *Vita Nuova* is the critical edition by Michele Barbi, *Le Opere di Dante*, 2d ed. (Florence: Società Dantesca Italiana, 1960). The edition by Kenneth McKenzie (Boston: Heath, 1922) supplies an English introduction, notes, and vocabulary. Among English translations, the free version by D. G. Rossetti (1861) retains historical interest, especially for students of Yeats; there is a graceful rendering by Barbara Reynolds in Penguin Classics (1969); and Mark Musa (Bloomington: Indiana University Press, 1973) includes extensive if tendentious notes.

ragione *Razos,* brief biographical comments on the poet's life, often accompany Provençal poetry, which many scholars believe may have influenced Dante. For a good summary of the issues, see Silvio Pellegrini, "Dante e la tradizione poetica volgare dai provenzali ai guittoniani," in *Dante nella critica d'oggi,* ed. Umberto Bosco (Florence: Le Monnier, 1965), pp. 27–35.

Cavalcanti On the relation of Dante to his predecessors and contemporaries, see Domenico De Robertis, *Il libro della "Vita Nuova"* (Florence: Sansoni, 1961), and Mario Marti, *Con Dante fra i poeti del suo tempo* (Lecce: Edizioni Milella, 1971).

a real woman The discussion by Erich Auerbach, *Dante: Poet of the Secular World,* tr. Ralph Manheim (Chicago: University of Chicago Press, 1961), pp. 60–63, first published in 1929, is interesting not only in itself but in its anticipation of Auerbach's later influential notion of "Figura" (1944) in *Scenes from the Drama of European Literature* (New York: Meridian, 1959), pp. 73–76.

23 **"you were raving"** "sol c'hai farneticato, sappie, intendo," in *Dante's Lyric Poetry,* ed. K. Foster and P. Boyde [Oxford: Clarendon Press, 1967], vol. 1, pp. 16–17. This text also prints the other replies, with translations and notes.

speculations Two currently popular interpretations view the sonnet as a Freudian dream of sex or sexual anxiety (see G. B. Squarotti, "L' 'ambiguità' della *Vita Nuova,*" *Psicoanalisi e Strutturalismo di fronte a Dante* 3 [1972]: 38–40) or as a religious allegory (see Barbara Nolan, "The *Vita Nuova* and Richard of St. Victor's Phenomenology of Vision," *Dante Studies* 92 [1974]: 37–44). These two views roughly correspond to the first responses by Da Maiano and Cavalcanti. J. T. S. Wheelock, "A Function of the *Amore* Figure in the *Vita Nuova,*" *Romanic Review* 68 (1977): 276–86, suggests that Dante's Love draws together the erotic and religious traditions of love poetry.

24 **glorified** The point is strongly emphasized by Singleton, *An Essay on the "Vita Nuova,"* pp. 6–24.

prove him a poet See J. A. Mazzeo, *Structure and Thought in the "Paradiso"* (Ithaca, N.Y.: Cornell University Press, 1958), pp. 25–49.

dreams or poems On the *Vita Nuova* as a visionary initiation, see Nicolò Mineo, *Profetismo e Apocalittica in Dante* (Catania: Università di Catania, 1968), pp. 103–41.

25 **great cruxes** For instance, J. E. Shaw's interpretation in *Essays on the "Vita Nuova,"* pp. 77–108, has been contradicted by Singleton, "*Vita Nuova* XII: Love's Obscure Words," *Romanic Review* 36 (1945): 89–102, and "The Use of Latin in the 'Vita Nuova,'" *MLN* 61 (1946): 108–12, replied to in turn by Shaw, " 'Ego Tanquam Centrum Circuli Etc.,' *Vita Nuova* XII," *Italica* 24 (1947): 113–18.

26 *la gente* xix. 5. On the relation of love to wisdom, see Kenelm Foster, "The Mind in Love: Dante's Philosophy," in *Dante: A Collection of Critical Essays,* ed. John Freccero (Englewood Cliffs, N.J.: Prentice-Hall, 1965), pp. 43–60.

27 **sweet new style** See J. A. Scott, "Dante's 'Sweet New Style' and the *Vita Nuova,*" *Italica* 42 (1965): 98–107.

new poetic heights Recent discussions of the crucial exchange between Dante and Bonagiunta include Giuseppe Mazzotta, "Dante's Literary Typology," *MLN* 87 (1972): 1–19, and M. D. B. Templer, *Itinerario di Amore: dialettica di Amore e Morte nella "Vita Nuova"* (Chapel Hill: University of North Carolina Press, 1973), pp. 64–79.

Guido Cavalcanti See Bruno Nardi, "Dante e Guido Cavalcanti," *Giornale Storico della Letteratura Italiana* 139 (1962): 481–512.

"miter thee" *Purgatorio* XXVII. 142.

28 **never-to-be-named ladies** The traditions of love poetry forbade such naming. Cavalcanti himself, it may be noted, had never mentioned Giovanna, and Dante refers to Beatrice's name in no other poem written before her death.

religious allegory Singleton's *Essay on the "Vita Nuova,"* pp. 20–24, stresses the importance of this transformation.

29 **"held in disdain"** *Inferno* X. 58–63.

one True Light See Carl Stange, *Beatrice in Dantes Jugenddichtung* (Göttingen: Musterschmidt-Verlag, 1959), esp. pp. 216–51.

donna gentile For a clear statement of the problems, see Umberto Cosmo, *A Handbook to Dante Studies,* tr. David Moore (Oxford: Blackwell, 1950), pp. 36–38.

30 **toward better reason** The case for an ironic reading of Dante the protagonist by Dante the author is strongly urged by Musa in the essay accompanying his translation, pp. 168–74.

31 **"in the *Vita Nuova*"** *Convivio* II. 13.

the lady Philosophy See J. E. Shaw, *The Lady "Philosophy" in the "Convivio"* (Cambridge, Mass.: Dante Society, 1938), and Etienne Gilson, *Dante the Philosopher,* tr. David Moore (London: Sheed & Ward, 1948), pp. 86–98.

a literary method H. R. Patch has noted the relation of Dante to *The Tradition of Boethius* (New York: Oxford University Press, 1935).

ordering the poems Various arrangements are discussed by Kenneth McKenzie, "The Symmetrical Structure of Dante's *Vita Nuova,*" *PMLA* 18 (1903): 341–55.

33 **the greater love** B. S. Levy, in "Beatrice's Greeting and Dante's 'Sigh' in the *Vita Nuova*," *Dante Studies* 92 (1974): 53–62, associates Dante's sigh with Christ's breathing-out of the Holy Spirit.

one bewilderment for another On the difficulties of rendering a vision, see Mazzeo, *Structure and Thought in the "Paradiso,"* pp. 84–110.

the present tense See Robert Hollander, "*Vita Nuova:* Dante's Perceptions of Beatrice," *Dante Studies* 92 (1974): 11–12.

34 **"where I read white"** "The Everlasting Gospel," in *William Blake's Writings,* ed. G. E. Bentley, Jr. (Oxford: Clarendon Press, 1978), p. 1058. Hereafter cited as *Writings*.

he prepares the way of the Lord The reference to John was omitted, along with many other allusions to Scripture, from the first edition of *La Vita Nuova* (1576). After the Council of Trent such allusions were considered sacrilegious.

a youthful John the Baptist The face resembles Blake's own; it might be considered a kind of signature, since his name does not appear.

35 **prophecy in his heart** Blake associates the Voice with the prophet Isaiah (40:3), its first source, more often than with John (1:23).

he being the Poetic Genius Principles 5–7, *Writings,* pp. 19–21.

"Genesis or Exodus" *Writings,* pp. 1413, 1418. The whole set of annotations (1798) is relevant to the *Marriage;* cf. "The Bible or Peculiar Word of God, Exclusive of Conscience or the Word of God Universal, is that Abomination which like the Jewish ceremonies is for ever removed & henceforth every man may converse with God & be a King & Priest in his own House" (p. 1414).

making the Bible anew John Beer discusses the evolution of Blake's attitudes toward the Bible in *Blake's Visionary Universe* (Manchester, Eng.: University of Manchester Press, 1969), pp. 30–38.

Swedenborg On Blake's debt to Swedenborg, see J. G. Davies, *The Theology of William Blake* (Oxford: Clarendon Press, 1948), pp. 31–53.

36 **Blake's subject and his object** In *Blake's Visionary Forms Dramatic,* ed. David Erdman and John Grant (Princeton, N.J.: Princeton University Press, 1970), p. 64, Grant has noted that the *Marriage* "is about the education of the Prophetic Character." The word "about," however, needs qualification: the *Marriage is* that education and that prophecy.

its essential point The appendix to Morton Paley's *Energy and Imagination: A Study of the Development of Blake's Thought* (Oxford: Clarendon Press, 1970), pp. 261–62, anticipates my argument in some respects.

Bishop Lowth Robert Lowth, *De sacra poesi Hebraeorum* (Oxford: Clarendon Press, 1753). The influence of Lowth's theory of "parallelism" on Blake is discussed by Murray Roston, *Prophet and Poet* (Evanston: Northwestern University Press, 1965), pp. 133–42, 159–71.

37 **"loss of Eden"** *Paradise Lost* I. 1–4.

the etching of the Argument My analysis presupposes that Blake's illuminated works must be read and studied in their original form: plates containing both pictures and texts. A good facsimile of *The Marriage of Heaven and Hell* is now available at a reasonable price (ed. Geoffrey Keynes; New York: Oxford University Press, 1975).

is it fruit? Fewer than half of the nine surviving copies of the *Marriage* support such a hypothesis, according to David Erdman (with Tom Dargan and Marlene Deverell-Van Meter), "Reading the Illuminations of Blake's *Marriage of Heaven and Hell*," in *William Blake: Essays in Honour of Sir Geoffrey Keynes,* ed. M. D. Paley and Michael Phillips (Oxford: Clarendon Press, 1973), p. 170.

a fortunate Fall? John Grant makes the case for this reading in a note on "Regeneration in *The Marriage of Heaven and Hell*," in *William Blake: Essays for S. Foster Damon,* ed. A. H. Rosenfeld (Providence, R.I.: Brown University Press, 1969), pp. 366–67.

39 **revolution is in the air** For a political reading of "The Argument," see David Erdman, *Blake: Prophet against Empire* (Princeton, N.J.: Princeton University Press, 1977), pp. 189–92.

its shocking humor The scourging apocalyptic rowdiness of the *Marriage* is stressed by Northrop Frye, *Fearful Symmetry,* pp. 200–201.

40 **to study with him** "I found them blind, I taught them how to see / And now they know neither themselves nor me" (Blake's Notebook, *Writings,* p. 945).

correcting Milton's version On the place of Milton in the *Marriage,* see J. A. Wittreich, Jr., *Angel of Apocalypse: Blake's Idea of Milton* (Madison, Wis.: University of Wisconsin Press, 1975), pp. 199–219.

"Go out" "Auguries of Innocence," lines 109–10, *Writings,* p. 1315.

"of his cavern" Plate 14. Blake revised Plate 11 more thoroughly than any other in the *Marriage;* see Erdman, "Reading the Illuminations," pp. 185–88.

"the Holy Ghost" *Writings,* p. 1340.

41 **"to have been"** *Writings,* pp. 1343–44.

42 **sting and taunt** Harold Bloom analyzes the Proverbs' ability "to break down orthodox categories of thought and morality" in *Blake's Apocalypse,* pp. 85–89.

Chatterton "How dydd I know thatt ev'ry darte / Thatt cutte the airie waie / Myghte notte fynde passage toe my harte / And close myne eyes for aie?" "Bristowe Tragedie," lines 133–36.

marriage of text and picture See W. J. T. Mitchell, *Blake's Composite Art* (Princeton, N.J.: Princeton University Press, 1978), pp. 3–39. I have discussed the designs at greater length in "Blake's Initiation: The Marriage of Heaven and Hell," in *Woman in the 18th Century and Other Essays,* ed. Paul Fritz and Richard Morton (Toronto: Hakkert, 1976), pp. 217–43.

"a Printing house in Hell" David Erdman's note, "The Cave in the Chambers," in *William Blake: Essays for S. Foster Damon,* pp. 410–13, ties the plate to Blake's own practice.

43 **chain of inspiration** In his commentary on Plate 15 in *The Illuminated Blake* (Garden City, N.Y.: Doubleday, 1974), pp. 112–13, Erdman stresses the positive implications of marrying the snake and bird—body and soul, craft and genius.

44 **"the Prophetic Characters"** Blake's Notebook, p. 83, in *Writings,* p. 1019. The preceding passage draws a clear moral: "If the Spectator could Enter into these Images in his Imagination approaching them on the Fiery Chariot of his Contemplative Thought . . . then would he arise from his Grave then would he meet the Lord in the Air & then he would be happy"; *Writings,* p. 1018.

"five prophets" Erdman, *The Illuminated Blake,* p. 121.

"another Mans" *Jerusalem,* Plate 10, line 20, *Writings,* p. 435.

45 **a single book** "A Song of Liberty" has often been regarded as a work separate from the *Marriage;* André Gide's charming translation (1922), for instance, omits the "Song," and the politics seem to date from 1792–93 rather than 1790. But all nine known copies of the *Marriage* include the "Song," and Blake did not publish the *Marriage* before 1793. The textual evidence, therefore, supports my argument from internal evidence: without the "Song" the *Marriage* would not be complete.

Book of Revelation In *Angel of Apocalypse,* Wittreich argues that the *Marriage* is a prophecy "whose structure is modeled upon that of the Book of Revelation" (p. 192). That seems to me untrue in any but a teleological sense.

46 **liberty can dawn** Cf. Erdman's political reading of the "Song," *Prophet against Empire,* pp. 192–95.

harvests to come The last line of the "Song of Liberty" is repeated in the two works that immediately followed it: *Visions of the Daughters of Albion* (1793), Plate 8, line 10, and *America a Prophecy* (1793), Plate 8, line 13.

47 **"that I remake"** *The Variorum Edition of the Poems of W. B. Yeats,* p. 778.

his late twenties Though the date of *La Vita Nuova* is still disputed, there is general agreement that Dante conceived the work about 1292, when he was twenty-seven.

the new discovery According to the classic *Life of William Blake* by Alexander Gilchrist (London: Macmillan, 1863), vol. 1, p. 69, Blake's new process was directly inspired by his dead brother: "In a vision of the night, the form of Robert stood before him, and revealed the wished-for secret."

48 **"into Paradise"** *Marriage*, Plate 3.

"the Artery" *Milton*, Plate 28, lines 1–3, *Writings*, p. 380.

"may find his pardon" *Mythologies* (London: Macmillan, 1959), pp. 331–33. Page numbers in the text refer to this edition.

49 **in his early fifties** Though sections of *Per Amica* date back at least to 1908–9, when Yeats compiled the journal eventually published in *Memoirs* (ed. Denis Donoghue [London: Macmillan, 1972]), he did not shape those thoughts into a book until after his fiftieth birthday, in 1915. *Per Amica* was finished in 1917 and published in January 1918.

"management of men" "The Fascination of What's Difficult" (1910), *Variorum*, p. 260.

"night and morning" "The People" (1916), *Variorum Yeats*, p. 171.

"uphold the world" "Ireland and the Arts" (1901), in *Essays and Introductions* (London: Macmillan, 1961), p. 210.

50 **"an European pose"** "Reveries over Childhood and Youth" (1914), in *Autobiographies* (London: Macmillan, 1926), p. 126.

"workaday Western world" Yeats quotes this, disapprovingly, from Arnold Toynbee in "A General Introduction for My Work" (1937), *Essays and Introductions*, p. 517.

might have told him Both men later disputed the remark; see Richard Ellmann, *Eminent Domain* (New York: Oxford University Press, 1967), pp. 37–38.

"set in the past" *The Letters of Ezra Pound, 1907–1941*, ed. D. D. Paige (London: Faber & Faber, 1951), p. 58.

"clear and natural" Quoted by A. N. Jeffares, *W. B. Yeats: Man and Poet* (New Haven: Yale University Press, 1949), p. 167.

"united by affection" Introduction to *A Vision* (New York: Macmillan, 1956), p. 3.

the occult See *Yeats and the Occult*, ed. G. M. Harper (Toronto: Macmillan, 1975).

51 **"your grovelling"** 25 July 1914, *Letters to W. B. Yeats*, ed. R. J. Finneran, G. M. Harper, and W. M. Murphy (New York: Columbia University Press, 1977), vol. 1, p. 297.

never happens *Autobiographies*, pp. 131–32.

proposed marriage Joseph Hone, *W. B. Yeats, 1865–1939* (London: Macmillan, 1967), pp. 302–6.

completed two years earlier According to M. C. Flannery, *Yeats and Magic: The Earlier Works* (New York: Harper & Row, 1978), p. 144, "manuscript evidence definitely indicates Yeats wrote it in 1912." Flannery transcribes an early draft, previously dated October 1915, but does not specify the evidence for dating it 1912. In any case, Yeats' final drafts of "Ego Dominus Tuus" are dated 5 December 1915, and he did not publish the poem until 1917.

the turn in his career See H. J. Levine, "Yeats at the Crossroads: The Debate of Self and Anti-Self in 'Ego Dominus Tuus,'" *Modern Language Quarterly* 39 (1978): 132–53.

52 *your blood and mine* *Variorum Yeats*, p. 270.

losing it in yearning Harold Bloom reads these lines in an antithetical way, as an ironic tribute to "the wisdom presumably of nineteenth-century liberal humanism, of those who could find themselves and not an image" (*Yeats*, p. 199). This seems a deliberate contradiction of the text.

"that beating breast" "Michael Robartes and the Dancer"(1920), *Variorum Yeats*, p. 386.

"Hic" and "Willie" Ellmann, *Eminent Domain*, p. 71. At the time when Yeats finished the poem, Pound was still serving as his secretary.

53 **belong to Ille** See Flannery, *Yeats and Magic,* pp. 135–36.

"a peasant" *Mythologies*, p. 271. On the use of Robartes in general, see M. J. Sidnell, "Mr. Yeats, Michael Robartes and Their Circle," in *Yeats and the Occult*, pp. 225–54.

54 **told it in *A Vision*** Pp. 8–25. Cf. B. S. Webster, *Yeats: A Psychoanalytic Study* (Stanford: Stanford University Press, 1973), pp. 169–72.

"rich, dark nothing" "The Gyres," *Variorum*, p. 565.

55 **"thine own soul within thee"** *The Works of Dante Gabriel Rossetti,* ed. W. M. Rossetti (London: Ellis, 1911), p. 553.

"some other Body" 27 October 1818, Keats' *Letters*, ed. H. E. Rollins (Cambridge, Mass.: Harvard University Press, 1958), vol. 1, p. 387.

56 **dark side of the mind** Robert Langbaum, *The Mysteries of Identity* (New York: Oxford University Press, 1977), pp. 158–74, discusses Yeats' search for an exterior self in *Per Amica.*

Great Memory The relations among the Platonic World Soul, Yeats' Great Memory, and Jung's collective unconscious are remarked by James Olney, "The Esoteric Flower: Yeats and Jung," in *Yeats and the Occult*, pp. 27–54.

57 **"roots of the hair"** *Autobiographies*, p. 395.

"luminous circle" Ibid., p. 396.

murdered by drowning "Clair de Lune," in Hugo's *Oeuvres Poétiques*, ed. Pierre Albouy (Paris: Gallimard, 1964), vol. 1, pp. 622–23. The poem derives from a similar incident in Byron's *Giaour,* supposed to be based on the Turkish punishment for infidelity.

the stigmata *"Per Amica Silentia,"* in *Parallèlement*, Verlaine's *Oeuvres Complètes* (Paris: A. Messein, 1908), vol. 2, p. 222.

"with the beasts" *Autobiographies*, pp. 421–22.

58 **from Verlaine** Ibid., p. 421.

"combat with circumstance" *A Vision*, p. 8.

cycles of history The comparison of Blake's wheel with Yeats' gyres is a central theme of Hazard Adams' *Blake and Yeats: The Contrary Vision* (Ithaca, N.Y.: Cornell University Press, 1955) and an important part of T. R. Whitaker's *Swan and Shadow: Yeats's Dialogue with History* (Chapel Hill: University of North Carolina Press, 1964).

59 **"sink in and forget"** "Introduction to *The Cat and the Moon*," *Explorations* (London: Macmillan, 1962), pp. 403–4. The poem and play of "The Cat and the Moon" were inspired by an incident recounted as the Prologue to *Per Amica* in 1917.

"more ancient world" *Memoirs*, p. 124.

60 **"impulse to create"** To J. B. Yeats, 14 June 1917, *Letters*, p. 627.

"fill the cradles right" "Under Ben Bulben," line 41, *Variorum Yeats*, p. 638.

"not less than everything" "Little Gidding," *Collected Poems, 1909–1962*, by T. S. Eliot (London: Faber & Faber, 1963), pp. 222–23.

61 **material for a new poem** Connections between sections of *Per Amica* and individual poems are traced at length by H. J. Levine, " 'Meditation upon a Mask': *Per Amica Silentia Lunae* and the Middle Poems and Plays of William Butler Yeats" (unpublished Ph.D. dissertation, Princeton University, 1977).

62 **"meanness of culture"** "William Blake" (1920), *Selected Essays* (London: Faber & Faber, 1951), p. 321.

obeyed his call *Variorum Yeats*, p. 576.

or to God *Collected Poems*, p. 199. The two passages are associated by Helen Gardner, *The Composition of "Four Quartets"* (London: Faber & Faber, 1978), p. 68.

"In a different form" "The Dry Salvages," *Collected Poems*, p. 208.

63 **to face the change** "Yeats," *On Poetry and Poets* (New York: Farrar, Straus & Cudahy, 1957), p. 301.

procession of ancestors A partial list of those suggested might include Shelley, T. E. Hulme, Swift, Mallarmé, Milton, Shakespeare, Tennyson, Laforgue, Henry James, Ezra Pound, and Samuel Johnson. Eliot himself admitted his indebtedness to Dante and Yeats; the lecture on Yeats was drafted on the same notepad used for drafts of *Little Gidding*. Gardner (p. 69) concludes that "at the close Eliot combines Dante with Yeats."

HARMONIUM

65 **"grossen Konfession"** *Dichtung und Wahrheit*, Book 7, in *Goethes Werke*, ed. Erich Trunz (Hamburg: Christian Wegner, 1949), vol. 9, p. 283.

66 **"his whole work"** "What Is Minor Poetry?" *On Poetry and Poets*, p. 47. "What Is a Classic?" follows immediately in the same volume, pp. 52–74.

"are readjusted" *Selected Essays*, p. 15.

"his place among the great" In Bernard Gheerbrant's catalogue of *James Joyce* (Paris: La Hune, 1949).

67 **"cease to matter"** All quotations in this paragraph appear in "East Coker," parts 2 and 5.

a face still forming *Collected Poems*, p. 217.

talking to himself Eliot's own comment that the passage contrasts Dante with "a hallucinated scene after an air-raid" ("What Dante Means to Me" [1950], in *To Criticize the Critic* [New York: Farrar, Straus & Giroux, 1965], p. 128) suggests that the bombing may have induced shell shock. On an earlier occasion, however, Eliot had emphasized the dangerous closeness of poetic dream-visions to hallucinations: "Note sur Mallarmé et Poe," tr. Ramon Fernandez, *Nouvelle Revue Française* 27 (1926): 524–26. In "A Note on *Little Gidding*," *Essays in Criticism* 25 (1975): 145–53, Christopher Ricks has argued that Eliot's "Note" anticipates the world of phantoms in "Little Gidding." The hallucinatory effect of being inhabited by another poet may be compared with my own discussion of Mallarmé's "Le Tombeau d'Edgar Poe" in part III, below.

68 **words in pain** John of Gaunt in *King Richard II*, II. i. 5–8.

"but to die" Reported (January 1744) by Joseph Spence, *Observations, Anecdotes, and Characters of Books and Men,* ed. J. M. Osborn (Oxford: Clarendon Press, 1966), vol. 1, p. 258.

"for other compositions" "Life of Milton," *Lives of the English Poets,* ed. G. B. Hill (Oxford: Clarendon Press, 1905), vol. 1, p. 170.

69 **survives from antiquity** The attribution dates from the second century A.D., when Suetonius reported hearing (at second hand) that Varius, Virgil's executor and editor, had removed the lines. Servius (fourth century) confirms the story, but the lines are not found in any ancient manuscript of the *Aeneid*. For the case against including them, see R. G. Austin, *"Ille Ego Qui Quondam," Classical Quarterly* 18 (1968): 107–15.

"sing unbidden" "non iniussa cano," *Eclogues* VI. 9.

70 **"ch'io vidi"** "O Muses, o high genius, . . / o memory which recorded what I saw" (*Inferno* II. 7–8). The delay of the invocation to Canto II probably indicates that Canto I is to be regarded as a prologue to the *Commedia* as a whole. It may also be worth noting that Statius, who succeeds Virgil in the *Commedia* as in life, ends the *Thebaid* with a personal avowal of his inferiority to the divine *Aeneid*.

his own left foot Blake's *Milton,* Plate 3, lines 1–10, Plate 14, lines 47–50, Plate 19, lines 4–14 (*Writings,* pp. 319, 348, 358).

Cavafy See Edmund Keeley, *Cavafy's Alexandria* (Cambridge, Mass.: Harvard University Press, 1976), pp. 135–52.

the unity of the world See E. R. Curtius, *European Literature and the Latin Middle Ages,* tr. W. R. Trask (New York: Pantheon, 1953), pp. 302–47.

"insects have sprung" To Harriet Monroe, 28 October 1922, *Letters of Wallace Stevens,* ed. Holly Stevens (New York: Knopf, 1966), p. 231.

USE HARMONIUM To Alfred A. Knopf, 23 March and 18 May, 1923, *Letters,* pp. 237–38.

W. S. To Herbert Weinstock, 6 May 1954, *Letters,* p. 831.

71 **"Negation"** *The Collected Poems of Wallace Stevens* (New York: Knopf, 1955), p. 97. For the circumstances of composition, see A. W. Litz, *Introspective Voyager: The Poetic Development of Wallace Stevens* (New York: Oxford University Press, 1972), pp. 71–77, 313.

"a supreme Fiction" *Collected Poems,* p. 403.

the whole poem R. A. Blessing, *Wallace Stevens' "Whole Harmonium"* (Syracuse, N.Y.: Syracuse University Press, 1970), attempts to read Stevens' *Collected Poems* as a single, unified, grand poem" (p. ix).

72 **"try to sleep"** The end of Browning's "Abt Vogler," *Dramatis Personae* (1864).

"While the music lasts" "The Dry Salvages," *Collected Poems,* p. 213.

"under the burden" "Burnt Norton," *Collected Poems,* p. 194.

Alice in Wonderland Eliot's own comparison; see the comments by L. L. Martz in *T. S. Eliot: A Selected Critique,* ed. Leonard Unger (New York: Rinehart, 1948), pp. 448–49.

Kipling's "They" Eliot's comparison of another Kipling story "with the opening passages of *Alice in Wonderland*: both depict external events which have exact nightmare correspondence to some spiritual terror" ("Rudyard Kipling" [1941], in *On Poetry and Poets,* p. 279n.) would apply equally well to "They" and "Burnt Norton."

73 **"that kind of poet"** *On Poetry and Poets,* pp. 301–2.

"shall survive or perish" *Reunion by Destruction: Reflections on a Scheme for Church Union in South India* (London: Pax House, 1943), p. 1. Cf. "The Classics and the Man of Letters" (1942) in *To Criticize the Critic,* pp. 145–61.

74 **"where one starts from"** From the conclusion to "East Coker."

"born with the dead" From the conclusion to "Little Gidding."

the poet's last testament Some critics would reserve that place for *The Elder Statesman* (1958)—though at the cost of allowing Eliot to empty his career of significance. See A. D. Moody, *Thomas Stearns Eliot: Poet* (Cambridge, Eng.: At the University Press, 1979), 279–85.

like Yeats before him Though "A Note on War Poetry" (*Collected Poems,* pp. 229–30) was written for a patriotic anthology, *London Calling,* ed. Storm

Jameson (New York: Harper & Bros., 1942), it seems more properly a response to Yeats' notorious attack on both Eliot and war poetry in the Introduction to *The Oxford Book of Modern Verse* (Oxford: Clarendon Press, 1936), pp. xxi–xxiii, xxxiv–xxxv. Against Yeats' charge that contemporary poets merely combine Eliot's "accurate record of the relevant facts" with the passive suffering of the war poets, Eliot maintains that the facts and the suffering can become poetry when they "create the universal, originate a symbol."

75 **"surrender of others"** "Johnson as Critic and Poet" (1944), *On Poetry and Poets*, p. 191.

"the complete man" "Virgil and the Christian World" (1951), *On Poetry and Poets*, p. 141. As Eliot himself admitted, his vision of a Virgil close to *anima naturaliter Christiana* is strongly influenced by Theodor Haecker, *Virgil, Father of the West*, tr. A. W. Wheen (New York: Sheed & Ward, 1934).

fired his lightnings *The Georgics of Virgil*, tr. C. Day Lewis (London: Jonathan Cape, 1940), p. 95.

over the original "The *Georgics*, as a technical treatise on farming, are both difficult and dull. . . . I shall only recommend them in the translation of Mr. Day Lewis" (*On Poetry and Poets*, p. 140).

"Dedicatory Stanzas" Lewis' *Georgics*, pp. 9–11.

76 **"who is right"** *On Poetry and Poets*, p. 142.

"a poet of unique destiny" "What Is a Classic?" in *On Poetry and Poets*, pp. 70–71. Eliot's observations on the classicism of Virgil furnish the starting place for Frank Kermode's interesting sketch of *The Classic* (New York: Viking, 1975).

"a new beginning" *On Poetry and Poets*, p. 143.

"conquered the world" *Georgics* I. 145–46. The early lives of Virgil have been edited by Colin Hardie, *Vitae Vergilianae antiquae* (Oxford: Clarendon Press, 1954). Useful modern biographies include Karl Büchner, *P. Vergilius Maro, der Dichter der Römer* (Stuttgart: A. Druckenmüller, 1955), and Tenney Frank, *Vergil* (New York: Henry Holt, 1922).

77 **"wheel" or pattern** The notion of "Virgil's wheel," dividing all poetry into a threefold hierarchy, was developed by medieval rhetoricians on the basis of ancient sources (especially Donatus) and further codified by sixteenth-century Italian critics, beginning with Badius Ascensius (1500). A full study of the "wheel" remains to be written, but see Bernard Weinberg, *A History of Literary Criticism in the Italian Renaissance* (Chicago: University of Chicago Press, 1961), vol. 1, pp. 82–84.

leaders The authorship of the epitaph is disputed, though it was attributed to Virgil himself in the oldest surviving life (Suetonius-Donatus) and was inscribed on his tomb near Naples.

Appendix Vergiliana Of the twenty-seven poems in the collection, few scholars currently accept more than a handful as Virgil's own work. The internal evidence is thoroughly discussed by Büchner in *P. Vergilius Maro*, pp. 41–160.

carmine Calliope Catalepton XV, ed. J. A. Richmond, in *Appendix Vergiliana* (Oxford: Clarendon Press, 1966), p. 146. The attribution to Virgil is usually doubted, and that to Varius is also doubtful despite the putative pun on *vario*.

78 **"Homer of a line"** "Suetonius' " Life of Virgil, in the Loeb Classical Library *Suetonius*, edited by J. C. Rolfe (Cambridge, Mass.: Harvard University Press, 1914) vol. 2, p. 482 (my translation). This life, our best source of information about Virgil, is now generally believed to have been extracted by Aelius Donatus (fourth century), with some additions, from an earlier life by Suetonius (ca. 100 A.D.).

the challenge that he poses Virgil's challenging of his predecessors is strongly emphasized by E. K. Rand, *The Magical Art of Virgil* (Cambridge, Mass.: Harvard University Press, 1931).

part of itself Carthage was the exception, of course, for both Rome and the *Aeneid*.

Reverence for Homer Virgil's use of and divergence from the *Odyssey* and *Iliad* is the central theme of Brooks Otis' *Virgil: A Study in Civilized Poetry* (Oxford: Clarendon Press, 1963).

"they had to refer" E. R. Curtius, *Essays on European Literature*, tr. Michael Kowal (Princeton N.J.: Princeton University Press, 1973), p. 7.

Propertius announced "cedite Romani scriptores, cedite Grai! / nescio quid maius nascitur Iliade," *Elegies* II. xxxiv. 65–66.

"threatening in jest" "minacibus per iocum," Suetonius 31 (Loeb vol. 2, p. 474).

79 **" 'tis all exactly planned"** Spence's *Observations*, 1:153. Pope's plan has been analyzed, with reference to the *Aeneid*, by D. J. Torchiana, "Brutus: Pope's Last Hero," *Journal of English and Germanic Philology* 61 (1962): 853–67, and, with reference to his life-work, by Miriam Leranbaum, *Alexander Pope's "Opus Magnum," 1729–1744* (Oxford: Clarendon Press, 1977), pp. 155–74.

80 **columns should arrive** Suetonius 23–25 (Loeb vol. 2, p. 472).

most scholars would agree For a brief survey and evaluation of theories about Virgil's plan, see Otis' *Virgil*, pp. 415–20.

a precise arithmetic Though the calculations of G. E. Duckworth, *Structural Patterns and Proportions in Vergil's "Aeneid"* (Ann Arbor: University of Michigan Press, 1962), have not been generally accepted, many other scholars have been led to make their own computations. Cf. W. F. J. Knight on "Vergil's Secret Art," *Roman Vergil* (Harmondsworth: Penguin Books, 1966), pp. 419–39.

a blueprint Duckworth's schemata, pp. 1–19, may be balanced by the more tempered account of W. A. Camps, *An Introduction to Virgil's "Aeneid"* (London: Oxford University Press, 1969), pp. 51–60.

81 **"genitore petivi"** "I yielded and, lifting up my father, set out for the mountains" (II. 804). *The Aeneid of Virgil,* ed. R. D. Williams (2 vols; London: Macmillan, 1972–73), has a good text and notes, and the Loeb *Virgil,* translated by H. R. Fairclough (2 vols; Cambridge, Mass.: Harvard University Press, 1935), is useful. Virgil's combination of beauty, pathos, and energy is notoriously untranslatable, but the energy at least has been captured in Dryden's classic version (1697) and in the recent version by Allen Mandelbaum (Berkeley: University of California Press, 1971).

alluded to Virgil See R. A. Brower, *Alexander Pope: The Poetry of Allusion* (Oxford: Clarendon Press, 1959), pp. 35–62.

the status of the present The question is a central concern of Sara Mack, *Patterns of Time in Vergil* (Hamden, Conn.: Archon Books, 1978), esp. pp. 3–5, 80–84.

82 **many modern critics** For instance, Adam Parry, "The Two Voices of Virgil's *Aeneid,*" *Arion* 2, 4 (1963): 66–80; M. C. J. Putnam, *The Poetry of the "Aeneid"* (Cambridge, Mass.: Harvard University Press, 1965), pp. 145–50; W. R. Johnson, *Darkness Visible: A Study of Vergil's "Aeneid"* (Berkeley: University of California Press, 1976), pp. 111–14.

the hero's nature The positive aspects of Aeneas' self-control are stressed by Richard Heinze, *Virgils Epische Technik* (Leipzig: B. G. Teubner, 1903), pp. 266–73, and by Viktor Pöschl, *The Art of Vergil,* tr. Gerda Seligson (Ann Arbor: University of Michigan Press, 1962), pp. 34–60.

83 **"piety"** On *pietas* see Cyril Bailey, *Religion in Virgil* (Oxford: Clarendon Press, 1935), pp. 79–87.

only the executioner It is possible to argue, of course, that Aeneas' words merely rationalize his bloodlust, and many critics have so argued; e.g., Kenneth Quinn, *Virgil's "Aeneid"* (Ann Arbor: University of Michigan Press, 1968), pp. 271–76.

never finished According to Suetonius, Virgil intended to spend three more years revising the *Aeneid.* Camps' *Introduction,* pp. 127–31, surveys the evidence for incompletion. The most celebrated "loose ends," Virgil's half-lines, often seem artistically justified, according to John Sparrow, *Half-Lines and Repetitions in Virgil* (Oxford: Clarendon Press, 1931). The legend that Virgil intended to compose *twenty-four* books has no ancient authority.

"burn it himself" Suetonius 39 (Loeb vol. 2, p. 478).

84 **"the victimization of Turnus"** Johnson, *Darkness Visible,* p. 116. Johnson's first chapter, pp. 1–22, describes the turn from optimism to pessimism in Virgilian interpretations.

many successors Early imitations of the *Aeneid* are discussed by A. J. Gossage, "Virgil and the Flavian Epic," in *Virgil,* ed. D. R. Dudley (London: Routledge & Kegan Paul, 1969), pp. 67–93. The most popular of all continuations, Maphaeus Vegius' "Thirteenth Book" (1428), was actually bound together with the *Aeneid* for almost two centuries; see A. C. Brinton, *Maphaeus Vegius and His Thirteenth Book of the Aeneid* (Palo Alto: Stanford University Press, 1930).

85 **its companion passages** The same experiment is performed, though with quite different conclusions, by Wendell Clausen, "An interpretation of the *Aeneid*," in *Virgil*, ed. Steele Commager (Englewood Cliffs, N.J.: Prentice-Hall, 1966), pp. 75–88.

reincarnated Aeneas See Michael Grant, *Roman Myths* (New York: Charles Scribner's Sons, 1971), pp. 44–90.

Eduard Norden *Aeneis Buch VI* (Leipzig: B. G. Teubner, 1903), pp. 175–231.

86 **destiny demands it** "To spare Turnus would have been the betrayal of the mission of Aeneas in Italy," according to W. W. Fowler, *The Death of Turnus* (Oxford: Blackwell, 1919), p. 156. For the view that the death of Turnus reveals the darkness inherent in Aeneas' mission, see Johnson, *Darkness Visible*, pp. 114–34, 144–49. An "uneasy truce" between these views is offered by M. A. Di Cesare, *The Altar and the City: A Reading of Vergil's "Aeneid"* (New York: Columbia University Press, 1974), pp. 198–239.

87 **in medium quaerebant** *Georgics* I. 125–27. On the centrality of this passage to the *Georgics* as a whole, see L. P. Wilkinson, *The Georgics of Virgil* (Cambridge, Eng.: At the University Press, 1969), pp. 132–45.

alter our gestures "Ode to Terminus," Auden's *Collected Poems*, ed. Edward Mendelson (New York: Random House, 1976), p. 609. Erasmus used the motto of Terminus, "cedo nulli" ("I yield to none") as his own seal; see Edgar Wind, *"Aenigma Termini," Journal of the Warburg Institute* 1 (1937): 66–69.

88 **Poor hero!** Turnus' character is brilliantly analyzed by Pöschl, *The Art of Vergil*, pp. 91–138, and by Otis, *Virgil*, pp. 317–19, 370–81.

"where we start" "Little Gidding," V (*Collected Poems*, pp. 221–22).

a type of himself See J. H. W. G. Liebeschuetz, *Continuity and Change in Roman Religion* (Oxford: Clarendon Press, 1979), pp. 82–85.

most inspired of seers J. W. Spargo has traced the legend of *Virgil the Necromancer* (Cambridge, Mass.: Harvard University Press, 1934).

89 **historian and prophet in one** The same poetic combination of history and prophecy characterizes *The Bard* of Thomas Gray.

Sibyl of Cumae Pierre Boyancé, *La Religion de Virgile* (Paris: Presses Universitaires de France, 1963), pp. 114–41, discusses Virgil's use of the Sibyl.

90 **the mastering god** see Bailey, *Religion in Virgil*, pp. 161–72.

91 ***he does not know himself*** "sed neque currentem se nec cognoscit euntem" (XII. 903).

reconciled to her fate On Dido's struggle against fate see Pöschl, *The Art of Vergil*, pp. 71–77.

subject to fate Bailey, *Religion in Virgil,* pp. 204–34, identifies fate with the will of Jupiter; but cf. Boyancé, *La Religion de Virgile,* pp. 39–57.

Sainte-Beuve *Etude sur Virgile* (Paris: Michel Lévy Frères, 1870), pp. 64–69. Kermode's discussion in *The Classic* (pp. 16–18, 26–28) notes the importance of Virgil for Sainte-Beuve and Haecker.

92 **a hopeless future tense** More precisely, "The sudden change to the indicative expresses certainty of the logical necessity of the apodosis" (H. E. Butler, *The Sixth Book of the "Aeneid"* [Oxford: Blackwell, 1920], p. 273). Both the punctuation and the meaning of these lines remain vexed questions. Recent editions tend to place the exclamation mark after *rumpas* rather than *eris,* which supports interpreting "Marcellus" simply as the dead heir, not as "*a* Marcellus" (i.e., a true hero like that other Marcellus, victor in the Second Punic War, described in the passage immediately preceding, VI. 855–59). A case can be made for either reading.

his mother, fainted Suetonius 32 (Loeb vol. 2, p. 474).

ambitious disciples George Sherburn's perception that *Amelia* (1751) is a modern version of the *Aeneid* ("Fielding's *Amelia*: An Interpretation," *ELH* 3 [1936]: 1–14) has been elaborated by several later scholars. Undoubtedly, the prize for the most ambitious of all Virgil's disciples, however, belongs to Victor Hugo, who worked on his immense epic, *La Légende des siècles,* for more than thirty years without completing it; its subject is the history of the human race from the Creation to the Last Judgment. Petrarch's *Africa,* Ronsard's *Franciade,* and Pope's *Brutus* are only a small sample of the many abortive Virgilian epics attempted by major poets; see the amusing discussion by Thomas Greene, *The Descent from Heaven* (New Haven: Yale University Press, 1963), pp. 1–7, 100–103. On the earlier reception and competition with Virgil, the standard work remains Domenico Comparetti, *Vergil in the Middle Ages,* tr. E. F. M. Benecke (Hamden, Conn.: Archon Books, 1966), whose first edition is now more than a century old.

93 **resumes a project** E. C. Mason, *Goethe's "Faust": Its Genesis and Purport* (Berkeley: University of California Press, 1967), supplies a large store of information about the stages through which the work evolved.

94 **(1699–1706)** Parenthetical numbers throughout this section refer to lines in the German text of *Faust;* I have used the text in volume 3 of *Goethes Werke,* ed. Erich Trunz (Hamburg: Wegner, 1949), (hereafter cited as *Werke*). No English translation of *Faust* can be recommended wholeheartedly, but the version by Walter Arndt, edited by Cyrus Hamlin (New York: Norton, 1976), includes useful materials and notes. For the reader with some German, the text edited by R.-M. S. Heffner, Helmut Rehder, and W. F. Twaddell, 2 vols. (Madison: University of Wisconsin Press, 1975), provides extensive notes and vocabulary.

Faust's pact On the terms of the pact and wager, see A. R. Hohlfeld, *Fifty Years with Goethe* (Madison: University of Wisconsin Press, 1953), pp. 3–28. The almost infinite complexity and ambiguity of the wager are stressed by Emil Staiger in his monumental critical biography, *Goethe* (Zurich: Atlantis, 1952–59), vol. 2, pp. 333–56.

the age of a hundred Goethe himself assured J. P. Eckermann that, in the fifth act, "I intended that Faust should be exactly a hundred years old" (6 June 1831, in Eckermann's *Gespräche mit Goethe,* ed. Ernst Beutler [Zurich: Artemis, 1948], p. 503).

be granted another Note, for instance, his comment to Eckermann, 1 September 1829: "I do not doubt our permanence, for nature cannot do without the entelechy. But we are not immortal in the same way, and he who would manifest himself as a great entelechy in the future must also be one now" (*Gespräche mit Goethe,* p. 371).

95 **In Memoriam** Tennyson himself declared that the first stanza of *In Memoriam,* section 1—"I held it truth, with him who sings / To one clear harp in divers tones, / That men may rise on stepping stones / Of their dead selves to higher things"—had been inspired by Goethe's phrase (see H. E. Shepherd, *A Commentary upon Tennyson's "In Memoriam"* [New York: Neale, 1908], p. 28), and that the second line affirmed that "Goethe is consummate in so many different styles."

As a scientist Among the vast literature on Goethe's advocacy of organic unity as the key to science, significant works include Rudolf Magnus, *Goethe as a Scientist* (1906), tr. Heinz Norden (New York: Collier Books, 1961); Rudolf Steiner, *Goethe the Scientist* (1926), tr. O. D. Wannamaker (New York: Anthroposophic Press, 1950); Karl Viëtor, *Goethe the Thinker* (Cambridge, Mass.: Harvard University Press, 1950); and Ernst Lehrs, *Man or Matter* (London: Faber & Faber, 1951).

Urlicht Properly speaking, Goethe believed that colors derive from a primal *(uranfänglicher)* opposition of light and darkness.

Urfaust Ed. R. H. Samuel (London: Macmillan, 1958.)

in deinem Geist *Werke,* 1:248. For commentary, see James Boyd, *Notes to Goethe's Poems* (Oxford: Blackwell, 1962), vol. 2, pp. 123–26.

96 **Substance and form** On the meaning of *Gehalt* see E. M. Wilkinson, "Goethe's Conception of Form," in *Goethe: Poet and Thinker* (New York: Barnes & Noble, 1962), pp. 180–81.

Goethe did not admire Virgil Goethe's patronizing attitude toward Virgil has been profoundly embarrassing to later German Virgilians like E. R. Curtius, Friedrich Klinger, and, most of all, Viktor Pöschl: "It is symptomatic of the ignorance of Vergil among Germans that he does not play a role in the discussion between Goethe and Schiller concerning the nature of the epic, even though the epic 'fulfills its nature' only in the *Aeneid*" (*The Art of Vergil,* p. 32). As a matter of fact, Goethe specifically ruled out the *Aeneid* as an epic model: "Virgil's rhetorical sentimental treatment cannot come into question here" (letter to Schiller, 23 December 1797, in *Goethes Briefe,* ed. K. R. Mandelkow [Hamburg: Wegner, 1964], vol. 2, p. 321). Pöschl's fine book repairs the balance by defending the *Aeneid* exclusively on Goethean principles. Thus, "The demand made by Goethe upon the drama, that each scene must symbolically represent the whole, is fulfilled in the exposition of the Vergilian epic in an ideal manner" (24); the *Aeneid* fulfills the nature of the epic "by bringing all parts under the law of the whole" (32); "Vergil meets Goethe's demand that the figures, while definitely separate and different from each other, should be of one kind" (90); Virgil "strives to make the whole plan present in every moment. . . . Indeed, this is the goal of every work of art, for as Goethe has said in his review of *Des Knaben Wunderhorn:* 'The work of art in whole and in part is a symbol of the universe' " (172). Even the major pattern of symbolism that Pöschl finds in the *Aeneid,* the opposition of light and darkness, comes directly from Goethe, who based not only his color theory but much of his philosophy on the same opposition.

"and the congealed" To Eckermann, 13 February 1829, *Gespräche mit Goethe,* p. 316.

Newton's optics . . . had been wrong It was Goethe, in fact, who was wrong. Richard Friedenthal, *Goethe: His Life and Times* (Cleveland: World, 165), pp. 285–91, 394–404, discusses the issues and their background. On Goethe's antiscientific attitudes in general, C. C. Gillispie, *The Edge of Objectivity* (Princeton: Princeton University Press, 1960), pp. 179–80, 192–201, administers a dash of cold water.

97 **"even about Virgil"** *Goethes Werke* (Weimar: Böhlaus Nachfolger, 1897), 1:xxxviii, 369.

Barker Fairley *Goethe as Revealed in His Poetry* (New York: Frederick Ungar, 1963), pp. 141–61.

Erich Heller *The Disinherited Mind* (New York: Harcourt, Brace, Jovanovich, 1975), pp. 35–63.

Goethe's hope of music To Eckermann, 12 February 1829, *Gespräche mit Goethe,* p. 313.

"a little space" *Werke,* 12:250.

98 **repeated reflections** Goethe's own brief essay, "Wiederholte Spiegelungen" (1823) (*Werke,* 12:322–23), has been used as an entrance into his whole work by L. A. Willoughby, "Literary Relations in the Light of Goethe's Principle of 'Wiederholte Spiegelungen'," *Goethe: Poet and Thinker,* pp. 152–66.

"within one another" Letter to C. J. L. Iken, 27 September 1827, *Goethes Briefe,* 4:250.

99 **of second love** Perhaps the clearest and most brilliant of all Goethe's treatments of this theme is the "Trilogie der Leidenschaft" (1825), whose first poem welcomes back the shade of Werther on the fiftieth anniversary of his first appearance, and whose second poem, the great "Marienbad Elegy," passionately expresses the failure of the seventy-four-year-old poet to reclaim love with a girl in her teens.

100 **the epic he had been planning** "The interest of my new epic plan is perhaps also evaporating into a haze of rhyme and strophe," Goethe confessed, and then suddenly wrote Schiller that, "Since it is highly necessary, in my current restless condition, that I give myself something to do, I have determined to go back to my Faust" (22 June 1797, *Briefe,* 2:279). The Dedication followed two days later.

the work as a whole For thematic justifications of the Dedication, see Stuart Atkins, *Goethe's Faust* (Cambridge, Mass.: Harvard University Press, 1958), pp. 11–12, and Paul Requadt, *Goethes "Faust I"* (Munich: Wilhelm Fink, 1972), pp. 28–33.

C. J. L. Iken 27 September 1827, *Goethes Briefe*, 4:250.

told Eckermann 20 December 1829, *Gespräche mit Goethe*, pp. 379–80.

101 **process or product** Mason, *Goethe's "Faust,"* exemplifies the camp of process; Harold Jantz, *The Form of Faust: The Work of Art and Its Intrinsic Structures* (Baltimore: Johns Hopkins University Press, 1978), an extreme commitment to the product. Recent criticism of *Faust* has been surveyed by H. G. Haile, *Invitation to Goethe's "Faust"* (University, Ala.: University of Alabama Press, 1978), pp. 158–86.

world literature Goethe himself coined the term; see Fritz Strich, *Goethe and World Literature* (New York: Hafner, 1949).

rhythm of his feelings Most translations of *Faust* are compromised right from the start by failing to adapt to its rapid changes of tone and style. Faust's first words are deliberately crude:

> Habe nun, ach! Philosophie,
> Juristerei und Medizin,
> Und leider auch Theologie
> Durchaus studiert, mit heissem Bemühn.

> (I've studied, alas! philosophy,
> Jurisprudence and medicine,
> And, sorry to say, theology
> Feverishly, the whole routine.)
>   [354–57]

But thirty lines later he has slid into an Ossianic or Klopstockian apostrophe to the moon:

> Ach! könnt' ich doch auf Bergeshöhn
> In deinem lieben Lichte gehn, .
> Um Bergeshöhle mit Geistern schweben,
> Auf Wiesen in deinem Dämmer weben

> (Ah, would that on some mountain height
> I walked amid your lovely light,
> Hovered with spirits in mountain caves,
> Floated at dusk on meadow waves!)
>   [392–95]

And by the end of the passage a new Romantic spirit invades the verse, breaking or extending the lines as the speaker's excitement rises:

> Ich fühl's, du schwebst um mich, erflehter Geist.
> Enthülle dich!
> Ha! wie's in meinem Herzen reisst!
> Zu neuen Gefühlen

215

> All' meine Sinnen sich erwühlen!
> Ich fühle ganz mein Herz dir hingegeben!
> Du musst! du musst! und kostet' es mein Leben!

> (I feel you hover round me, conjured spirit.
> Reveal yourself!
> Oh! how it tears my heart!
> Though what I feel
> Beginning, all my senses reel!
> I feel my heart give way to your control!
> You must! you must! though it should cost my soul!)
> [475–81]

Even in the 1770s, when Goethe wrote these lines, he evidently considered Faust a one-man anthology of historical and poetic styles: a puppet in a morality play; a Man of Sentiment; and perhaps—anticipating the future—a Romantic hero. Ontogeny recapitulates phylogeny. And the verse must also show a capacity for growth. Hence the monologue may be said to epitomize the whole work, in Goethe's fashion, by shifting the poetic framework of the *Faust* story from external to internal meanings, from allegory to symbol.

102 **"this way and that"** To Sulpiz Boisserée, 22 October 1826, *Goethes Briefe*, 4:207.

"part of the whole" 23 September 1800, *Der Briefwechsel zwischen Schiller und Goethe*, ed. Paul Stapf (Berlin: Tempel, 1960), p. 698.

"the present day itself" 5 July 1827, *Gespräche mit Goethe*, p. 256.

wedded and brought forth Goethe himself was justifiably proud of the final series of choral songs, in which the chorus gradually disperses into nature—trees, mountains, rivers, vines.

> ALLE: Ewig lebendige Natur
> Macht auf uns Geister,
> Wir auf sie vollgültigen Anspruch.

> (Ever-living nature
> Holds on us spirits,
> As we on her, a fully binding claim.)
> [9989–91]

The Ovidian metamorphosis blends into a drunken Dionysian spree and romantic nature worship. Hence the new kind of verse suggests that poetry, whether classic or romantic, is immanent in the elements of earth. The act ends at the beginning of the world, in a fertile chaos or pantheism where consciousness merges with the unconscious and the gods of poetry live everywhere around us.

103 **to myself a phantom** On Helen's phantom aspect, see Wilhelm Emrich, *Die Symbolik von Faust II* (Frankfurt am Main: Athenäum, 1964), pp. 312–25, and Katharina Mommsen, *Natur- und Fabelreich in Faust II* (Berlin: Walter de Gruyter, 1968), pp. 1–10.

104 **vocable and prayer** *The Collected Poems of Hart Crane,* ed. Waldo Frank (New York: Liveright, 1933), p. 99.

105 **dynamic tension** The tension is related by Georg Lukács to class as well as sexual conflicts; see his *Goethe and His Age,* tr. Robert Anchor (New York: Grosset & Dunlap, 1969), pp. 217–34.

as Nietzsche charged "Der Wanderer und sein Schatten," no. 124 in *Werke,* ed. Karl Schlechta (Munich: Carl Hanser, 1966), vol. 1, p. 927.

106 **dominated by Mothers** See *Faust II,* esp. lines 6212–306, 6421–500, and the commentary by Harold Jantz, *The Mothers in "Faust"* (Baltimore: Johns Hopkins University Press, 1969).

107 **"form and solidity"** 6 June 1831, *Gespräche mit Goethe,* p. 504.

a secular bargain On the Christian symbolism of Faust's redemption, see A. P. Cottrell, *Goethe's "Faust": Seven Essays* (Chapel Hill: University of North Carolina Press, 1976), pp. 50–67.

"love comes to his aid" 6 June 1831, to Eckermann, *Gespräche mit Goethe,* p. 504.

"sustain my spirit" 4 February 1829, to Eckermann, ibid., p. 308.

108 **"drunk enough"** To Wilhelm von Humboldt, 1 December 1831, *Goethes Briefe,* 4:463–64.

109 **Danube with the Rhine** To Eckermann, 21 February 1827, *Gespräche mit Goethe,* pp. 599–600.

110 **revision of the story** On Goethe's deliberate departure from the Faust tradition, see E. M. Butler, *The Fortunes of Faust* (Cambridge, Eng.: At the University Press, 1952), pp. 262–65.

the author himself Goethe himself acknowledged that the "mockery and bitter irony of Mephistopheles" showed a side of his own character (to Eckermann, 3 May 1827, *Gespräche mit Goethe,* p. 627).

111 **the paradox of existence** See Walter Kaufmann, *From Shakespeare to Existentialism* (Boston: Beacon Press, 1959), pp. 56–70.

112 **the inaccessible** Emil Staiger (*Goethe,* vol. 3, p. 466) points out that "inaccessible," rather than the modern sense of "insufficient," is the proper reading of *Das Unzulängliche;* but the full force of the paradox can accommodate both.

Torquato Tasso *Werke,* 5:166.

experience controlled The process is described by Goethe in *Dichtung und Wahrheit,* Book 7 (*Werke,* 9:282–84).

"astounds the world" 17 March 1832, *Goethes Briefe,* 4:480.

113 **refused even to comment** Staiger, *Goethe,* 3:466.

"He whose life is symbolic" Quoted by Maynard Mack as the epigraph to his study of Pope, *The Garden and the City* (Toronto: University of Toronto Press, 1969), p. vi.

"incipient disintegration" Curtius, *Essays on European Literature,* pp. 89–90. A similar analysis informs Frank Kermode's *The Classic,* which contrasts the "imperial classic" with "the modern classic, which offers itself only to readings which are encouraged by its failure to give a definitive account of itself" (p. 114).

project its destiny forward Goethe himself seems to have considered Byron the aspiring author of such a poem; see the Euphorion section of *Faust* (9598–9961) and the comments to Eckermann, especially those of 24 February 1825 (*Gespräche mit Goethe,* pp. 145–50). In these terms *Don Juan* might be considered the first "modern classic" or "antiharmonium."

114 **"does the greatest poet bring"** "Preface 1855" to the first edition of *Leaves of Grass;* from *Leaves of Grass: Comprehensive Reader's Edition,* ed. H. W. Blodgett and Sculley Bradley (New York: New York University Press, 1965), p. 727. Citations from *Leaves of Grass* in the text refer to this edition.

"the throes of birth" From *Democratic Vistas* (1871), in *Prose Works 1892,* ed. Floyd Stovall (New York: New York University Press, 1964), vol. 2, p. 371.

Emerson, "The Poet" *Essays,* Second Series (Boston: Houghton, Mifflin, 1904), p. 10.

Richard Bucke Quoted by Horace Traubel, *With Walt Whitman in Camden* (New York: Mitchell Kennerley, 1915), vol. 2, p. 378. Dr. Bucke was Whitman's friend and executor.

"remain to be sung" *Leaves of Grass,* p. 574.

no truck with them On Whitman's attitudes toward Goethe, see Floyd Stovall, *The Foreground of "Leaves of Grass"* (Charlottesville, Va.: University Press of Virginia, 1974), pp. 129–37.

115 **"for America to-day at all"** *Prose Works,* 2:664–65.

"the same experience" *With Walt Whitman,* 3:159

"truly on record" "A Backward Glance," *Leaves of Grass,* pp. 573–74.

116 **"a great forthcoming Poet"** Quoted by Stovall, *Foreground,* p. 3.

"desire to be primitive" "The Poetry of Barbarism," in *Essays in Literary Criticism of George Santayana,* ed. Irving Singer (New York: Scribner's, 1956), pp. 159–60.

117 **the United States** *Prose Works,* 2:373n.

one of the people The struggle is traced by Roger Asselineau, *The Evolution of Walt Whitman* (Cambridge, Mass.: Harvard University Press, 1962), vol. 2, pp. 129–78.

Fanny's Port-Folio Sarah Payson Willis Parton, in her character of "Fanny Fern," greeted Whitman as a fellow gatherer of Leaves in a flattering review, "Fresh Fern Leaves: Leaves of Grass," reprinted in *New York Dissected by Walt Whitman,* ed. Emory Holloway and Ralph Adimari (New York: R. R. Wilson, 1936), pp. 162–65.

his role as Frankenstein See J. B. Moore, "The Master of Whitman," *Studies in Philology* 23 (1926): 77–89.

"this land today" *Leaves of Grass,* p. 731.

118 **"likely to be"** *Walt Whitman: The Critical Heritage,* ed. Milton Hindus (London: Routledge & Kegan Paul, 1971), p. 45.

"hurry or compromise" *Leaves of Grass,* p. 731.

a single one See G. W. Allen, *The Solitary Singer* (New York: New York University Press, 1967), pp. 150–51.

thirty-eight *Leaves of Grass,* pp. 320–21.

"self-will'd record" "A Backward Glance," ibid., p. 563.

119 **I contain multitudes** *Leaves of Grass: The First (1855) Edition,* ed. Malcolm Cowley (New York: Viking, 1959), p. 85.

its elemental form *With Walt Whitman,* 3:355.

Andrew Jackson Davis See Stovall, *Foreground,* pp. 154–55. Davis, a Swedenborgian and Spiritualist, also had some influence on Yeats; see Yeats, "Swedenborg, Mediums, and the Desolate Places" (1914), reprinted in *Explorations* (London: Macmillan, 1962), pp. 45–48.

All these and more Several of these possibilities, each of which may be supported by some of Whitman's own words, are explored in F. O. Matthiessen's path-breaking study, *American Renaissance* (New York: Oxford University Press, 1941), pp. 517–625.

"my own poems" "An Egotistical 'Find' " (1879), *Prose Works,* 1:210. On this occasion it was the Rocky Mountains that had taught him the law.

Malcolm Cowley "Introduction" to *Leaves of Grass: The First (1855) Edition,* pp. vii–xxxvii.

120 **Roy Harvey Pearce** "Introduction" to *Leaves of Grass: Facsimile Edition of the 1860 Text* (Ithaca, N.Y.: Cornell University Press, 1961), pp. vii–li.

a variorum Leaves *Leaves of Grass: A Textual Variorum of the Printed Poems,* ed. Sculley Bradley, H. W. Blodgett, Arthur Golden, and William White, 3 vols. (New York: New York University Press, 1980), has appeared after twenty years of preparation, with all variants included. G. W. Allen supplies a detailed study of the sequence of *Leaves* in *The New Walt Whitman Handbook* (New York: New York University Press, 1975), pp. 67–159.

a constantly revised edition The effort was first made in 1933 by Frederik Schyberg, *Walt Whitman,* tr. E. A. Allen (New York: Columbia University Press, 1951).

filter them through yourself *The First (1855) Edition,* p. 26.

121 **"reader of the book does"** *Prose Works,* 2:424–25.

organizing principle See, for instance, Part Two of J. E. Miller's *A Critical Guide to "Leaves of Grass"* (Chicago: University of Chicago Press, 1957).

A similar logic See S. A. Black, *Whitman's Journeys into Chaos* (Princeton: Princeton University Press, 1975).

122 **Cowley argues** *The First (1855) Edition*, pp. xxxii–xxxvi.

and to none else "Chants Democratic," *Facsimile Edition*, p. 193.

123 **is ever complete** In the first three editions, for instance, Whitman supplied the information that he "was born on the last day of May 1819" (or "the Year 43 of America") and "that I grew six feet high" (lines 21, 22), but in later editions he omitted the personal data.

told Horace Traubel *With Walt Whitman*, 1:156.

every where *Leaves of Grass*, p. 745.

"dicker and adventure" *The First (1855) Edition*, p. 60.

explorer enough In 1856, however, Whitman strongly identified *Emerson* with Columbus, as shown in the letter to his Master: "Those shores you found, I say you have led The States there—have led Me there. . . . [I]t is yours to have been the original true Captain who put to sea, intuitive, positive, rendering the first report, to be told less by any report, and more by the mariners of a thousand bays, in each tack of their arriving and departing, many years after you" (*Leaves of Grass*, p. 739).

124 **"visionary fervour"** Washington Irving, *History of the Life and Voyages of Christopher Columbus* (Philadelphia: Carey, Lea, and Blanchard, 1837), vol. 2, p. 204. Whitman reviewed Irving's *Columbus* in 1847; see *Uncollected Poetry and Prose of Walt Whitman*, ed. Emory Holloway (Garden City, N.Y.: Doubleday, Page, 1921), vol. 1, p. 133.

125 **has become explicit** "My 'song of *the redwood tree*,' in last Harpers is copied a little, & abused & sneered at in the newspaper criticisms, a good deal, (from what I glean)—*of course*, that last makes me feel *very bad*—I expect to have another piece in February Harpers—(but am not certain)—'prayer of Columbus'—as I see it now I shouldn't wonder if I have unconsciously put a sort of autobiographical dash in it" (letter to Ellen O'Connor, 3 February 1874, in Walt Whitman, *The Correspondence*, ed. E. H. Miller [New York: New York University Press, 1961], vol. 2, p. 272).

"the latest posterity" Irving, *Life of Columbus*, 2:205.

126 **"shows the Great Master"** Stovall, *Foreground*, p. 262. Edward Carpenter heard Whitman recite "Ulysses" in 1877: "The subtle harmonies of the Tennysonian verse effloresced under the treatment, but the sterner qualities of the poem stood out finely. We expressed admiration. He said: 'I guess it is about the best Tennysonian poem'" (*Days with Walt Whitman* [London: Allen & Unwin, 1906], p. 25).

"the struggle of life" *The Poems of Tennyson*, ed. Christopher Ricks (London: Longmans, 1969), p. 560.

127 **when I move** "Ulysses," lines 18–21, *Poems*, p. 563.

"went forth every day" *Leaves of Grass*, p. 366.

immense distance of time On Tennyson's approach to myth, see A. D. Culler, *The Poetry of Tennyson* (New Haven: Yale University Press, 1977), pp. 90–99.

129 **"flesh and blood woman"** Quoted in *Leaves of Grass*, p. 5n. Though others stressed the first syllable of the word, Whitman insisted on stressing the second.

material particulars "Of the best of events and facts, even the most important, there are finally not the events and facts only, but something flashing out and fluctuating like tuft-flames or eidólons, from all" (Whitman's "Note at Beginning" of the 1888 edition of his *Complete Poems and Prose;* in *Prose Works,* 2:732).

on the ether According to an interesting note by W. S. Kennedy, *The Fight of a Book for the World* (West Yarmouth, Mass.: Stonecroft Press, 1926), pp. 180–83, the idea of Whitman's poem (except for the word "eidólon") derives from a popular contemporary book, *The Unseen Universe,* by Balfour Stewart and P. G. Tait (New York: Macmillan, 1875). "This facsimile register we can conceive of as a living and immortal part of the immortal Soul of the Universe" (Kennedy, p. 182).

130 **as much worth saving** Whitman did eliminate about 10 percent of his earlier work, however, from the final *Leaves.*

"poems of the morning" "Backward Glance," *Leaves of Grass,* p. 572.

131 **his last words** *In Re Walt Whitman,* ed. Horace Traubel, R. M. Bucke, and T. B. Harned (Philadelphia: David McKay, 1893). Whitman's actual last words, "Warry, shift" (asking Warren Fritzinger to turn him to a more comfortable position), did not satisfy the disciples but may stand as an emblem of the poet's need to stay in motion.

she would not engage The deliberateness of the choice is a central theme of Ruth Miller, *The Poetry of Emily Dickinson* (Middletown, Conn.: Wesleyan University Press, 1968): "Emily Dickinson knew the sacrifice she was making, knew why, and was willing to gamble on an imitation of Christ for the sake of a victory like His—immortality" (p. 3).

"End of a Culture" Broch's own long letter on the genesis of *The Death of Virgil* was first published in translation by H. J. Weigand, "Broch's *Death of Vergil:* Program Notes," *PMLA* 62 (1947): 551–54; it is reprinted in slightly fuller form in Broch's *Briefe,* ed. Robert Pick (Zurich: Rhein-Verlag, 1957), pp. 242–47. The account differs slightly from the one in Broch's *Massenpsychologie,* ed. Wolfgang Rothe (Zurich: Rhein-Verlag, 1959), p. 51, which dates the start of *Virgil* in 1937. "Erwägungen zum Problem des Kulturtodes" ("Reflections on the Problem of the Death of Culture," 1936) is reprinted in Broch's *Essays,* ed. Hannah Arendt (Zurich: Rhein-Verlag, 1955), vol. 2, pp. 103–10.

"old religious forms" *Briefe,* p. 243.

"my own dying" Ibid., p. 244. On the centrality of the moment of death to Broch's work, see Beate Loos, *Mythos Zeit und Tod* (Frankfurt: Athenäum, 1971), pp. 142–82.

132 **"No longer and not yet"** As Hannah Arendt points out, in "The Achievement of Hermann Broch," *Kenyon Review* 11 (1949): 476–83, this refrain "permeates the work like a leitmotif."

"in every single part" *The Death of Virgil*, tr. Jean Starr Untermeyer (New York: Pantheon Books, 1945), p. 325. Despite some deficiencies in this translation, it has a special authority because Broch himself supervised it (the English and German versions were published simultaneously in 1945). Untermeyer supplies a full account of her role as "Midwife to a Masterpiece" in *Private Collections* (New York: Alfred Knopf, 1965), pp. 218–77.

Virgil, Father of the West The dependence of Broch on Haecker is rightly emphasized by Manfred Durzak, *Hermann Broch: Dichtung und Erkenntnis* (Stuttgart: Kohlhammer, 1978), pp. 98, 222, 225. In his afterword to the German edition of *Der Tod des Vergil*, Broch notes that all his citations from the *Eclogues* are taken from Haecker's version (1932); and the Elegies on Fate, the very center of Broch's work, clearly derive from Haecker's chapter on *fatum* (*Virgil, Father of the West*, pp. 82–91). The difference between the positions of the two men—Haecker a Christian minister and Broch a nonpracticing Jew—is wittily summarized in a remark by Broch's friend and publisher, Daniel Brody: "It was Virgil, certainly, who was the father of Western culture (the mother was the synagogue!)" (*Hermann Broch–Daniel Brody Briefwechsel 1930–1951*, ed. Bertold Hack and Marietta Kloss [Frankfurt: Buchhändler-Vereinigung, 1971], p. 770).

disapproves of Virgil Broch was not, in fact, a learned Virgilian. He relied on a few standard sources and, for his own adaptations of Virgil's poetry, the help of his friend Erich Kahler.

133 **the form of the book** A starting place for analysis is Broch's own series of comments, collected as "Bemerkungen zum 'Tod des Vergil,' " *Essays*, 1:265–75. Walter Hinderer outlines the "Grundzüge des 'Tod des Vergil' " in *Hermann Broch: Perspektiven der Forschung*, ed. Manfred Durzak (Munich: Wilhelm Fink, 1972), pp. 89–134 (a good collection of essays). In English, in addition to Weigand's "Program Notes," cited above, Ernestine Schlant provides a useful introduction in *Hermann Broch* (Boston: Twayne, 1978), with selected bibliography, as does Theodore Ziolkowski in a brief survey, *Hermann Broch* (New York: Columbia University Press, 1964).

"the mind with itself" Matthew Arnold's phrase, in the "Preface" to the First Edition of his *Poems* (1853), where he explains that he has omitted "Empedocles on Etna" because "the suffering finds no vent in action" (*The Poems of Matthew Arnold*, ed. Kenneth Allott [London: Longmans, 1965], pp. 591–92). Compare Broch's refrain, "No longer and not yet," with the famous lines from "Stanzas from the Grande Chartreuse": "Wandering between two worlds, òne dead, / The other powerless to be born" (*Poems*, p. 288).

mortal name *The Death of Virgil,* pp. 387–94; *Der Tod des Vergil* (Zurich: Rhein-Verlag, n.d.), pp. 426–35. Virgil's decision can be "explained" by two motives—his earlier philosophical discovery that love is greater than power, and his later appeal for the emancipation of his slaves—but Broch himself chooses to emphasize the arbitrary about-face of the submission.

companion is chance *Der Tod des Vergil,* p. 224 (my translation).

134 **"on the syntax"** *Essays,* 1:250. The essay, composed in English as an introduction to Rachel Bespaloff, *On the Iliad,* tr. Mary McCarthy (New York: Pantheon Books, 1947), complements Broch's earlier essay "Die mythische Erbschaft der Dichtung" ("The Heritage of Myth in Literature"), published in 1945.

"of all existence" *Essays,* 1:250.

the structure of the universe Broch's view of Goethe approximates that of his correspondent Wilhelm Emrich (see *Briefe,* p. 414), whose *Die Symbolik von Faust II* is cited above. By forcing Virgil to become a type of Goethe, Broch was ironically anticipating the contemporaneous argument of Viktor Pöschl, whose *Art of Vergil* (I have suggested above) interprets Virgil as Goethe's precursor. The powerful resemblance between the symbol systems of the *Aeneid,* as Pöschl reads it, and those of *The Death of Virgil,* as Broch constructs it, seems a coincidence attributable to both men's love of Goethe.

"lack of pity" *Essays,* 1:263.

135 **"rebirth of myth"** Ibid., p. 260.

"bestowed upon him" Ibid., p. 263. In a later essay on Hofmannsthal, Broch developed the theme of man's attempt to tame the horrors of modern life: "It is a situation of utter helplessness and Kafka, not Joyce, did it justice; in Kafka we find the germ of an adequate counter-myth" ("Introduction," tr. Tania and James Stern, to Hugo von Hofmannsthal, *Selected Prose* [New York: Pantheon Books, 1952], p. xxvi). It is also worth noting Broch's great admiration for Hofmannsthal's brief "Letter of Lord Chandos," in which a young Englishman is represented as "apologizing for his complete abandonment of literary activity."

"my poetic career" Letter to Weigand, *Briefe,* p. 247.

"Bill of Duties" Despite his intention to abandon literature, however, Broch was pressed by his publishers to continue writing fiction and became involved in two further projects: *Die Schuldlosen* (The Guiltless), a collection of prewar stories expanded and threaded into a "novel" (1949), and the long, much revised, and never finished "Mountain Novel" *(Der Bergroman),* also known as "The Tempter" or "Demeter." They stand as an Appendix Brochiana.

136 **literary greatness** See Joseph Strelka, "Hermann Broch: Comparatist and Humanist," *Comparative Literature Studies* 12 (1975): 76–78.

"artist of old age" *Essays,* 1:251.

"Homecoming" The full title is "Äther—Die Heimkehr." "Air" completes the four-part cycle of the book through "Water," "Fire," and "Earth"; but the German word also suggests the Greek "ether" or realm of the ethereal. See Schlant, *Hermann Broch,* p. 116 and n.

137 **again and again. . . .** *The Death of Virgil,* p. 481.

the word beyond speech Ibid., pp. 481–82.

TOMBEAU

138 **"patimur Manes"** "We must suffer our own shades"; Anchises to Aeneas, *Aeneid* VI. 743.

will be remembered A remarkable collection of photographs and sketches of the tombs of a hundred poets, from "Virgil to Klingsor," has been assembled (with accompanying verses) by Maurice d'Hartoy in *Les Tombeaux des Poètes,* 2 vols. (Paris: Grassin, 1961, 1968).

139 **design their own memorials** Whitman's design of his tomb, after a Blake engraving, is reproduced by Justin Kaplan, *Walt Whitman, A Life* (New York: Simon & Schuster, 1980), opposite page 321.

this powerful rhyme Sonnet 55. The boast is conventional, of course, with possible sources not only in Horace and Ovid but in Sonnet 69 of Spenser's *Amoretti.*

"or eyes can see" Sonnet 18.

140 *my* **Shakespeare** The possessive pronoun had first been used by Jonson (lines 19 and 56), but in affectionate familiarity rather than appropriation. Milton's poem is only the first of many that ambitious young poets have addressed to Shakespeare, trying to capture his spirit but at ever-increasing distance. Consider, for example, Matthew Arnold's early "Shakespeare" (1844): "Others abide our question. Thou art free. / We ask and ask—Thou smilest and art still, / Out-topping knowledge"; or Gerard Manley Hopkins' "Shakespere" (1865): "In the lodges of the perishable souls / He has his portion."

spiritual competition A splendid if unintentionally comic example is Lamartine's *Le dernier Chant du Pèlerinage d'Harold* (1825), in which the French poet employs Byron's own hero and rhetoric in order to deny the dead Byron entrance into heaven (Christ himself turns Harold down!). Lamartine seems not to have known that he was writing a reverse parody (a dis-parody?) of Byron's *Vision of Judgment.*

"invidious panegyric" Dryden, "A Discourse concerning the Original and Progress of Satire," *Essays,* ed. W. P. Ker (Oxford: Clarendon Press, 1900), vol., 2, p. 18.

141 **"been so too"** Jonson's *Works,* ed. C. H. Herford and Percy and Evelyn Simpson (Oxford: Clarendon Press, 1947), vol. 8, p. 584.

if at all, to thee Ibid., p. 396.

covert satire J. W. Hebel, "Drayton's *Sirena,*" *PMLA* 39 (1924): 830–32.

Friend to thee *Works,* 8:398.

seem'd to raise Ibid., p. 390.

142 **to contrast his poem** William Basse's "Elegy on Shakespeare" had requested Spenser, Chaucer, and Beaumont to close ranks in their graves, making room for Shakespeare in the Poet's Corner; Jonson's dig insists that Shakespeare deserves a place of his own.

to new hammering Jonson, lines 623–28 (Horace, 438–41), *Works*, 8:333.

143 **true-filed lines** Lines 55–68, *Works*, 8:392.

144 **"triumphal forms"** Though my observation about the center of Jonson's poem is (so far as I know) original, the general method of analysis draws on Alastair Fowler, *Triumphal Forms* (Cambridge, Eng.: At the University Press, 1970).

145 **"or haughty *Rome*"** *Works*, 8:591.

the new constellation Cygnus Both the christening of the poet as swan (as in Pindar, the Dircaean Swan) and the elevation of that swan into Cygnus (the son of Neptune, made a constellation by Apollo) were of course thoroughly conventional. Jonson's earlier cygnification of Hugh Holland (1603; in Jonson's *Works*, 8:365–69) contains a good deal of swan lore.

the last word The poem ends, in fact, on a highly self-conscious pun. Since the flight of its swan, the stage "hath mourn'd like night, / And despaires day, but for thy Volumes light." Modernized texts, which require an apostrophe in "Volume's," forgo the possibility of reading "light" as an adjective. But Jonson probably intends to remind us both that the Folios are anything *but* light in weight and that their comic spirit makes them nimble and amusing. At any rate, by the end Shakespeare's volumes have thoroughly superseded Shakespeare, even in the heavens.

146 **muse his praise** The last line of Thomson's "A Hymn on the Seasons" (*Poetical Works*, ed. J. L. Robertson [London: Oxford University Press, 1908], p. 249).

the soothing Shade *The Works of William Collins*, ed. Richard Wendorf and Charles Ryskamp (Oxford: Clarendon Press, 1979), pp. 53–54.

an eloquent Druid bard See A. L. Owen, *The Famous Druids* (Oxford: Clarendon Press, 1962), pp. 172–78.

147 **popularize it** A. D. McKillop discusses Thomson's role in reinventing the Aeolian harp in *The Castle of Indolence* (Lawrence: University of Kansas Press, 1961), pp. 206–9.

it cannot be mistaken In *Precious Bane: Collins and the Miltonic Legacy* (Austin: University of Texas Press, 1977), pp. 105–9, P. S. Sherwin reads the "Ode" as a subversion of "Lycidas" rather than a tribute to Thomson; given this premise, it is not surprising that he finds Collins' pastoral elegy utterly unlike Milton's.

"confer no honor" *Lives of the English Poets*, ed. G. B. Hill (Oxford: Clarendon Press, 1905), vol. 1, pp. 163–64.

"Richmond by water" John Langhorne's comment (1765) serves as the basis for a structural analysis by E. M. W. Tillyard, "William Collins's 'Ode on the Death of Thomson,' " *Review of English Literature* 1 (1960): 30–38.

arranged symmetrically Stanzas 1 and 11, the Druid's grave; 2 and 10, nature as a rural tomb; 3 and 9, distant sounds and fading views; 4 and 8, the haunted Thames; 5 and 7, the nearby spire or shrine (Ease and Health, Fancy and Joy); 6, the earthy bed itself. The structure and theme of the "Ode" are sensitively described by Richard Wendorf in a forthcoming book on Collins.

148 **forget my heart to beat!** Thomson, *Poetical Works,* pp. 248–49.

"want of an epitaph" Sidney, *Miscellaneous Prose,* ed. Katherine Duncan-Jones and Jan van Dorsten (Oxford: Clarendon Press, 1973), p. 121. Versions of this curse are conventional in pastoral elegies; see, especially, Spenser's *The Ruines of Time,* lines 344–57.

149 **Critics have differed** See *The Poems of Gray, Collins, and Goldsmith,* ed. Roger Lonsdale (London: Longmans, 1969), p. 490n.

"Daphnis loved" "Amavit nos quoque Daphnis" (*Eclogues* V. 52).

150 **"pointed clay"** The word "pointed" has been the subject of debate; it may mean "pointed out" (most probable); a jointure in brickwork; "piercing"; or the shape of the tomb (see Lonsdale, 491n). Perhaps Collins intended some combination of these. But what gives the phrase its force is the word "clay," which suggests not only a primitive building material but the poet's body recycled into the soil.

"simple as truth" *The Poetical Works of Mr. William Collins,* ed. A. L. Barbauld (London: Cadell & Davies, 1797), p. xliii.

151 **religiously instructive** Thomson's beliefs are described by A. D. McKillop, *The Background of Thomson's "Seasons"* (Minneapolis: University of Minnesota Press, 1942), pp. 1–42.

152 **the human mind again** "Under Ben Bulben," lines 23–24, *Variorum Yeats,* p. 637.

translated by Yeats *Variorum,* p. 493. On Yeats' burial and reburial, see Joseph Hone, *W. B. Yeats, 1865–1939* (London: Macmillan, 1967), pp. 477–80.

153 **ancestral associations** See Hone, pp. 1–22, and Yeats' own "Reveries over Childhood and Youth," *Autobiographies* (London: Macmillan, 1926).

we are told T. R. Henn, *The Lonely Tower* (London: Methuen, 1950), pp. 318–22.

154 **unfamiliar affections** W. H. Auden, *Collected Poems,* ed. Edward Mendelson (New York: Random House, 1976), p. 197.

"possible in neither" *The Dyer's Hand* (New York: Random House, 1962), p. 19.

155 **rejected Auden himself** Richard Ellmann emphasizes the incompatibility of Yeats and Auden in *Eminent Domain* (New York: Oxford University Press, 1967), pp. 97–126.

"journalists and groundlings" *Essays and Introductions* (London: Macmillan, 1961), p. 523.

"materially unchanged" *Partisan Review* 6 (Spring, 1939): 51.

"prayed for war" Ibid., p. 48.

156 **He was silly** In the *New Republic* version (8 March 1939) this line ended the first section. On Yeats' "silliness," cf. Auden's remarks in *Partisan Review*, p. 48. Samuel Hynes discusses the historical context of Auden's argument with Yeats in *The Auden Generation* (New York: Viking, 1977), pp. 349–53.

"shop of the heart" "The Circus Animals' Desertion," *Variorum Yeats*, p. 630.

"the English shot" "The Man and the Echo," ibid., p. 632.

"most dishonest" *Partisan Review*, p. 47.

lonely as they die *Collected Poems*, p. 218.

157 **indomitable Irishry** "Under Ben Bulben," *Variorum Yeats*, p. 640. Many years later, at the end of "Academic Graffiti," Auden expressed his criticism more succinctly:

> To get the Last Poems of Yeats,
> You need not mug up on dates;
> All a reader requires
> Is some knowledge of gyres
> And the sort of people he hates.
> [*Collected Poems*, p. 518]

a mouth *Collected Poems*, p. 197.

"out of my own dark" *Essays and Introductions*, p. 526.

"one's prejudices" "Foreword" (1965) to *Collected Poems*, p. 15.

"to overcome it" *Partisan Review*, p. 51.

158 **"as a master"** Ibid.

"language into his meaning" "The Metaphysical Poets" (1921), *Selected Essays* (London: Faber & Faber, 1951), p. 289.

"The book of the people" "Coole Park and Ballylee, 1931," *Variorum Yeats*, p. 492.

159 **the cradles right** Ibid., p. 638.

160 **formal innovation** "He transformed a certain kind of poem, the occasional poem, . . . into a serious reflective poem of at once personal and public interest" ("Yeats as an Example," *Kenyon Review* 10 [1948]: 193). The other formal trait singled out by Auden, Yeats' revitalization of the traditional stanza, also seems appropriate to "In Memory of W. B. Yeats."

"incurable dishonesty" "Foreword," by B. C. Bloomfield, to *W. H. Auden: A Bibliography* (Charlottesville, Va.: University of Virginia Press, 1964), p. viii. The extent to which Auden associated Yeats with dishonesty is shown dramatically in some remarks to Stephen Spender (May 1964): "I am incapable of saying a word about W. B. Yeats because, through no fault of his, he has become for me a symbol of my own devil of authenticity, of everything which I must try to eliminate from my own poetry, false emotions, inflated rhetoric, empty sonorities.

> No poem is ever quite true,
> But a good one
> Makes me desire truth.

His make me whore after lies" (quoted by Charles Osborne, *W. H. Auden: The Life of a Poet* [New York and London: Harcourt, Brace, Jovanovich, 1979], pp. 280–81).

the same in bed "Heavy Date" (1939), *Collected Poems,* p. 208.

161 **imitate the life** "Sir *Philip Sidney,* that exact image of quiet, and action: happily united in him, and seldome well divided in any; being ever in mine eyes, made me thinke it no small degree of honour to imitate, or tread in the steps of such a Leader" (*Sir Fulke Greville's Life of Sir Philip Sidney,* ed. Nowell Smith [Oxford: Clarendon Press, 1907], p. 150).

through excellent desart *Spenser Variorum: The Minor Poems,* vol. 2, ed. C. G. Osgood and H. G. Lotspeich (Baltimore: Johns Hopkins University Press, 1947), p. 46. Spenser, it should be noted, was two years *older* than Sidney but was so widely regarded as the younger poet's successor that he seems to have felt considerable embarrassment about his delay in providing a memorial.

so many good poets A short list might include John Ford, James Shirley, Robert Herrick, Edmund Waller, Owen Felltham, and John Cleveland, authors whose only common denominator is their claim of kinship to Jonson.

162 **The sequence stretches on** It has been continued to the present moment by Joseph Brodsky's fine *tombeaux* to Eliot, Auden, and especially Robert Lowell: "Elegy: for Robert Lowell" (1977), in *A Part of Speech* (New York: Farrar, Straus & Giroux, 1980), pp. 135–37.

163 **"someday to replace"** *Oeuvres complètes,* ed. Henri Mondor and G. Jean-Aubry (Paris: Gallimard, 1945), p. 662. All quotations from Mallarmé refer to this edition and all translations are my own. Austin Gill, *The Early Mallarmé* (Oxford: Clarendon Press, 1979), discusses the debts of Mallarmé's juvenilia to Béranger and other poets.

tries to find himself Gardner Davies has provided full exegeses of each of *Les "Tombeaux" de Mallarmé* (Paris: José Corti, 1950).

What is there left? "I am quite sure that the great Hugo, dying, was persuaded that he had buried all poetry for a century; yet Paul Verlaine had already written *Sagesse*" (Mallarmé, "On Literary Evolution" [1891], *Oeuvres,* p. 866).

l'enferme tout entier "Toast Funèbre," ibid., p. 54. For the circumstances and significance of the poem, see Wallace Fowlie, *Mallarmé* (Chicago: University of Chicago Press, 1953), pp. 171–91. Conscientious translations of all the poems, with facing originals, are available in *Mallarmé: The Poems,* tr. Keith Bosley (Harmondsworth: Penguin Books, 1977).

164 **"mystery of a name"** "éveille / Pour la Rose et le Lys le mystère d'un nom" (*Oeuvres*, p. 55). On Mallarmé's theory of language, see Guy Delfel, *L'Esthétique de Stéphane Mallarmé* (Paris: Flammarion, 1951), pp. 134–57, and G. L. Bruns, *Modern Poetry and the Idea of Language* (New Haven: Yale University Press, 1974), pp. 101–17.

165 **dans le futur** *Oeuvres*, p. 70.

later recollection Ibid., p. 1492. Clearly Mallarmé was misremembering, since he agreed to write the poem in April 1876, five months *after* the monument was dedicated. The circumstances of composition are discussed by E. Noulet, *Vingt Poèmes de Stéphane Mallarmé* (Geneva: Droz, 1967), pp. 43–53.

166 **an earlier version** *Oeuvres*, p. 1493. Mallarmé's own translation of this version is reproduced by Noulet, pp. 52–53, and R. G. Cohn, *Toward the Poems of Mallarmé* (Berkeley: University of California Press, 1965), pp. 156–57.

Baudelaire had said "Edgar Poe, sa vie et ses oeuvres" (1856), in Baudelaire's *Oeuvres complètes*, ed. Claude Pichois (Paris: Gallimard, 1976), vol. 2, p. 297.

"never reappear" *Oeuvres*, p. 1493.

168 **shaping of the phrase** Ibid., p. 366. Bradford Cook has translated this text and others in *Mallarmé: Selected Prose Poems, Essays, & Letters* (Baltimore: Johns Hopkins University Press, 1956).

without its encumbrance The French "purification" of Poe is remarked by T. S. Eliot, "From Poe to Valéry," *To Criticize the Critic*, pp. 27–42.

painstakingly noticed See especially Davies, *Les Tombeaux*, pp. 89–114, and Cohn, *Toward the Poems of Mallarmé*, pp. 153–57.

dim mid . . . **"never"** I owe these observations to remarks by Mr. Humbert Humbert and Mr. Roman Jakobson.

169 **an autonomous "Image"** *Romantic Image* (London: Routledge & Kegan Paul, 1957).

Alleluia *Oeuvres*, p. 264.

"cold and intellectual" Davies, *Les Tombeaux*, p. 187.

a premature report See Georges Lafourcade, *Swinburne* (New York: William Morrow, 1932), p. 194.

170 **too sweet for comfort** J. J. McGann offers a spirited defense of "Ave Atque Vale" in *Swinburne: An Experiment in Criticism* (Chicago: University of Chicago Press, 1972), pp. 292–312.

praised its music Mallarmé's *Correspondance*, ed. Henri Mondor and L. J. Austin (Paris: Gallimard, 1965), vol. 2, pp. 100, 122.

découche *Oeuvres*, p. 70. The committee proposal is described in the notes, pp. 1494–95.

171 **"bloating and bending"** *Les Mots anglais*, ibid., p. 929. On the significance of such effects for the poet, see Jacques Michon, *Mallarmé et "Les Mots anglais"* (Montreal: L'Université de Montréal, 1978), pp. 113–43.

172 **to modify "soir"** That is the reading of Fowlie (*Mallarmé*, pp. 67, 87); but Davies (*Les Tombeaux*, p. 176) takes "votif" to modify "feuillage."

"at his vanishing" Wallace Stevens, "The Idea of Order at Key West," line 34.

173 **"the hero remains"** *Oeuvres*, pp. 510–11.

incongruities of the scene The occasion is described in detail by Henri Mondor, *L'Amitié de Verlaine et Mallarmé* (Paris: Gallimard, 1939), pp. 239–52.

calomnié la mort *Oeuvres*, p. 71.

174 **a wedding veil** See Noulet, *Vingt Poèmes*, p. 263, and Cohn, *Toward the Poems*, p. 173.

175 **any religious pieties** In his commentaries on Mallarmé's poems, Charles Mauron stresses the "pagan wisdom" of both poets in opposition to the deadly beliefs of Christianity. See Mallarmé, *Poems*, tr. Roger Fry (New York: New Directions, 1951), pp. 252–56.

"of the Earth" "Autobiography," *Oeuvres*, p. 663.

176 **"aboutir à un livre"** "Le Livre, instrument spirituel," ibid., p. 378; cf. p. 872. The idea has been expounded at length by Jacques Scherer, *Le "Livre" de Mallarmé* (Paris: Gallimard, 1957), pp. 7–24.

"his own proper tomb" Mallarmé, "On Literary Evolution," *Oeuvres*, p. 869. As Scherer points out (pp. 53–55), the tomb itself may be regarded as the symbol of a book.

"possesse his gost" Henry Howard, Earl of Surrey: "Epitaph on Sir Thomas Wyatt," line 38.

177 **the lightest Ground** John Dryden, "To the Pious Memory of . . . Mrs. Anne Killigrew," lines 188–90.

the dancers forget themselves Mallarmé, "Ballets," *Oeuvres*, pp. 303–4. The metaphor of an "ideal dance of constellations," a favorite of Mallarmé, contributed to Yeats' later effort to tell the dancer from the dance.

"the starry sky" Paul Valéry, "Le *Coup de dés*" (1920), reprinted in *Ecrits divers sur Stéphane Mallarmé* (Paris: Gallimard, 1950), p. 18.

A similar destiny On the relations of death, the absolute, and the destiny of the poet, see Albert Thibaudet, *La Poésie de Stéphane Mallarmé* (Paris: Gallimard, 1926), pp. 152–79.

178 **die Mütter bedeutet** Rilke, Tenth Elegy, lines 94–96 (*Duino Elegies*, ed. and tr. J. B. Leishman and Stephen Spender [London: Hogarth Press, 1948], p. 96; the symbols are interpreted on pp. 145–46).

palmistry Siegfried Mandel, *Rainer Maria Rilke* (Carbondale, Ill.: Southern Illinois University Press, 1965), pp. 155–56.

ENDING

180 **"greatest ambition"** 17 November 1819, Keats' *Letters*, 2:234.

towards you— Stillinger, in *The Poems of John Keats* (Cambridge, Mass.: Harvard University Press, 1978), p. 503, has regularized the text by substituting a period for the dash after "calm'd," capitalizing "see," following it with a comma, and replacing the final dash with a period. Though editorially proper, these emendations have the subtle effect of making the fragment seem a finished *poem*.

181 **until 1898** H. B. Forman first found the fragment and published it in his sixth edition of Keats' *Poetical Works* (London: Reeves & Turner, 1898). The manuscript page is reproduced opposite page 740 of C. L. Finney, *The Evolution of Keats's Poetry* (Cambridge, Mass.: Harvard University Press, 1936).

play or melodrama The further possibility that Keats did not compose the lines at all but copied them from someone else's play cannot be absolutely ruled out, though no source has ever been found.

as has been suggested Keats had been studying the story of Elizabeth and Leicester as a "promising" subject for a great play (letter of 17 November 1819, *Letters*, 2:234).

back to life In Book XI of the *Odyssey* the spirits of the dead are able to speak to Odysseus only after sipping the blood of the ewe and ram he has sacrificed to them. The great German classicist Wilamowitz is said to have interpreted this passage as an allegory of the act of reading: by filling the shades of dead authors with our blood, we bring them momentarily to life.

182 **"that we can see it"** Jonathan Culler, "Apostrophe," *diacritics* 7 (Winter, 1977): 69.

someone other than "us" If the fragment were a speech in a play, of course, Culler's argument would have to be withdrawn. In general his interpretation shows both the strengths and the weaknesses, it seems to me, of a criticism founded on a theory of reading uncomplemented by a theory of authorial intention. The reader's understanding of the fragment clearly depends on a prior assumption about what Keats intended the fragment to be.

"this warm scribe my hand" Keats, "The Fall of Hyperion," Canto I, line 16.

183 **even closure** As the end of a speech in a play, on the other hand, the broken line would invite the listener to reply, completing the line and hence refusing to be bound by the speaker's self-serving fancy. Thus a logical conclusion to the line might be such words as "You are not dead."

wrote Ezra Pound *The Translations of Ezra Pound* (London: Faber & Faber, 1970), p. 407. This version of Horace (*Odes* III. 30), dated 1964, may be the last poem that Pound intended for publication.

184 **"a high romance"** "When I have fears that I may cease to be," line 6.

"a record of an event" Robert Lowell, quoted by Helen Vendler in a collection of remarks from Lowell's lectures, *New York Times Book Review*, 3 February 1980, p. 28.

"direct address" The two quoted phrases are identical in Culler's "Apostrophe" (p. 68) and Lowell's remarks (p. 28). Though Professor Vendler recalls no reference to Culler (which would be unnecessary, of course, in the class-room), Professor Culler has informed me that "I delivered 'Apostrophe' as a Morris Gray lecture at Harvard in Feb. or March 1977, and I believe Lowell was there." Considering the rarity of the word "eschews," it seems likely that Lowell was consciously or unconsciously remembering Culler's phrase. I am grateful to Professors Culler and Vendler for supplying this information.

my open coffin Lowell, *History* (New York: Farrar, Straus & Giroux, 1973), p. 194.

185 **"the eel fighting"** "Dolphin," *The Dolphin* (New York: Farrar, Straus & Giroux, 1973), p. 78.

imitation of it *Imitations* (New York: Farrar, Straus and Cudahy, 1961), pp. 125–27.

borrowed from Rilke The connection with Rilke is drawn by Philip Cooper, *The Autobiographical Myth of Robert Lowell* (Chapel Hill: University of North Carolina Press, 1970), p. 154, though the conclusion that "Lowell is actually doing what Rilke taught" seems extravagant to me.

"The line must terminate" "Fishnet," *The Dolphin,* p. 15. Lowell comments on his attempt to "avoid the themes and gigantism of the sonnet" in *Notebook 1967–68* (New York: Farrar, Straus & Giroux, 1969), p. 160.

derives from Whitman's E.g., J. E. Miller, Jr., *The American Quest for a Supreme Fiction* (Chicago: University of Chicago Press, 1979), pp. 2–11.

resembling "thousands" The earliest version of "Reading Myself" (*Notebook 1967–68,* p. 128) began "Like millions." The higher number probably reflects a momentary optimism, in June or July 1968, about the power of poets to sway the multitude (in Eugene McCarthy's campaign). In this form, "Reading Myself" appeared as the third in a sequence ("We Do What We Are") on the problematic involvement of poets in a world of change. The version in *History* was reprinted unchanged in *Selected Poems* (New York: Farrar, Straus & Giroux, 1976), p. 177.

186 **burying him alive** The image of the honeycomb is regarded more benignly ("charming, witty," and sweet) by Irvin Ehrenpreis in a review of Lowell's *Selected Poems* in *The New York Review of Books* 23 (28 October 1976): 6.

"to die is life" *Selected Poems,* p. 40.

"forward like fish" "For the Union Dead" (*Selected Poems,* p. 137).

187 **"for the first time"** The final paragraph of "Little Gidding" (*Collected Poems,* p. 222).

without approving it According to S. G. Axelrod, *Robert Lowell: Life and Art* (Princeton, N.J.: Princeton University Press, 1978), the end of "Dolphin" shows that "Lowell, in a moment of spiritual insight, unconditionally accepts his world and himself" (p. 232). But Lowell's own view of the relations between life and art is hardly so positive and unproblematical.

188 **"shop of the heart"** "The Circus Animals' Desertion," *Variorum Yeats,* p. 630.

"bees of the invisible" *Letters of Rainer Maria Rilke 1910–1926,* tr. J. B. Greene and M. D. Herter Norton (New York: Norton, 1948), p. 374.

189 **"im Kerne Eins"** J. J. L. Mood, *Rilke on Love and Other Difficulties* (New York: Norton, 1975), p. 68. The unity of life and death is stressed by William Rose, "Rilke and the Conception of Death," *Rainer Maria Rilke: Aspects of His Mind and Poetry,* ed. William Rose and G. C. Houston (London: Sidgwick & Jackson, 1938), pp. 41–84. William Butler Yeats was so annoyed by this essay, he wrote Dorothy Wellesley (15 August 1938, *Letters,* p. 913), that it prompted his own epitaph, with its disdain for those like Rilke who look on death with fear.

"that were good" Rilke, *Sämtliche Werke* (Frankfurt am Main: Insel-Verlag, 1966), vol. 6, pp. 723–24; *The Notebook of Malte Laurids Brigge,* tr. John Linton (London: Hogarth Press, 1930), p. 19.

the work becomes invisible Cf. Rilke's "Mausoleum" (October 1924), *Sämtliche Werke,* 2:500–501.

more practical poet Robert Frost, in "Birches" (line 52).

"I want my freedom" Quoted by J. R. von Salis, *Rainer Maria Rilke: The Years in Switzerland,* tr. N. K. Cruickshank (London: Hogarth Press, 1964), p. 280.

190 **"subjected to him"** Letter to Nanny Wunderly-Volkart, 29 July 1920, published in J. B. Leishman's translation of Rilke's *Sonnets to Orpheus* (London: Hogarth Press, 1946), p. 149. The Swiss poet Carl Spitteler (1845–1924) was much admired by Rilke.

"wenn es singt" "Once and for all / it's Orpheus, when there's singing" (*Sonnets to Orpheus,* I. v. 5–6).

better than Rilke On "The Difficulty of Dying" and Rilke's epitaph, see Mood, *Rilke on Love and Other Difficulties,* pp. 101–11.

"anonymous pain" To Rudolf Kassner, 15 December 1926, *Letters of Rainer Maria Rilke,* p. 395.

191 **brenn in dir** *Sämtliche Werke,* 2:511. Walter Kaufmann has translated and commented on the last poem in "Rilke: Nirvana or Creation," *Rilke: The Alchemy of Alienation,* ed. Frank Baron, E. S. Dick, and W. R. Maurer (Lawrence: Regents Press of Kansas, 1980), pp. 26–27. R.i.p.

Index

Abrams, M. H., 196
Accius, 145
Achilleis (Goethe), 92
adab, 15
Adam, 8, 37, 47, 164; "red clay," 38
Adams, Hazard, 205
Aeneas, character of, 73, 74–76 passim, 82–83, 84–93 passim, 161
Aeneid (Virgil), 57, 67, 97, 100, 108, 140, 208–12; constraints on action in, 88–93; ending of, 83–88; plan of, 79–82; as poetic model, 76–79; as signature-epic, 68–69
—as viewed by: Broch, 130–37; Eliot, 76, 208; Goethe, 93, 96–97, 213–14; Whitman, 130
Aeolian harp, 99, 147, 148, 150, 225
Aeschylus, 102, 139
Aesculapius, 83
Africa (Petrarch), 92, 212
Aherne, Owen, 53
Alice in Wonderland (Carroll), 72, 207
Allen, G. W., 219
alphabet, 16, 59
Amelia (Fielding), 92, 212
America as source of poetry, 114–19, 121, 123–26, 127, 128, 130
anatomy, 16, 197
Anchises, 81, 85, 89, 90, 92, 161, 224
ancients and moderns, Jonson on, 144–45

Anima Hominis, 14, 17, 48, 55, 140, 156, 178; defined, 56
Anima Mundi, 14, 17, 19, 48, 56–61, 140, 156, 178; defined, 56
Anubis, 170–72
Apollo, 3, 5, 7, 10, 88, 89, 90, 189, 225
Apuleius, 197
Arendt, Hannah, 221, 222
Aristophanes, 139
Arnold, Matthew, 133, 193, 222, 224
Ascensius, Badius, 208
Asselineau, Roger, 218
Atkins, Stuart, 215
Auden, W. H.: "In Memory of W. B. Yeats," 152, 154–60, 226–28; "Ode to Terminus," 87, 211
Auerbach, Erich, 198
Augustine, x
Augustus, 78, 80, 85, 88, 89, 91–92, 130, 133, 135
Austin, R. G., 206
Axelrod, S. G., 232

b, Mallarmé on, 171
Bach, J. S., 134
Bacon, Sir Francis, 145
Bailey, Cyril, 210, 211, 212
Balboa, V. N., 6, 9
Barbauld, A. L., 150
Barbi, Michele, 198
Barthes, Roland, vii, 193

Basse, William, 142, 225
Bate, W. J., 195
Baudelaire, Charles, 138, 163, 166, 176, 177, 195; Mallarmé on, 169–72, 229–30; Swinburne on, 169–70, 229
Beatrice, 13–34 passim, 53, 90, 106, 199, 200; as number nine, 25; as type of Christ, 21, 25, 28–29, 30–34
Beaumont, Francis, 225
Beer, John, 200
Beethoven, Ludwig van, 134
Ben Bulben, 153–54, 157
Béranger, Pierre-Jean de, 163, 228
Berlioz, Hector, 97
Bible, Blake's version of, 17–18, 19, 34–41, 44–47, 200
Black, S. A., 220
Blackmore, Richard, 68
Blake, Robert, 202
Blake, William, 13–15, 58, 61, 62, 70, 98, 158, 196, 197, 205, 206, 224; as initiate, 16–20; as printer, 42–43; as prophet, 34–47; as reader 36–46; "Argument," 17, 36–39; *The Marriage of Heaven and Hell,* 16–20, 34–48, 56, 63–64, 200–203; "A Song of Liberty," 17, 45–47. *See also Marriage of Heaven and Hell*
Blessing, R. A., 207
Bloom, Harold, 195, 197, 201, 204
Boccaccio, Giovanni, 17
Boethius, 31, 197
Bonagiunta da Lucca, 27, 199
Bonnycastle, John, 5, 6, 195
book as symbol, 9, 17–18, 207
Books of New Life, 13–20; defined, 16
Bosley, Keith, 228
Boyancé, Pierre, 211, 212
Boyd, James, 213
Brawne, Fanny, 181, 182
Brinton, A. C., 211
Broch, Hermann: as poet of death, 131—32, 136–37; on Virgil, xi, 130–37, 162, 179, 221–24; *The Death of Virgil,* 131–37, 221–24; "The Style of the Mythical Age," 134–35. *See also Death of Virgil*

Brodsky, Joseph, 228
Brody, Daniel, 222
Brower, R. A., 210
Browning, Robert, 20, 72, 207
Bruns, G. L., 229
Brutus (Pope), 68, 79, 92, 209, 212
Büchner, Karl, 208
Bucke, Richard, 114, 218
Butler, E. M., 217
Butler, H. E., 212
Byron, Lord, vii, 102, 177, 204, 218, 224. *See also* Euphorion

Camps, W. A., 209, 210
Can Grande, 24
career (destiny, vocation), idea of a, ix–xiii, 76, 117–18, 130–32, 187–88, 194
careerism, xi–xiii, 194
Carew, Thomas, 139, 140, 162
Carpenter, Edward, 220
Cavafy, C. P., 72, 206
Cavalcanti, Guido, 21, 22–23, 24, 27–29, 198, 199
Chapman, George, 3–11; as poet, 7, 8
Charon, 83
Chatterton, Thomas, 42, 201
Chaucer, Geoffrey, 79, 136, 142, 162, 225
Chavannes, Puvis de, 163
Clarke, C. C., 3, 5, 7, 195
Claudel, Paul, 158
Clausen, Wendell, 211
Cleveland, John, 228
Cohn, R. G., 229
Coleridge, S. T., 17, 193, 195, 197
Collins, William, "Ode Occasion'd by the Death of Mr. Thomson," 146–51, 225–26; contrasted to Thomson, 150–51
Columbus, Christopher, 123–28, 220
Comparetti, Domenico, 212
constellation, idea of a, 142, 177–79, 225, 230
Cook, Bradford, 229
Cooper, Philip, 232
Cortez, Hernando, 3, 6, 7, 8, 9

Cosmo, Umberto, 198, 199
Cottrell, A. P., 217
Cowley, Abraham, 162
Cowley, Malcolm, 119, 122, 219, 220
Crane, Hart, 104
Crashaw, Richard, 162
Culler, A. D., 221
Culler, Jonathan, 182, 184, 231, 232
cummings, e. e., 152
Curtius, E. R., 78, 113, 131, 206, 209, 213, 218
Cygnus, 145, 177, 225

daimon, 53, 56, 57–58, 61, 94
Da Maiano, Dante, 23, 198
Damon, S. Foster, 197
Dante Alighieri, 4, 15, 45, 51, 57, 61, 63, 66, 80, 97, 106, 132, 133, 136, 162, 187, 190, 205; and Beatrice, 25–26, 28–30, 33, 34; and Cavalcanti, 27–29; growth of, as interpreter and poet, 20–34; principles of initiation of, 16–20; *Commedia,* viii, x, 13, 14, 20, 25, 27, 28–29, 33, 40–41, 47, 69–70, 90, 94–95, 101, 111, 206; *La Vita Nuova,* xi, 16–34, 47, 55, 63, 196–200, 202. *See also Vita Nuova*
Davies, Gardner, 228, 229, 230
Davies, J. G., 200
Davis, A. J., 119, 219
The Death of Virgil (Broch), xi, 162, 179, 221–24; conception of, 130–32; form of, 133–34, 222; as poem of death, 132–37
Deiphobe (Sibyl), 90
Delfel, Guy, 229
Denham, John, 162
De Robertis, Domenico, 198
Díaz, Bernal, 196
Di Cesare, M. A., 211
Dickinson, Emily, xiii, 131, 221
Dido, 82, 90–91, 93, 211
Diogenes, 41
Diomedes, 86–87
Doktor Faustus (Mann), 15
dolce stil nuovo, 26–30

Donatus, 208–9
donna gentile, 29–32
Donne, John, 139, 140, 162
Dostoevski, Fyodor, 113
Drayton, Michael, 141, 224
druids, 40, 146, 147, 149, 150, 151, 225
Dryden, John, 81, 140, 177, 210, 224, 230
Duckworth, G. E., 209
Durzak, Manfred, 222
Duval, Jeanne, 171

Eckermann, J. P., 100, 102, 107, 213–18 passim
Eddas, 68
"Ego dominus tuus," meaning of, 24, 51
Ehrenpreis, Irvin, 193, 232
eidolon, 103, 128–30, 221; defined, 129
Eliade, Mircea, 193
Eliot, T. S., 131, 136, 158, 193, 197, 207, 228, 229; on initiation, ix–x, 62–64; on poetic redemption, 72–76; as self-reader, 62–67; *Four Quartets,* 62–67, 72–76, 205–8; "Little Gidding," 63–64, 67, 73–76, 88, 124, 187, 205, 206; "Note on War Poetry," 74–75, 207–8. *See also Four Quartets*
Elizabeth I, 181, 182, 231
Ellmann, Richard, 203, 204, 226
Emerson, R. W., 114, 116, 117, 118, 119, 121, 128, 219, 220
Emrich, Wilhelm, 216, 223
epic, modes of, xi, 68–70, 73, 79, 92, 97–98
Erasmus, Desiderius, 211
Erdman, David, 200, 201, 202
Erikson, Erik, 194
"Eternal Feminine," 107, 110, 111, 112, 137
Euphorion, 101, 102, 177, 218
Euripides, 102, 139
Evans, B. I., 195

Fairley, Barker, 97, 214

Faust, 115, 117; character of, 93–94, 102–7, 213, 217; death and burial of, 109–11

Faust (Goethe), 67, 132, 178, 212–18; form of, 95–101; genre of, 97–98; "Helena," 101–4; problem of ending, 93–95, 104–13

—viewed by: Broch, 134, 223; Whitman, 113–15

Faustbuch, 109

Felltham, Owen, 228

Fern Leaves from Fanny's Port-Folio (Parton), 117, 218

Ferrar, Nicholas, 76

Fielding, Henry, 15, 92, 212

"Figura," 198

Finney, C. L., 195, 231

Flannery, M. C., 203

Ford, John, 228

Forman, H. B., 231

Foster, Kenelm, 199

Foucault, Michel, 193

Four Quartets (Eliot): as harmonium, 65–67, 72–76, 205–8; as initiation, 62–64, 74

Fowler, Alastair, 225

Fowler, W. W., 211

Fowlie, Wallace, 228, 230

Franciade (Ronsard), 92, 212

Frank, Tenney, 208

Frazer, Sir James, ix, 193

Freudian analysis, x, 194, 198

Friedenthal, Richard, 214

Fritzinger, Warren, 221

Frost, Robert, 10, 189, 196

Frye, Northrop, 16, 18, 197, 201

Fucci, Vanni, 13–14, 44, 196

Gardner, Helen, 205

Gautier, Théophile, 163–64

Gennep. See Van Gennep, Arnold

Gide, André, 202

Gilchrist, Alexander, 202

Gilgamesh, 68

Gill, Austin, 228

Gillispie, C. C., 214

Gilson, Etienne, 199

Gittings, Robert, 195

Goethe, J. W. von, xi, 4, 16, 20, 54, 65, 92, 123, 136, 162, 177, 223; and organic unity, 94–96, 101, 112–13, 213–14; as poet of returning, 98–101, 107–8, 214; and problem of ending, 93–95, 104–13; "Dauer im Wechsel," 95; Faust, 93–115, 134, 178, 212–18; "Helena," 101–4, 216. See also Faust

Golden Section, 80

Gonne, Iseult, 51. See also "Maurice"

Gonne, Maud, 51

Gossage, A. J., 210

Goya, F. J. de, 134

Grant, John, 200, 201

Grant, Michael, 211

"Grass, Walt," 117

Graves, Robert, xii, 194

Gray, Thomas, 211

The Great Harmonia (A. J. Davis), 119

Greene, Thomas, 212

Gregory, Lady Augusta, 50

Gretchen, 104, 105, 106–7

Greville, Fulke, 161, 228

Guinicelli, Guido, 21, 26–27

Haecker, Theodor, 91, 131, 132, 208, 212, 222

Haile, H. G., 215

Hallam, Arthur, 126, 127

harmonia mundi, 71, 95

harmonium (reed organ), 71–72

Harmonium, ix, 206–24; as completed destiny, 76–92; deconstructed, 130–37; defined, xi, 70–72; as endless beginning, 114–30; as great confession, 65, 92–114; modern pattern of, 135–36; as poetic summing-up, 65–76

d'Hartoy, Maurice, 224

Hebel, J. W., 224

Heinze, Richard, 210

Helen of Troy, 57, 102–4, 129–30

Heller, Erich, 97, 214

Henn, T. R., 226

Heraclitus, 95, 174

Herder, J. G., 114

Herodiade, 57
Herrick, Robert, 162, 228
Herschel, William, 6, 9
Hesiod, viii, 77
Hic, 52–53
Hinderer, Walter, 222
Hofmannsthal, Hugo von, 223
Hohlfeld, A. R., 212
Holland, Hugh, 225
Hollander, Robert, 200
Homer, viii, 3–11, 68, 77, 78, 80, 81,
    85, 86, 87, 97, 99, 114, 126, 134,
    138, 161, 195, 231; as poetic spirit,
    10–11
Homunculus, 95, 106
Hone, Joseph, 203, 226
Hopkins, G. M., 224
Horace, 142, 145, 183, 224, 231
Horton, W. T., 50–51
Hugo, Victor, 57, 113, 204, 212, 228
Hulewicz, Witold von, 188
Hulme, T. E., 205
Humbert, Humbert, 229
Humboldt, Wilhelm von, 112
Hunt, Leigh, 3, 5, 194
Hynes, Samuel, 227

Iken, C. J. L., 100
Ille, 52–53
Initiation, 13–14; defined, xi, 15–20; as
    harmonium, 114, 116, 119, 121, 128;
    and initiation ceremonies, ix, 193; as
    method of interpretation, 20–34; as
    personal sacred code, 34–47; as
    regeneration 47–64
Ireland, Yeats' view of, 19, 49–50,
    156–57
Irving, Washington, 124, 125, 220

Jakobson, Roman, 229
James, Henry, 205
Jantz, Harold, 215, 217
Jeffares, A. N., 203
Jehovah (in Blake), 36, 39, 46
Jews, Blake's view of, 35, 37
John the Baptist, 28–29, 34, 43, 200

Johnson, Samuel, vii, x, 68, 147, 150,
    193, 194, 205, 208
Johnson, W. R., 210, 211
Jonson, Ben, 161, 162, 228; on
    Shakespeare, 139–46, 169, 177,
    224–25
Joyce, James, 16, 20, 50, 66, 197, 223
Juan de la Cruz, 15
Jung, C. G., 204

Kafka, Franz, 135, 223
Kahler, Erich, 222
Kaplan, Justin, 224
Kaufmann, Walter, 217, 233
Keats, John, 53, 55, 71, 126, 140, 149,
    177; end of, as poet, 180–84, 230–31;
    as reader, 6–8, 183; realizing a
    dream, 8–10, 181–83; self-discovery
    of, as poet, 3–11, 194–96;
    "Chapman's Homer," 3–11, 126,
    194–96; "This Living Hand," 180–84
Keeley, Edmund, 206
Kennedy, W. S., 221
Kermode, Frank, 169, 208, 212, 218
Killigrew, Anne, 177
King, Edward, 140
Kipling, Rudyard, 72, 158, 207
Klinger, Friedrich, 213
Klingsor, Tristan, 224
Klopstock, F. G., 215
Knight, W. F. J., 209
Knittelvers, 101
Kyd, Thomas, 143

labor, 76
Laforgue, Jules, 205
Lafourcade, Georges, 229
Lamartine, A. M. L. P., 224
Landaff, Bishop of (R. Watson), 35
Langbaum, Robert, 204
Langhorne, John, 226
Leaves of Grass (Whitman), 15, 186,
    218–21; diversity of, 119, 121,
    128–30; as national poem, 114–17; as
    poem of beginnings, 114–15; as
    poem of death, 121–30; as poem of

the self, 115–19, 128; unity of, 119, 121, 128–30
Lehrs, Ernst, 213
Leicester, Earl of, 181, 182, 231
Leranbaum, Miriam, 209
Levine, H. J., 204, 205
Levy, B. S., 200
Lewis, C. Day, 75–76, 208
Liebeschuetz, J. H. W. G., 211
Li Po, vii
Litz, A. W., 207
Lonsdale, Roger, 226
Loos, Beate, 222
Love, personified by Dante, 20–33, 51
Lowell, Robert, 228; end of career of, 184–88, 231–32; *The Dolphin*, 187–88; "Reading Myself," 184–87, 232
Lowth, Robert, 36, 200
Lukács, Georg, 217
Lydgate, John, 162
Lyly, John, 143

Mack, Maynard, 217
Mack, Sara, 210
The Magic Flute, 18
Magnus, Rudolf, 213
Mallarmé, Stéphane, 57, 68, 136, 138, 205
—*tombeaux:* in practice, 163–79, 228–30; in theory, 163–64, 175–78, 230; "Toast Funèbre" (Gautier), 163–64; "Le Tombeau de Charles Baudelaire," 169–72, 176, 195; "Le Tombeau d'Edgar Poe," 164–69, 175, 190, 206; "Tombeau" (Verlaine), 173–76
Mandel, Siegfried, 230
Mandelbaum, Allen, 210
Mann, Thomas, 15, 113
Marcellus, 91–92, 212
The Marriage of Heaven and Hell (Blake), 48, 56, 63–64, 200–203; "Argument," 17, 36–39; as bible, 34–41, 44–47; genre of, 16–20; "A Song of Liberty," 17, 45–47; as trial by vision, 41–44

Marlowe, Christopher, 94, 143
Marti, Mario, 198
Martz, L. L., 207
Marvell, Andrew, 158
Mason, E. C., 212, 215
Mater Gloriosa, 105, 108
Matthiessen, F. O., 219
"Maurice" (Iseult Gonne), 17, 59
Mauron, Charles, 230
Mazzeo, J. A., 198, 200
Mazzotta, Giuseppe, 199
McCarthy, Eugene, 232
McGann, J. J., 229
McKenzie, Kenneth, 198, 199
McKillop, A. D., 225, 226
Mephistopheles (Goethe), 93, 94, 102–3, 109–11, 112, 115, 121, 217
Michon, Jacques, 229
Miller, J. E., 219, 232
Miller, Ruth, 221
Milton, John, viii, x, xi, xii, 4, 9, 38, 39, 40, 45, 68, 70, 136, 138, 140, 146, 147, 148, 150, 194, 197, 201, 205, 224, 225; epic signature of, 69; on Shakespeare, 139–40
Mineo, Nicolò, 198
Misenus, 85
Mitchell, W. J. T., 202
Mommsen, Katharina, 216
Mondor, Henri, 230
Monroe, Harriet, 50
Montale, Eugenio, 185
Mood, J. J. L., 233
Moody, A. D., 207
Moore, J. B., 219
Moore, Sturge, 18
More, Henry, 56
Mothers, The, 106, 114, 178, 188, 217
Murry, J. M., 195
Musa, Mark, 198, 199

Nebuchadnezzar, 44
Newton, Sir Isaac, 95, 96, 151, 214
Nietzsche, Friedrich, 105, 113, 217
Nolan, Barbara, 197, 198
Norden, Eduard, 85, 211
Noulet, E., 229, 230

old age, style of, 65–68, 134–36
Olney, James, 204
Orpheus, 145, 166, 175, 176, 190, 233
Osborne, Charles, 228
Ossian, 99, 128, 215
Otis, Brooks, 209, 211
Ovid, 216, 224
Owen, A. L., 225
Oxford English Dictionary, 161

Pacuvius, 145
Paley, Morton, 200
Palinurus, 85
Pallas, 83, 84, 86
Parry, Adam, 210
Parton, S. P. W. ("Fanny Fern"), 218
Patch, H. R., 199
Pearce, Donald, 197
Pearce, R. H., 120
Pellegrini, Silvio, 198
Per Amica Silentia Lunae (Yeats),
    196–98, 202–5; genre of, 16–20; as
    ritual of initiation, 47–51, 60–63;
    struggle with Daimon in, 57–60; title
    of, 56–57; "Ego Dominus Tuus," 17,
    51–55, 204
"persona," viii, 193
Petrarch, F. P., 68, 79, 92, 212
The Phoenix Nest, 162
Pilgrim's Progress, 50
Pindar, 225
pius, defined, 78
Plath, Sylvia, viii
Plato, 40
Poe, Edgar Allan, 138, 163, 175, 176,
    177, 229; Mallarmé on, 164–69
Pöschl, Viktor, 210, 211, 213–14, 223
Poet: death of the, vii, 193; as focal
    point of history, 9–10, 18–19, 37–40,
    49–50, 114–17, 156, 160, 176, 186; as
    hero of epic, 68–69; idea of a,
    viii–ix, 4–11, 35–36, 65–66, 74–79,
    88–90, 92–93, 96, 112–13, 116–17,
    127, 134–35, 143, 153, 154–58,
    160–63, 164, 168–69, 172, 176–79,
    186, 190, 194; life of the, defined,
    viii–xi, 183–91

Pope, Alexander, xi, 68, 73, 79, 81,
    92, 136, 152, 206, 209, 210, 212, 217
Pound, Ezra, xi–xii, 50, 52–53, 68, 79,
    183, 194, 197, 205, 231
Primavera (Giovanna), 27–29, 34, 199
principia, 16, 197
Propertius, Sextus, xii, xiii, 78, 194,
    209
prophecy, preauthenticated, 88–89, 211
prudentia, 76, 89
"pure poetry" *(la poésie pure),* 76, 164,
    166, 168
Putnam, M. C. J., 210
Pythagoras, 80

Quinn, Kenneth, 210
Quintilius, 142

Rabelais, François, 197
"race" (Shakespeare's), 143, 145
Rand, E. K., 209
razos, 198
"realms of gold," 7
recantation, 136
Rembrandt, 134
Requadt, Paul, 215
Revelation, Book of, 16, 45–46, 202
"reverie," 16
Reynolds, Barbara, 198
rhyming (in Goethe), 102, 104, 106
Richards, I. A., xii
Ricks, Christopher, 206
Rilke, R. M., 15, 185, 197, 232;
    destiny and death of, 188–91, 233;
    last notebook entry by, 190–91, 233;
    on "Mothers," 178, 230
Rintrah, 36, 39
rites of passage, ix, 193
Robartes, Michael, 53, 204
Robertson, William, 5, 8, 196
Roe, Albert, 196
Ronsard, Pierre, 79, 92, 212
Rose, William, 233
Der Rosenkavalier, 111
Rossetti, D. G., 17, 55, 198, 204
Roston, Murray, 200

Sachs, Hans, 101
Said, Edward, 194
Sainte-Beuve, C. A., 91, 212
Santayana, George, 116, 220
Sappho, vii
Scaliger, 97
Scherer, Jacques, 230
Schiller, J. C. F., 97, 102, 104, 213, 214
Schlant, Ernestine, 222, 224
Schyberg, Frederik, 227
Scott, J. A., 199
"serene," 8, 195
Servius, 206
Shaffer, E. S., 196
Shakespear, Olivia, 14
Shakespeare, William, viii, 5, 66, 67–68, 101, 169, 177, 205; Jonson on, 138–46, 224–25; Milton on, 139–40, 224
Shaw, J. E., 197, 199
Shelley, P. B., 140, 177, 190, 205
Sherburn, George, 212
Sherwin, P. S., 225
Shirley, James, 228
Sibyl of Cumae, 89–90, 211
Sidnell, M. J., 204
Sidney, Sir Philip, 7, 148, 161–62, 195, 226, 228
signature-epics, 68–70
simulacrum, 29, 30, 103, 129–30
Singleton, Charles, 17, 197, 198, 199
Smith, Alexander, 116
Spargo, J. W., 211
Sparrow, John, 210
Spence, Joseph, 206, 209.
Spender, Stephen, 75, 228
Spenser, Edmund, 79, 142, 146, 151, 224, 225, 226, 228; epic signature of, 69; on Sidney, 161–62
Spitteler, Carl, 190, 233
Squarotti, G. B., 198
Stabat Mater, 105
Staiger, Emil, 113, 212, 217
Stange, Carl, 199
Statius, 13, 92, 206
Steiner, Rudolf, 213

Stevens, Wallace, 15, 172, 207; as maker of harmonium, 70–72
Stewart, Balfour, 221
Stillinger, Jack, 194, 231
Stovall, Floyd, 218, 219, 220
Strelka, Joseph, 223
Strich, Fritz, 215
Stuart, Mary, 197
Suetonius, 79–80, 83, 89, 206, 208, 209, 210, 212
Suez Canal, 109, 123
Sullivan, J. P., 194
Surrey, Earl of, 162, 230
Swedenborg, Emanuel, 18, 35, 42, 47, 200, 219
Swift, Jonathan, 152, 205
Swinburne, A. C., 229; "Ave Atque Vale," 169–70
Symons, Arthur, 57

Tagore, Rabindranath, 197
Tait, P. G., 221
The Tale of Genji (Murasaki), 15
Tasso, Torquato, 112, 146, 162
Templer, M. D. B., 199
Tennyson, Alfred, Lord, 95, 205, 213; "Ulysses," 126–27, 220–21
Terminus, 87, 211
Thebaid (Statius), 92, 206
Theocritus, 77
Thibaudet, Albert, 230
Thomas, Dylan, viii
Thompson, Lawrance, 196
Thomson, James, 195; Collins on, 146–51, 225–26; contrasted to Collins, 150–51
Thoreau, H. D., 19, 197
Tillyard, E. M. W., 226
Titian, 134
Tolstoy, L. N., 135
tombeau, ix, xi, 224–30; as aesthetic challenge, 163–79; characterized, 138–40, 175–78; as form of opposition, 151–60; as form of tribute, 146–51; as literary history, 160–63; tension of the form, 140–46
Tom Jones (Fielding), 15
Torchiana, D. J., 209

Toynbee, Arnold, 203
tradition (Eliot), x, 66
Traubel, Horace, 115, 123, 127
Trees of Knowledge and Life, 14, 37
"triumphal forms," 144, 147, 225
Turnus, death of, 81, 83–88, 90–91, 210, 211
"tutelary," 172, 195

"Ulysses" (Tennyson), 126–27, 220–21
Untermeyer, J. S., 134, 222
Urphänomen (Goethe), 95

Valéry, Paul, 169, 177, 185
Van Gennep, Arnold, 193
Varius, 77, 206, 209
vates, 88, 90
Vegius, Maphaeus, 211
Vendler, Helen, 197, 231, 232
Verlaine, Paul, 58, 138, 163; Mallarmé on, 173–76, 177, 228, 230; "Per Amica Silentia," 57, 203
Vida, M. G., 68
Viëtor, Karl, 213
Virgil, 13, 27, 53, 75, 98, 113, 120, 138, 149, 161, 162, 179, 188, 194, 206, 221–24, 226; death of, 83, 130–37; as pattern of poetic career, xi, xiii, 69, 76–80, 92–93, 96, 130–32, 135–37, 208; as poet-prophet, 88–90, 211; Aeneid, 57, 67, 68–69, 76–93, 96, 97, 100, 108, 130, 132, 133, 134, 136, 137, 140, 208–12. See also Aeneid
"Virgil's wheel," 77–78, 97, 208
La Vita Nuova (Dante), xi, 47, 55, 63, 196–200, 202; genre of, 16–20, 197; meaning of title, 16, 197; as method of interpretation, 21–33; subject of, 20–21, 33–34
Vulcan's shield, 81, 82

Wagner, Richard, 163
Waller, Edmund, 228
Ward, Aileen, 195
Webster, B. S., 204
Weigand, H. J., 221, 222
Weinberg, Bernard, 208

Wellesley, Dorothy, 233
Wendorf, Richard, 225, 226
Werther (Goethe), 98–99, 112, 113, 214
Wheelock, J. T. S., 198
Whitaker, T. R., 205
Whitman, Walt, xi, 113, 131, 132, 136, 185, 187, 224; as poet of death, 121, 122–30; as poet of democracy, 114–18; as subject of Leaves of Grass, 115, 116, 117, 118–19, 120, 123–27, 130; "Eidólons," 128–30, 221; Leaves of Grass, 15, 114–30, 186, 218–21; "Passage to India," 123–25; "Prayer of Columbus," 125–27, 220; "A Thought of Columbus," 127–28. See also Leaves of Grass
"Wiederholte Spiegelungen," 98–100, 105, 214
Wilamowitz-Moellendorff, Ulrich von, 231
Wilkinson, E. M., 213
Wilkinson, L. P., 211
Williams, W. C., 197
Willoughby, L. C., 214
Wind, Edgar, 211
Winters, Yvor, xii, 194
Wittreich, J. A., 201, 202
Woodring, Carl, 195
Wordsworth, William, viii, 5, 48, 61, 70, 79, 149, 188; Keats on, 9
Wyatt, Sir Thomas, 162

Yeats, George Hyde-Lees, 54
Yeats, William Butler, 70, 74, 79, 140, 185, 188, 208, 219, 230; Auden on, 151–60, 161; on death, 152–54, 226–28, 233; as initiate, 16–20, 47–62; as self-reader, 13–15, 54–61; "Ego Dominus Tuus," 17, 51–55, 203, 204; Per Amica Silentia Lunae, 16–20, 47–64, 196–98, 202–5; "Sailing to Byzantium," 13–15; "Under Ben Bulben," 152–54, 157, 158–59, 226–27, 233. See also Per Amica Silentia Lunae

Ziolkowski, Theodore, 222